Interpreting
Together

Interpreting Together

Essays in Hermeneutics

Edited by
Peter Bouteneff &
Dagmar Heller

WCC Publications, Geneva

Cover design: Rob Lucas

ISBN 2-8254-1333-X

© 2001 WCC Publications, World Council of Churches
150 route de Ferney, P.O. Box 2100
1211 Geneva 2, Switzerland
Website: http://www.wcc-coe.org

Faith and Order Paper no. 189
Printed in Switzerland

Contents

vii   Preface

1   Hermeneutics and Ecumenism: The Art of Understanding
a Communicative God   *Anton Houtepen*

19   BEM and the Eucharist: A Case Study in Ecumenical
Hermeneutics   *William Tabbernee*

47   Hermeneutics and Ecumenical Dialogue:
BEM and Its Responses on "Apostolicity"   *William Henn*

92   "Scripture, Tradition and traditions": A Reflection
on the Studies of This Issue in the 1960s   *Martin Cressey*

98   Tradition Revisited   *Nicholas Lossky*

102   The Pneumatological Dimension in the Hermeneutical Task
Michael Prokurat

111   Ecumenical Hermeneutics: Suspicion versus Coherence?
Rudolf von Sinner

122   Hermeneutics: An Instrument for an Ecumenical Reflection
on the Search for Church Unity
Metropolitan Gennadios (Limouris) of Sassima

128   Reflections on "A Treasure in Earthen Vessels:
An Instrument for an Ecumenical Reflection on Hermeneutics"
Pablo R. Andiñach

134   A Treasure in Earthen Vessels: An Instrument for an
Ecumenical Reflection on Hermeneutics

161   Contributors

163   Participants in the Consultations

Preface

Since the very outset of the modern ecumenical movement, hermeneutics clearly has been a significant factor in Christian division. The ways in which Christians from different confessional, regional and cultural contexts interpret certain key words and concepts, such as "gospel", "scripture" and "tradition", not to mention how they interpret scripture itself, have a profound effect on Christian life and doctrine. Divided Christians do well to examine the ways in which their different hermeneutical approaches have effectively caused or perpetuated their division.

The Faith and Order commission has recently devoted special attention to the idea of ecumenical hermeneutics, in the understanding that Christian unity would be served if churches could agree on certain hermeneutical principles. In November 1998, after a five-year study process, Faith and Order published *A Treasure in Earthen Vessels: An Instrument for an Ecumenical Reflection on Hermeneutics.*[1] This text represents the first published result of what is to be an ongoing study process. It is a preliminary attempt to set out some of the issues surrounding the role of hermeneutics in ecumenical work, and seeks to provide some directions in developing ecumenical principles of interpretation.

The document has been received and studied with considerable interest in seminaries, theological faculties and theological institutes, many of whom have enquired whether Faith and Order might make additional study materials available. The present book seeks to "open out" the study process that shaped the *Treasure* text by publishing the essays and studies which were contributed along the way.

Before introducing them, however, we would like to set out the wider context out of which the current work on hermeneutics emerges.

Hermeneutics in Faith and Order history

The first world conference on Faith and Order (Lausanne 1927) was one of the first attempts in modern history to identify what different churches held in common and what their differences were. Coming to matters of interpretation, the conference report defined the gospel as "the message of the church to the world". It is "the joyful message of redemption, both here and hereafter, the gift of God to sinful man in Jesus Christ".[2] The Lausanne report revealed a consciousness of the fact that changed contexts might demand new forms of expression of the truths of revelation.[3] Ten years later, the second world conference on Faith and Order in Edinburgh suggested that we have this gospel in the texts of the Old and New Testaments: "We have this treasure in earthen vessels," the report said,[4] raising the significant question of "right interpretation":

...if it is conscious of its true nature, such [biblical] research can render the church important services in bringing about a right interpretation of the scripture, provided that the freedom needed for carrying out its work is not denied to it.[5]

The report further points to "the problem of the Tradition of the church and its relation to holy scripture", noting already the divergent approaches to this question.

The issue of the interpretation of scripture appeared concurrently in other areas of ecumenical work. In the years following the second world war the Study Department of the WCC organized several conferences on the ethical and political message of the Bible for the modern world, culminating in "Guiding Principles for the Interpretation of the Bible", published in 1949. Three years later, Faith and Order revisited hermeneutical questions at its third world conference (Lund 1952), this time addressing differences in approach to the authority of the Bible.

Issues that had been raised at Edinburgh, those concerning the relationship of scripture and Tradition, received concerted attention at the fourth world conference in 1963 in Montreal. Perhaps the most memorable and oft-cited paragraphs from Montreal are those that address "scripture, Tradition and traditions". The section with that title in the Montreal report attempted a step forward in what was emerging as an important tension between two approaches to scripture and its authority in the doctrine and life of the church. One emphasized "scripture alone" *(sola scriptura)*; the other insisted on a balance between scripture and Tradition. Montreal also attempted to define what was meant by Tradition ("the *paradosis* of the *kerygma*, testified in scripture, transmitted in and by the church through the power of the Holy Spirit").

Montreal marked the beginning of what was to be a new and more deliberate phase of study on hermeneutical questions within the WCC. One year later, Faith and Order authorized an examination of the hermeneutical problem that produced a report (Bristol 1967) on "The Significance of the Hermeneutical Problem for the Ecumenical Movement". The next step was a look at the authority of the Bible, leading to a report at the Louvain meeting of 1971. In Bangalore in 1978 another report was approved on "The Significance of the Old Testament in its Relation to the New".

After 1978, hermeneutical questions retreated somewhat into the background. All energies went into the production of the convergence document on *Baptism, Eucharist and Ministry* (BEM). To a certain extent, BEM represented a practical application of the results from the Montreal meeting. But as we shall shortly see, it raised as many hermeneutical questions as it answered, a fact that was made explicit at the fifth world conference on Faith and Order (Santiago de Compostela 1993). It was there that hermeneutics again took a central place in Faith and Order work.

Santiago and the current study process on ecumenical hermeneutics

Between the fourth and fifth world conferences on Faith and Order the situation of the ecumenical movement, and especially in the WCC, changed considerably. The number of WCC member churches had doubled since its founding, now encompassing virtually all the Orthodox churches together with the so-called "young" churches from the southern hemisphere. The Roman Catholic Church had become a full participant in the Faith and Order commission in 1968. This new landscape was the main impetus for a call for further work in ecumenical hermeneutics. Yet in fact there were several factors that influenced the Santiago meeting to press for this work:

- The BEM process had revealed several questions that were left unaddressed by Montreal's section on "Scripture, Tradition and traditions".
- BEM also showed that the reading of ecumenical texts, especially "convergence documents", is affected by different interpretations of the Bible.
- The BEM process finally indicated the need for hermeneutical reflection on the nature of convergence texts, which themselves are open to different ways of being read and interpreted.
- The rise of the so-called "young" churches in the South has raised in a fresh way the issues of inculturation and context, together with intercultural and intercontextual hermeneutics.
- All of the above led to a deepening of investigation into ecumenical methodology in general. Many participants at the fifth world conference suggested that the field of hermeneutics ought to serve as a framework for broader questions of ecumenical methodology.

The study process requested by Santiago took form in three consultations (Dublin 1994, Lyon 1996, Bossey 1997), and two smaller drafting meetings (Boston 1994, Faverges 1998). As interim texts were produced, each was discussed with recommendations from larger Faith and Order meetings, notably at the 1996 plenary commission meeting held in Moshi, and at the annual meetings of the standing commission (also known as the Faith and Order board). It was also sent at different stages to scholars from different contexts and confessions for comments and suggestions. In this way the process encompassed a participation far wider than at the official consultations and drafting meetings. The November 1998 text, *A Treasure in Earthen Vessels,* has been distributed widely and translated so far into German, French, Italian and Russian.

The essays here published

As stated previously, this book seeks to provide the background that contributed to the current Faith and Order study process, in the hope that this could be useful for further reflection on the issue. Included are papers presented at consultations and commission meetings on ecumenical hermeneutics. Some of the issues treated in the *Treasure* text can be explicitly recognized in these essays. For example, the relationship between "suspicion" and "coherence" (*Treasure* §§6-10) is treated by Rudolf von Sinner; the issue of Tradition and traditions (§§14ff.) is examined by Nicholas Lossky and Martin Cressey; questions surrounding the definition of ecumenical hermeneutics (§5) are dealt with in the contributions of Anton Houtepen and Michael Prokurat.

The essays are of independent value as well. In Dublin (1994) Houtepen gave an introduction into the issue of hermeneutics within the history of the ecumenical discussion in Faith and Order, focusing on some of the enduring questions of the study. In Lyon (1996) William Tabbernee and William Henn had been asked to present two case studies – one on "eucharist" and one on "apostolicity" – in order to uncover the implicit hermeneutics at work in the BEM text and its reception.

Several shorter papers helped to shape the discussion at Bossey (1997): Cressey discusses the issues that were not addressed, or addressed insufficiently, at Montreal on "Scripture, Tradition and traditions". Lossky reflects on the notion of Tradition and its role in the ecumenical discussion, with particular attention to the life of the Orthodox church. The importance of pneumatology for hermeneutics is pointed out by Michael Prokurat. And von Sinner analyzes a tension already existing in the different recommendations for a study on hermeneutics at the Santiago conference. Finally, Gennadios Limouris and Pablo Andiñach reflect on *A Treasure in Earthen Vessels* in its published form, in papers addressed to the Faith and Order standing commission (Toronto 1999).

Naturally, this collection cannot provide complete documentation of the five-year study process. It gives insights into just some of the issues raised. In reviewing this study process, two persons ought to be mentioned whose written contributions are not represented here but who have contributed in a considerable way to the process of the whole study. The two co-moderators of the study, Turid Karlsen Seim and Emmanuel Clapsis, gave generously of their time and energy, contributing immeasurably through their reflections as well as in planning and leading the discussions. We would like to thank them for the fruitful collaboration and friendship that has developed through the process. They have been supported by several members of the hermeneutics sub-committee of the Faith and Order standing commission: Melanie May, Evangelos Theodorou, Mary O'Driscoll, Kyung Sook Lee, Araceli Rocchietti and Martin Cressey. Ultimately the results of this study would not have been possible without all the participants in the different consultations[6] and the reactions by correspondence to the different stages of the draft text. Neither would it have been realized without the able and professional assistance of Renate Sbeghen, Monica Schreil and Carolyn McComish.

We hope that the Faith and Order study process on ecumenical hermeneutics, which after all represents only a beginning, will inspire further work which may be of assistance to the churches on their way to unity, by making them aware of the hermeneutical questions involved along this way, and by helping them to find criteria for recognizing in each other the one, holy, catholic and apostolic church.

Dagmar Heller   Peter Bouteneff

NOTES

[1] While it is reproduced in the present volume (pp.134-60), this text is also available separately from the WCC secretariat on Faith and Order and on the internet at www.wcc-coe.org/wcc/what/faith/treasure.html
[2] Cf. Lukas Vischer, ed., *A Documentary History of the Faith and Order Movement 1927-1963*, St Louis, MO, Bethany, 1963, p.29.
[3] Cf. *op. cit.*, p.33.
[4] *Op. cit.*, p.44.
[5] *Ibid.*
[6] A complete list is given on pp.163-64.

Hermeneutics and Ecumenism: The Art of Understanding a Communicative God

ANTON HOUTEPEN

Hermeneutics: salvific interpretation and communication

The interpretation and communication processes that come under the heading "hermeneutics" present concrete challenges to ecumenical dialogue. Some basic insights from the history of hermeneutical theory can help prepare us for those challenges.[1]

In classical Greek literature, from Plato onwards at least, the term hermeneutics *(hermeneutike techne)* referred to the interpretation of divine signs and oracles as they related to the fate and destiny of people or individuals. Hermeneutics paralleled the work of Hermes, the messenger of the gods, who brought good tidings to people and protected their commerce and markets. But at an even deeper level, Hermes was the god of orientation in life: *hermai* were the signposts at crossroads or bifurcations, pointing in the right direction and surrounded by stones. Passers-by added stones to the sign, to keep up its function and out of reverence for Hermes. In this sense *hermeneia* meant guidance on our way.[2] It has, one could say, a soteriological thrust: *hermeneia* and *euaggelion* belong to a similar symbolical universe. For the Greek philosophers like for Plato and Aristotle, however, *hermeneuein* meant the re-reading of the old myths in the light of reason, in other words, in the tragedies.[3]

In early Jewish and Christian tradition, hermeneutics dealt with the application of the holy scriptures in view of new circumstances and problems of life. Origen *(Peri Archoon)* and Augustin *(De Doctrina Christiana)* wrote on the rules for such *interpretation* (which is the Latin translation of *hermeneia*, focusing on texts) and on the various senses or perspectives of the scriptures. Their findings were further refined by medieval scholars like Hugo of St Victor and summarized in a little verse, ascribed to Nicholas of Lyra (d. 1349) or to Augustin of Denmark (d. 1285):

littera gesta docet	*The letter teaches facts*
quid credas allegoria	*allegory what one should believe*
moralis quid agas	*tropology what one should do*
quo tendas anagogia	*anagogy where one should aspire*
	(tr. K. Froehlich)[4]

Several problems of interpretation are contained in this verse: the relation of a text to certain historical facts; to our actual system of belief; to its practical application and to its final eschatological orientation for life. One could call these four perspectives an ecumenical quadrilateral, at least as important as the famous Lambeth Quadrilateral.[5]

In the context of the European Enlightenment this quadrilateral drifted apart. Allegory and anagogy were reserved for preaching and piety. The literal sense became the exclusive field of scientific exegesis. The moral sense, or tropology, was secularized into civil morality, which turned Bible texts into illustrations for moral instruction about the common good. In scholarly exegesis all emphasis was laid on philology and on the historical-critical approach to the text of the Bible and the Tradition in what one could call a hypertrophy of the literal sense. Hermeneutics developed, from its original soteriological function, through an appeal to autonomous reason, into a theory about theological principles, into fundamental or foundational theology. Friedrich Schleiermacher is usually mentioned as the founding father of such a hermeneutical theory, which deals with the problem of human encounter with God and with the way God may communicate with us through scripture, Tradition and inner experience.[6] Hermeneutics becomes the part of systematic theology that deals with the way God may reveal and disclose divine care for us and how we come to know about it. It becomes synonymous with theological epistemology: it answers the question "How do you know?"

In secularized form, this type of hermeneutics began to be used as a metaphor in the so-called "philosophy of life" (Dilthey),[7] which was the mother of phenomenology and the father of existentialist and French post-modernist philosophy.

The art of understanding

Wilhelm Dilthey, the father of modern Western hermeneutics and hermeneutical philosophy (which includes phenomenology, existentialism and European post-modernism), defined hermeneutics as "the theory about the art of understanding of scripturally fixated expressions of life *(die Kunstlehre des Verstehens schriftlich fixierter Lebensäußerungen)*".[8]

When hermeneutics is a theory of art, or rather the theoretical exposition about the skills of interpretation, it implies not only explication but also application. In a theory of art, the rules of perspective, for example, must be applicable in painting or architecture. It is not a psychological or philosophical theory of perception, or an epistemology of signs and imagination. Neither is such a theory of art itself the method or the technique of painting or building. Likewise, hermeneutics deals with the performative process of interpretation and communication between the reader and the text and between the reader and his or her audience. In several other definitions of hermeneutics we find similar emphases.[9]

Three things are important in Dilthey's definition, if we apply it to Christian faith and to the ecumenical movement.

First of all we should recognize that the faith of the church through the ages and in six continents, insofar as it is an interpretative and communicative event, is more like a work of art or a practical skill than a system of thought or a pattern of knowledge. Of course this does not mean that faith has no cognitive aspects, but that it is first and foremost a practice, a discipline and obedience, a way of living one's life.

From the very beginning the hermeneutics of faith – as an interpretative and communicative process – had a performative character, as in the Jewish *halacha* or in the New Testament reinterpretation and application of Old Testament texts or even of Hellenistic wisdom. The ongoing Tradition – the faith of the church through the ages – is a dynamic and living process of interaction between the inherited faith of the past, with all its feasts and rites, hymns and stories, holy scriptures and canonical regulations, and the contextual demands springing from the real-life issues of people in all parts of the world. Modern ecumenical dialogue is just one form of such ongoing *halacha* for the encounter with various Christian traditions and with people of other living faiths.

Characterizing hermeneutics as a theory of art might be, therefore, appropriate for our study of ecumenical hermeneutics. If the mutual understanding of the various traditions of the past and the many contextual expressions of faith in our own times is the absolute precondition for a fruitful dialogue among the churches in the ecumenical movement, it is essential to be aware of the art-like character of any separate or specific tradition as well as of any convergence, reconciliation, consensus or re-union. Ecumenism is, like Christian faith as such, an artistic endeavour or rather an artistic event, based on the art of understanding, which we call hermeneutics. With Paul Ricoeur[10] we may consider our different ecclesial traditions as historical *configurations*: a mosaic of memories, practices, rituals, confessions and social structures, an amalgam of spiritualities, devotions, festivals, world-views; in short, of specific *cultures*. Instead of calling all of these *non-theological* factors, these factors are the basic expressions of life, in which the gospel becomes inculturated. As we cannot separate form and content in a piece of art, so we cannot isolate faith from our expressions of faith. Nor can we find expressions of faith without expressions of life itself. As we cannot separate fact and interpretation, so we cannot isolate a "deposit" or a sum of tenets of faith from the living communities where they are honoured and lived.

In our search to communicate and interpret the one faith in koinonia it might be fruitful to practise a more narrative approach to matters of faith and Christian discipline, to refer to iconography (as was done with regard to the doctrine of God's trinitarian life), to the *vitae* of the martyrs and saints of past and present, to the parables and performances of the prophets and of Jesus, and to the life-and-death stories of people from various contexts and cultures.

The second important feature of Dilthey's definition is that the art of understanding relates, in the end, to life itself. He called his hermeneutics a hermeneutics of life. Understanding is an act of the living communities of life. It is relational and it serves life. This primacy of life itself in its many expressions relates the act of understanding and the ecumenical endeavour to communicate such understanding across the boundaries of time and space, across generations and contexts for those who believe in God, to the life-giving reality of the Holy Spirit. Dilthey himself may have, perhaps, understood the emphasis on life from an Enlightenment perspective, reducing the idea of life to its autonomous biological and cultural forms of expression and refusing any heteronomous dependence of life on God as its creative Father and Spirit. While his insights might not concur with faith and religion, they can be very well applied to the life of faith.

The ecumenical movement lives from the art of understanding of the life forms of people, interpreting both these forms and the way we share them as the creative gifts, or charisms, of the Spirit. Any "fusion of horizons", a term used by Hans-Georg Gadamer to describe the essential core of the art of understanding, may be seen by believers to be the gratuitous result of divine creativity, opening up our narrow-mindedness and imprisonment in our languages, imaginations, interests and worldviews. Any "disclosure" or "revelation" of sense and meaning comes by way of communication with other people. The church, therefore, should be an inviting and communicative community, where people can open themselves to others and may learn from others. Such a *hermeneutical community* should be open for "salvific conversation" (L. Mudge) on all possible life-issues, for all those who look for a way between intolerant fundamentalism and indifferent scepticism or between the apathy of the rich and the despair of the poor.

A third element is as important. Hermeneutics in Dilthey's definition relates to the *scriptural fixations* of the expressions of life. For Dilthey, as for modern philosophy in general, *language* and *texts* became the main theme of reflection, the only "objective" domain of the human spirit that can compete with the objects of science. Theologians, grown up with the heritage of sacred scriptures and conciliar definitions of doctrine, have easily accompanied the philosophers in their "linguistic turn". By way of opposition against the 19th-century emphasis on history, they redefined theology as the interpretation of the kerygma, as the science of the Word (with a capital W). By way of a certain competition with the natural sciences they concentrated on propositional truth and articulated faith. In ecumenical dialogue the end result became convergence- and consensus-*texts*. Semiotic and structuralist approaches to reality seemed to undergird this focusing on language, symbols, signs as textual phenomena caught up in a continuous process of intertextuality. Various factors now seem to question such focusing on the text. Post-modernist deconstructivism affirms the primary role of oral communication and the primacy of the *voice* as the real key to phenomenology. Too long we have suffered from logocentrism (Derrida against Habermas). The home of meaning may be opened, but is not constituted by texts (Ricoeur). Fixation on the text produces protocollism, as in biblicist interpretations of the *sola scriptura*.[11] *Scriptures are not texts*, says Wilfred Cantwell Smith in his comparative hermeneutical study about the sacred scriptures of the Hindu, Jewish, Buddhist, Christian and Muslim traditions.[12] By that he means that the texts are rather narratives or scenarios about episodes of life, which ask for performances and iconography more than reading only. Doctrine functions more like a cultural-linguistic field of symbols and metaphors for use in a faith community's communication among themselves and with God.[13] Who Jesus is and what the message about the reign of God really implied, cannot be fixed in definitions of faith, but can only be disclosed in the stories told, both by Jesus, like the parables of the kingdom, and by people who have met the secret of the reign of God in some new and liberating experiences of a gratuitous presence of God.[14] The appeal to contextual and cultural expressions of life – like poverty, gender, oppression, deprivation, authenticity, agnosticism – as the starting point for any theological reflection on value or meaning, on the holy or on human destiny or, finally, on God produces a certain scepsis. This scepsis refuses to rely on any "scriptural fixation" of life-expressions and denies all "grand stories" as illusive meta-structures, including the Christian gospel of God's salvation in Jesus Christ.

The church as a hermeneutical community

This is only a very brief pointer to the hermeneutical landscape we inhabit today. Whether reading and hearing or speaking and expressing ourselves in language, we are caught up in a massive network of grammatical rules, symbolic compounds, contextual presuppositions, which together form what we call "traditions" and "cultures". Is understanding and communication possible at all? Is not diversity and pluralism so overwhelming that the ecumenical project of *koinonia and reconciliation* among the Christian churches or even among the world's living faiths must be considered illusive, a *grand story* (Lyotard) like so many others? In the light of such questions it may become very clear that the hermeneutical problem of interpretation and communication relates directly to the ecclesiological issues of unity and reconciliation, mission and dialogue.

In fact, the concept of *ekklesia* is the concrete answer to this depressing scepticism. The narrative of Jesus' life and death, interpreting his message as the message of the reign of God and of God's creative power stretching out beyond death, brings together from division various modalities of Jewish culture, invites Jews, Samaritans, Hellenists and all the nations of the earth (Acts 1:8) to build one community of faith, and overcomes barriers of gender, race, culture, social position or caste in all generations to come (Gal. 3:28). From the very beginning, therefore, the church of Jesus Christ is a hermeneutic community, recollecting people from the diaspora and bringing them together before God as disciples (Matt. 28:18-20) of Jesus, looking after the reign of God, promised to the whole of the inhabited world (Matt. 24:14).

Koinonia and the rule of faith

The concept of koinonia as developed by the fifth world conference on Faith and Order in Santiago de Compostela, in 1993, is meant as a community dynamic – created by God, lived out and transmitted through Israel, renewed by Jesus and the apostolic community of his first disciples and present by Tradition among those who believe and are baptized, which makes them into a hermeneutical community searching for the reign of God. The scriptures of both testaments are a gift of God to that community dynamic, together with the constitutive sacramental signs of God's covenant, baptism and the eucharist, and a ministry of servants who may interpret the scriptures as the living Word of God as well as celebrate the sacraments as configurations of the reign of God. Though the churches are divided, they share already in this common hermeneutical dynamic: their search for the reign of God. The apostolicity and catholicity of the church are measured by the faithful communication of the same "rule of faith" from ages unto ages, the koinonia-founding factor of the reign of God proclaimed to and sought by people from all nations.

This is a dynamic concept, because, as Santiago said, "not all of what God is and the [full extent of the] divine blessings may be received in [their] fullness by us until the end. God remains greater than our comprehension".[15]

A common criteriology?

It is not for the first time that Faith and Order contributed to the theme of ecumenical hermeneutics. Thus far, however, the main field of attention has been the elaboration of a common criteriology for the authoritative interpretation of the Christian faith as it was written down in the texts of the scriptures, in the creeds and confessions of the early church or in later confessional articulations of doctrine. Such criteriology had to deal with the *hierarchia auctoritatum* among those different sources of authoritative teaching – the relation between scripture and Tradition, or between the creeds of the 4th century and those of later times. Vatican II reflected this approach by pointing to a *hierarchia veritatum*, a difference in the value of doctrines according to their nexus to the fundamental articles of the faith, which turned out to be an important criteriological tool in ecumenical dialogues after Vatican II.[16]

Santiago, however, seems to have had in mind a thorough study of the ways in which the Christian faith would gain *credibility* through fresh understanding, and a study of the ways of *communication to and exchange with the real life of people* in various contexts. Of course we should not construct any opposition between these two tasks. A solid common criteriology and a missionary realism leading to credible configurations of the faith of the church must go hand in hand.

Written standards?

Already in Lausanne in 1927 Faith and Order dealt with the problem of an ecumenical criteriology in the section on "The Church's Common Confession of Faith". *Nemine contradicente* one could state:

> Notwithstanding the differences in doctrine among us, we are united in a common Christian faith which is proclaimed in the holy scriptures and is witnessed to and safeguarded in the ecumenical creed, commonly called the Nicene, and in the Apostles' Creed, which faith is continuously confirmed in the spiritual experience of the church of Christ.
>
> We believe that the Holy Spirit in leading the church into all truth may enable it, while firmly adhering to the witness of these creeds (our common heritage from the ancient church), *to express the truths of revelation in such other forms as new problems may from time to time demand* (author's italics).
>
> Finally, we desire to leave on record our solemn and unanimous testimony that no external and written standards can suffice without an inward and personal experience of union with God in Christ.[17]

So Lausanne was already aware of the problem of written standards: newer expressions of faith might be necessary; without a living personal faith (*fides qua*), formulated texts as such are insufficient to uphold the faith.

Scripture and/or Tradition

In 1937 at Edinburgh, section II, "The Church of God and the Word of God", went into the question of scripture and Tradition, the concept of revelation and the value of scholarly exegesis. There was no full agreement on either issue, however. The one point of agreement on criteriology was expressed as follows in the final report:

> We are at one in recognizing that the church, enlightened by the Holy Spirit, has been instrumental in the formation of the Bible.[18]

But then the disagreement starts:

> But some of us hold that this implies that the church under the guidance of the Spirit is entrusted with the authority to explain, interpret and complete *(sumpleroun)* the teaching of the Bible, and consider the witness of the church as given in tradition as equally authoritative with the Bible itself. Others, however, believe that the church, having recognized the Bible as the indispensable record of the revealed Word of God, is bound exclusively by the Bible as the only rule of faith and practice and, while accepting the relative authority of Tradition, would consider it authoritative only in so far as it is founded upon the Bible itself.[19]

The lack of a common criteriology

The final report from Lund in 1952 included this statement on unity and diversity:

> All accept the holy scriptures as either the sole authority for doctrine or the primary and decisive part of those authorities to which they would appeal. Most accept the ecumenical creeds as an interpretation of the truth of the Bible or as marking a distinctive stage in the working out of the orthodox faith. Some assign a special importance to the credal documents of the early ecumenical councils. Some would say that to found unity on any creeds is to found it on something human, namely our understanding of the gospel and our theological work in formulating its meaning. Some judge in accordance with the Inner Light and the leadings of the Spirit and are therefore concerned to witness against the use of outward creeds when these are held to be necessary or sufficient. Many denominations possess confessional documents in which they express the Christian faith as they read it in the Bible. It would generally be admitted, however, that these last documents would not be regarded as irreformable and they do not in fact occupy the same position in the rule of faith of all churches which possess them.[20]

The lack of a common criteriology could not be formulated more sharply, and the Roman Catholic position had not yet been presented!

The breakthrough of Montreal

Then in 1963 the fourth world conference in Montreal seemed to arrive at a breakthrough. After serious theological homework on "Scripture, Tradition and traditions" from 1952 to 1963, the leading idea became the salvation history paradigm of revelation:

> As Christians we all acknowledge with thankfulness that God has revealed himself in the history of the people of God in the Old Testament and in Christ Jesus, his Son, the mediator between God and man. God's mercy and God's glory are the beginning and end of our own history. The testimony of prophets and apostles inaugurated the Tradition of his revelation. The once-for-all disclosure of God in Jesus Christ inspired the apostles and disciples to give witness to the revelation given in the person and work of Christ. No one could, and no one can "say that Jesus is Lord, save by the Holy Spirit" (1 Cor. 12:3). The oral and written tradition of the prophets and apostles under the guidance of the Holy Spirit led to the formation of scriptures and to the canonization of the Old and New Testaments as the Bible of the church. The very fact that *Tradition precedes the scriptures points to the significance of tradition, but also to the Bible as the treasure of the word of God.*[21]

In our present situation, we wish to reconsider the problem of scripture and Tradition, or rather that of Tradition and scripture. And therefore we wish to propose the following statement as a fruitful way of reformulating the question. Our starting point is that we are all *living* in a tradition which goes back to our Lord and has its roots in the Old Testament, and are all *indebted* to that tradition inasmuch as we have *received* the revealed truth, the gospel, through its being *transmitted* from one generation to another. Thus we can say that we *exist* as Christians by the Tradition of the gospel (the *paradosis* of the kerygma) testified in scripture, transmitted in and by the church through the power of the Holy Spirit. Tradition taken in this sense is *actualized* in the preaching of the word, in the administration of the sacraments and worship, in Christian teaching and theology, and in mission and witness to Christ by the lives of the members of the church.[22] (author's italics).

Vatican II

In a similar way the Constitution on Divine Revelation, *Dei Verbum*, of Vatican II had stated:

> God graciously arranged that the things he had once revealed for the salvation of all peoples should remain in their entirety, *throughout the ages*, and be transmitted to all generations. Therefore, Christ the Lord, in whom the entire revelation of the most high God is summed up (cf. 2 Cor. 1:20; 3:16-4:6), commanded the apostles to preach the gospel, which had been promised beforehand by the prophets, and which he fulfilled in his own person and promulgated with his own lips. In preaching the gospel they were to communicate the gifts of God to all men. This gospel was to be the source of all saving truth and moral discipline. This was faithfully done: it was done by the apostles who *handed on, by the spoken word of their preaching, by the example they gave, by the institutions they established, what they themselves had received –* whether from the lips of Christ, from his way of life and his works, or whether

they had learned it at the prompting of the Holy Spirit; it was done by those apostles and other men associated with the apostles who, under the inspiration of the same Holy Spirit, committed the message of salvation to writing.[23](author's italics)

A living Tradition

Such formulations tried to give expression to a common ecumenical conviction about the inner relation between the preceding prophetic and apostolic tradition, from which the scriptures emerged, and the successive ecclesiastical traditions, which are bound to explain and to proclaim the Tradition of the gospel, testified in scripture as the primary instrument of the transmission of the gospel. So they tried to solve the Reformation and Counter-Reformation dispute on the sola scriptura versus the so-called *two sources theory* of scripture and Tradition as being an addition or sum of two separate tenets of revelation. But at the same time the idea of revelation was corrected from being a mainly rationalistic, cognitive source of supranatural knowledge about things not accessible to human experience. For Montreal and for Vatican II revelation means an event and a salvation process, reaching from the history of Israel, through the life, death and resurrection of Jesus Christ into the very ecclesial life of word and sacrament, mission and service of the faithful, that history being the work of the Holy Spirit of God. To quote Montreal once more:

> What is transmitted in the process of tradition is the Christian faith, not only as a sum of tenets, but as a living reality transmitted through the operation of the Holy Spirit. We can speak of the Christian Tradition (with a capital T), whose content is God's revelation and self-giving in Christ, present in the life of the church. But this Tradition which is the work of the Holy Spirit is *embodied in traditions* (in the two senses of the word, both as referring to diversity in forms of expression, and in the sense of separate communions). The traditions in Christian history are distinct from, and yet connected with, the Tradition. They are the expressions and manifestations in diverse historical forms of the one truth and reality which is Christ.[24]

The hermeneutical deficit of Montreal and Vatican II

The three main ecumenical breakthroughs at Montreal towards a common criteriology of a faithful transmission of the gospel were thus:
- the emphasis on the event-character of revelation and Tradition, as processes guided by the Holy Spirit in the *history* of Israel and the church – but nowhere in wider humanity or in other religions – over against a mere *verbal, oral or doctrinal* ("tenets") understanding of it;
- the *paradosis*-context of the whole Tradition process, which gave a nearly sacramental character to it and characterized the ecclesiastical

teaching and preaching of the "transmissioners" as a work of the Holy Spirit;

- the scriptures are part of this Tradition process, but are not, as such, *the gospel*; and it is not through the scriptures *alone* that the gospel is transmitted to every generation.

This high view of the transmission process of the gospel within the church through the power of the Holy Spirit did not solve, however, the hermeneutical problem of the relation between scripture and authoritative ecclesiastical traditions or between those traditions and Tradition (meaning the transmission of the gospel as a whole, including scripture). The tension between the diverse and separated ecclesiastical traditions with regard to preaching and teaching, sacraments and ministerial structures, mission and Christian life, all of them appealing to scripture and Tradition in the sense of Montreal, could not be solved by Montreal. Montreal could go no further than mere juxtaposition of three factors in the transmission process: the preceding events and testimonies leading to scripture, the scriptures themselves, and the ecclesiastical preaching and teaching.

Likewise the Second Vatican Council, though abandoning the *two sources theory*, did not answer the question of the *hierarchia auctoritatum* between the scriptures – read in the liturgy, reflected upon in theology, spelled out in Christian life, informing prayer and spirituality – and the scriptures as interpreted in dogmatic articulations of the faith by the ecclesiastical magisterium. The continuing debate after Vatican II on theological epistemology, on the value of the *consensus fidelium* (LG 12), on the reception of dialogue results, on the task of the theologians and on the teaching authority of the ecclesiastical magisterium are proof of this lack of clarity and hermeneutical deficit of Vatican II.

From Montreal to Bangalore

Several bilateral dialogues took up the question (ARCIC I,[25] Anglican-Orthodox dialogue,[26] Lutheran-Roman Catholic dialogue in the USA[27]), as well as Faith and Order in its multilateral approach. In various studies on the hermeneutical problem (Aarhus 1964, Bristol 1967, Louvain 1971) important insights from church history were established: the flexibility and frequency of the conciliar praxis of the early church and its later developments in East and West; the importance of "reception" of conciliar decisions by the local churches; the problem of continuity and change, diversity and unity, *consensio antiquitatis et universalitatis*.[28] Aarhus dealt also with the question of the selectivity in reading the Bible, and Bristol with the problem of a central key to the scriptures *(Mitte der Schrift)*.

In Louvain, in the report on the studies that were initiated at Montreal on the "Authority of the Bible", we may find a fair summary of the growing consensus in those years on the inter-relatedness of the Bible text and its interpretation in the church:

> The question about the authority of the Bible is inseparable from the interpretative process in the church. To speak of inspiration, therefore, means reopening the question of the Spirit in the community of the church. Whenever contemporary interpretation leads men to know the Bible as the work of the Spirit, we have to remember the long line of inspired witnesses which has influenced this interpretation. The first witnesses were called and inspired by the Spirit, but their testimony once it has been given its final form does not become independent of that same Spirit. *To be handed on it has to be read in the Spirit.* Just as the Spirit once called his witnesses, so today will he also awaken faith, obedience and witness as he opens up to us indispensable witnesses... Do we not have to affirm that it is *only within the community of the church* that scripture can be read and really heard as God's word created by the Spirit?[29]

And a still more explicit quotation reads:

> The contemporary interpretative process is in fact simply the continuation of the interpretative process which begins in the Bible itself.[30]

At Louvain such statements were warmly welcomed. They would lead to the hermeneutics of ecclesiastical tradition, applied in the *Baptism, Eucharist and Ministry* (BEM) document.

From a somewhat different angle hermeneutical questions came up in the study of the teaching authority of the church in 1976 (Geneva) and 1977 (Odessa). Here again the problem of continuity and change and the role of the people of God *(consensus fidelium)* came to the fore. Here the emphasis on *communicatio fidei* (how to communicate the faith of the church through the ages) started to correct the hermeneutical approaches thus far, which had concentrated on *determinatio fidei* (how can authoritative doctrine be defined and who is responsible for its definition).[31] It is not by authority as such that the proclaimed faith becomes credible. Through credibility or the self-authenticating truth of the gospel, the faith of the church can be taught with authority. The teaching authority of the church has to do with the living testimony of the members of the church. It is not based on power, nor on the logic of propositional truth. It is there for the faithfulness of the church to the truth once transmitted to the saints (Jude 3). It serves the tradition of life and must be seen as an antidote against any protocollism. Many hermeneutical problems remained unsolved, thus far, in this field.

From the Faith and Order commission meeting in Accra 1974 and the fifth assembly of the World Council of Churches in Nairobi 1975 onwards, keen interest awoke in the multifold ways Christians in different contexts lived their faith and found new credal forms of witness.[32] The study project on "Giving Account of Our Hope" collected such forms of witness from all parts of the world and Bangalore produced even "A Common Account of Hope". But how to relate such newer forms of expression to the classical creeds of the church? Must there not be a more *definite rule of faith*? Should not one of the creeds become the *ecumenical creed* of the una sancta? What kind of authority is needed to select and possibly correct the particular and sometimes rather private and peculiar credal expressions of recent times? Who should decide on what conditions they may be received?

The ongoing debate on the role of authoritative teaching – within Faith and Order, but elsewhere as well – resulted in a common conviction, formulated at Bangalore in 1978:

> Before the church performs acts of teaching, she exists and lives. Her existence and her life are the work of the triune God who calls her into being and sustains her as his people, the body of Christ, the fellowship of the faithful in the Spirit. The authority of the church has its ground in this datum of her being. The whole church teaches by what she is, when she is living according to the gospel.
>
> The gospel we proclaim is the gospel of God's free grace. He calls us into his grace which sets us free. Therefore, the authoritative teaching of the church assumes the form of a *joyful witness to God's liberating truth*. This truth is its own criterion as it leads us into the glorious liberty of the children of God. We obey the truth because we have been persuaded by it.[33]

> The ultimate authority is that of the Holy Spirit who makes Christ present and shall guide us into all truth. He is at work in all other manifestations of authority in the life of the church and prevents them from being opposed to each other. The Spirit-given authority of the church, the scriptures, the teaching ministry of the church and the confessional statements are authoritative on the basis of the truth of the gospel as received by the whole church. Although conflicts happen, there should be no false alternatives between the scriptures and the Tradition, the ordained ministry and the laity, the truth of the past and the truth of the present, the faith of the corporate body of the church and of the individual person, as these dimensions are constitutive elements of the revealed truth of the whole church.[34]

The Lima text: applied ecumenical hermeneutics

Following that same line of thought, the preface to BEM in 1982 stated:

> On the way towards their goal of visible unity, however, the churches will have to pass through various stages. They have been blessed anew through lis-

tening to each other and jointly returning to the primary sources, namely "the Tradition of the gospel testified in scripture, transmitted in and by the church through the power of the Holy Spirit" (Faith and Order world conference, Montreal, 1963).

In leaving behind the hostilities of the past, the churches have begun to discover many promising convergences in their shared convictions and perspectives. These convergences give assurance that despite much diversity in theological expression the churches have much in common in their understanding of the faith. The resultant text aims *to become part of a faithful and sufficient reflection of the common Christian Tradition on essential elements of Christian communion.* In the process of growing together in mutual trust, the churches must develop these doctrinal convergences step by step, until they are finally able to declare together that they are *living in communion with one another in continuity with the apostles and the teachings of the universal church.*[35]

It was with this theological understanding of a given, common, apostolic tradition and of a received, partially shared and growing universal communion, that the first question, put before the churches, was phrased as follows: "the extent to which your church can recognize in this text the faith of the church through the ages".

The formulation was chosen to broaden the scope of the particular teaching of any given tradition towards the wider idea of a common, future-oriented Christian tradition, from which the divided churches would draw, through the ecumenical movement, the opportunities for renewal and enrichment in their understanding of sacraments and ministry.

The same understanding had led to the description of the leading idea of "apostolic tradition" in §34 and commentary of the Ministry text:

In the creed, the church confesses itself to be apostolic. The church lives in continuity with the apostles and their proclamation. The same Lord who sent the apostles continues to be present in the church. The Spirit keeps the church in the apostolic tradition until the fulfilment of history in the kingdom of God. Apostolic tradition in the church means continuity in the permanent characteristics of the church of the apostles: witness to the apostolic faith, proclamation and fresh interpretation of the gospel, celebration of baptism and the eucharist, the transmission of ministerial responsibilities, communion in prayer, love, joy and suffering, service to the sick and the needy, unity among the local churches and sharing the gifts which the Lord has given to each.[36]

Apostolic faith

In a similar way a consultation of Faith and Order in Rome 1983 underlined the continuity of the apostolic faith in the life of the church:

The term "apostolic faith"... does not refer only to a single fixed formula or a specific moment in Christian history. It points to the dynamic, historical *(geschichtlich)* reality of the central affirmations of the Christian faith which are *grounded* in the witness of the people of the Old Testament and the normative testimony of those who preached Jesus in the earliest days ("apostles") and of their community, as attested in the New Testament. These central affirmations were further *developed* in the church of the first centuries. This apostolic faith is expressed in various ways, i.e. in individual and common confession of Christians, in preaching and sacraments, in formalized and received credal statements, in decisions of councils and in confessional texts. Ongoing theological explication aims at clarifying this faith as a service to the confessing community. Having its centre in the confession of Jesus as Christ and of the triune God, this apostolic faith is to be ever confessed anew and interpreted in the context of changing times and places in continuity with the original witness of the apostolic community and with the faithful explication of that witness throughout the centuries.[37]

The key words in this understanding of Tradition and apostolic faith, going far beyond the scope of the Montreal hermeneutical debate in its section II on scripture, Tradition and traditions, refer to the *ecclesial* implications of Tradition:
– apostolic *continuity* (in proclamation, mission, interpretation of the gospel, celebration of the sacraments, transmission of ministerial responsibilities);
– *communion* (sharing in the gifts of God, in prayer, service, unity); and
– *fulfilment of history in the kingdom of God.*

Both the diachronic aspect (continuity in the apostolic faith) and the synchronic meaning (solidarity, reconciliation, unity of the local churches in a universal community) are expressed in the idea of "Tradition" *(paradosis)* and of "communion" (koinonia). In the commentary to §34 of the Lima text on Ministry the content of this ecclesial Tradition is once more described as a "transmission process", which relates the actual church and its ministries to the gospel and to "the saving words and acts of Jesus Christ which constitute the *life* of the church". In the opening paragraphs of the text on Baptism and Eucharist and at many other places in BEM (e.g. in M1-6,8-14,15-16,19-23) this same basic idea of tradition as transmission of the salvific gifts of Christ in and by the church through the power of the Holy Spirit has been expressed.

Some conclusions
The responses to the Lima text[38] make it quite clear that the different Christian cultures with regard to the place of the Bible, creeds, confessional writings, teaching authority or actual appeal to reason and experi-

ence are far from overcome. But they no longer seem bound to specific confessional traditions. The same responses demonstrate at the same time the hermeneutical gap between the language of faith, coined in the course of the controversies and biblical interpretations in the West and the need, expressed by several churches in Asia, Africa and Latin America, to develop "new language". In a way BEM had tried out new language already by drawing heavily upon quotations of ecumenical conferences.

This, apparently, is inadequate for newer generations of Christians, who are not familiar at all with the controversies of the past and who long for creative and challenging "configurations" of the work and the word of God in the hermeneutic community which is the church. Postmodern scepsis about any binding formulation of truth or even about the possibility of truth claims at all enhance the difficulties of communicating faith convictions with our contemporaries in agnostic and secularized society. So many different expressions of life in multiform contexts and various cultures are the living tools of communicating the language of faith, but how to cope with them within the conciliar community of the ecumenical movement? This is the challenge: how to witness to a communicative God? The continuity or apostolicity of the faith of the church is rooted in the intention to search for the reign of God and to hear "what the Spirit says to the churches". The only common "ontological object of reference" we have in the continuous exchange of communications with other Christians past and present, which is the ecumenical movement, is the confidence in the Holy God JHWH of the covenant with Israel, in the message and the mission of Jesus and in the experience of the Spirit of God in our midst.

The "hermeneutical key" of this confidence cannot be history as such, nor a history of salvation. It cannot be inner awareness *(gnosis)*, nor any concept of human profit (progress, personal growth, retribution), but only the vision of the reign of God in the teachings of Jesus. It is the vision of a communicative God and the outpouring of the Holy Spirit at Pentecost: and all of them *understood* the same gospel in their own languages.

NOTES

[1] Several introductions to the field of theological hermeneutics may be mentioned here: R. Palmer, *Hermeneutics: Interpretation Theory in Schleiermacher, Dilthey, Heidegger, and Gadamer*, Evanston, Northwestern UP, 1969; H. Frei, *The Eclipse of Biblical Narrative: A Study in Eighteenth and Nineteenth Century Hermeneutics*, New Haven, Yale UP, 1974; G. Lindbeck, *The Nature of Doctrine: Religion and Theology in a Postliberal Age*, Philadelphia,

Westminster, 1984; D. Tracy, *The Analogical Imagination: Christian Theology and the Culture of Pluralism*, New York, Crossroad, 1981; D. Tracy, *Plurality and Ambiguity: Hermeneutics, Religion, Hope*, San Francisco, Harper & Row, 1987; J. Bleicher, *Contemporary Hermeneutics: Hermeneutics as Method, Philosophy and Critique*, London, Routledge & Kegan Paul, 1987; Cl. von Bormann, "Hermeneutik", in *Theologische Realenzyklopädie*, vol. 15, Berlin/New York, De Gruyter, 1986, pp.108-37; J. Grondin, *Einführung in die philosophische Hermeneutik*, Darmstadt, Wissenschaftliche Buchgesellschaft, 1991; J. Grondin, *Der Sinn für Hermeneutik*, Darmstadt, Wissenschaftliche Buchgesellschaft, 1994; W. Jeanrond, *Theological Hermeneutics: Development and Significance*, London, SCM Press, 1991; W. Nethöfel, *Theologische Hermeneutik: Vom Mythos zu den Medien*, Neukirchen Vluyn, Neukirchener Verlag, 1992.

[2] W. Fauth, "Hermes", in K. Ziegler et al., *Der Kleine Pauly*, vol. 2, Munich, DTV, 1979, 1069-1076.

[3] von Bormann, "Hermeneutik".

[4] Cf. H. de Lubac, *Exégèse médiévale: Les quatres sens de l'ecriture*, Paris, Aubier, 1964; and H. Brinkmann, *Mittelalterliche Hermeneutik*, Darmstadt, Wissenschaftliche Buchgesellschaft, 1980, p.243.

[5] For a further elaboration of this comparison see A. Houtepen, "Ökumenische Hermeneutik. Auf der Suche nach Kriterien der Kohärenz im Christentum", in *Ökumenische Rundschau*, 39, 1990, pp.279-96.

[6] On F. Schleiermacher, see Jeanrond, pp.44ff., and Frei, pp.287ff. For Schleiermacher's text see H. Kimmerle, ed., *Fr. D.E. Schleiermacher: Hermeneutik*, Heidelberg, Winter, 1974.

[7] On W. Dilthey see Palmer, pp.115ff.; Jeanrond, pp.51ff. His texts on hermeneutics in W. Dilthey, *Gesammelte Schriften*, vol. 5, Stuttgart, Vandenhoeck & Ruprecht, 1964. Cf. J. de Mul, *De tragedie van de eindigheid. Diltheys hermeneutiek van het leven*, Kampen, Kok Agora, 1993.

[8] His text, taken from the article "The Understanding of Other Persons and Their Life-Expressions", in K. Mueller-Vollmer, ed., *The Hermeneutics Reader*, London, Blackwell, 1986, pp.152-64, runs as follows: "As the life of the mind only finds its complete, exhaustive and therefore objectively comprehensible expression in language, explication culminates in the interpretation of the written records of human existence. This art is the basis of philology. The science of this art is hermeneutics." Dilthey, though, was not the first to speak of hermeneutics as a theory of art. He could have borrowed it from Schleiermacher, cf. Grondin, *Einfuhrung*, p.22.

[9] E.g., *Cambridge Dictionary of Philosophy*, Cambrige, 1995, s.v. "Hermeneutics": "... the art or theory of interpretation, or... the interaction between interpreter and text that is part of the history of what is understood"; *Europäische Enzyklopädie zu Philosophie und Wissenschaft*, Hamburg, 1990, s.v. "Hermeneutik": "Eine Methodologie des rechten Verstehens und der sinngemässen Auslegung und Anwendung von Texten"; *Enzyklopädie Philosophie und Wissenschaftstheorie*, Mannheim/Wien/Zürich, Bibliographisches Institut, 1980-96, s.v. "Hermeneutik": 1. "Die Praxis der Auslegung (Interpretation), die zum Verstehen führt; 2. die Theorie der Auslegung als einer Reflexion auf die Bedingungen und Normen des Verstehens und seiner sprachlichen Kundgabe."

[10] P. Ricoeur, *Time and Narrative*, vol. I-III, Chicago, Chicago UP, 1984-88.

[11] K. Schori, *Das Problem der Tradition. Eine fundamentaltheologische Untersuchung*, Stuttgart, Kohlhammer, 1992.

[12] W. Cantwell Smith, *What Is Scripture? A Comparative Approach*, London, SCM Press, 1993.

[13] G. Lindbeck, *The Nature of Doctrine: Religion and Theology in a Postliberal Age*, London, SPCK, 1984.

[14] C.S. Song, "Five Stages Towards Christian Theology in the Multi-Cultural World", in A. Houtepen, ed., *The Living Tradition: Towards an Ecumenical Hermeneutics of the Christian Tradition*, IIMO Research Publication 41, Zoetermeer, Meinema, 1995, 87-110.

[15] *On the Way to Fuller Koinona*, Thomas F. Best and Günther Gassmann, eds, Geneva, WCC, 1994, report of section II, para. 20, p.241.

[16] W. Henn, "The Hierarchy of Truths Twenty Years Later", in *Theological Studies*, 48, 1987, pp.439-71.

[17] H.N. Bate, ed., *Proceedings of the World Conference Lausanne, August 3-21, 1927*, Garden City, NY, Doubleday, Doran & Co, 1928, Section IV, final report, pp.467-68. The latter part of this quotation was a redraft of an earlier, sharper statement, saying: "... our solemn and unanimous testimony that no external and written standards *can take the place* of that inward

and personal experience of union with the living Christ, *which is the only evidence of spiritual vitality, and that the object of our faith is not any statement about Christ but the Lord Jesus Christ Himself*" (author's itals). Orthodox representatives (Zankov, *ibid.*, p.192) objected to this opposition between *fides quae* (the creed) and *fides qua* (personal adherence to Christ).

Edinburgh, second world conference on Faith and Order, 3-18 August 1937, final report, section III, in L. Vischer, ed., *A Documentary History of the Faith and Order Movement 1927-1963*, St Louis, Bethany Press, 1963, p.44.

Ibid., pp.44-45.

Lund, third world conference on Faith and Order, final report, in Vischer, *Documentary History*, p.100.

Montreal, fourth world conference on Faith and Order 1963, final report on scripture, Tradition and traditions, §42, in G. Gassmann, ed., *Documentary History of Faith and Order, 1963-93*, Geneva, WCC, 1993, pp.10-11.

Montreal report, section II §45, in Gassmann, *Documentary History*, p.11.

Constitution on Divine Revelation, *Dei Verbum* §7, in A. Flannery, ed., *Vatican Council II: The Conciliar and Post Conciliar Documents*, Dublin, 1975.

Montreal, section II §§46-47, in Gassmann, *Documentary History*, p.11.

Authority in the Church (I Venice statement 1976; II Windsor statement 1981), in H. Meyer and L. Vischer, eds, *Growth in Agreement*, F&O Paper no. 108, New York/Geneva, 1984, pp.88-118.

Moscow statement 1976, *Growth in Agreement*, pp.41-46.

Peter in the New Testament 1973; Papal Primacy and the Universal Church 1974. Further dialogues listed in N. Ehrenström and G.Gassmann, *Confessions in Dialogue*, F&O Paper no. 74, pp.144-64. See also M. Haudel, *Die Bibel und die Einheit der Kirche*, Göttingen, 1993.

H.J. Sieben, *Die Konzilstheorie der Alten Kirche*, Paderborn, 1979.

Louvain report, "Interpreting the Sources of Our Faith", section IV, in *Faith and Order, Louvain 1971*, study reports and documents, Geneva, WCC, 1971, p.21.

Ibid., p.23.

How Does the Church Teach Authoritatively Today?, F&O Paper no. 91, Geneva, WCC, 1979. Cf. A. Houtepen, "Lehrautorität in der ökumenischen Diskussion", in *Verbindliches Lehren der Kirche heute*, Beiheft zur Ökumenischen Rundschau, no. 33, Frankfurt, Lembeck, 1978, pp.120-207.

Cf. *Giving Account of the Hope Today*, F&O Paper no. 81, Geneva, WCC, 1976; *Giving Account of the Hope Together*, F&O Paper no. 86, Geneva, WCC, 1978; *Confessing Our Faith Around the World I-IV*, F&O Paper nos 104, 120, 123, 126, Geneva, WCC, 1980-85.

Sharing in One Hope, F&O Paper no. 92, Geneva, WCC, 1978, p.258.

Ibid.

Baptism, Eucharist and Ministry, F&O Paper no. 111, Geneva, WCC, 1982, preface, p.ix.

Ibid., p.28.

The Roots of Our Common Faith, F&O Paper no. 119, Geneva, WCC, 1984, p.20.

M. Thurian, ed., *Churches Respond to BEM*, vols I-VI, Geneva, WCC, 1986-88; *Baptism, Eucharist & Ministry 1982-1990. Report on the Process and Responses*, F&O Paper no. 149, Geneva, WCC, 1990, part V: "Major Issues Demanding Further Study: Provisional Considerations", pp.131-42; A. Houtepen, "The Faith of the Church through the Ages", in A. Houtepen, ed., *The Living Tradition*, pp.49-56.

BEM and the Eucharist:
A Case Study in Ecumenical Hermeneutics

WILLIAM TABBERNEE

1. There are no uninterpreted texts. All texts (including scripture) are the products of interpretative communities and are read (and interpreted) by people who belong to and whose perspectives are shaped by interpretative communities. Ecumenical convergence documents, such as *Baptism, Eucharist and Ministry*,[1] are produced jointly through the collaboration of people who come from a large number of distinct interpretative communities, are read (and, one hopes, "received") by people within their separate interpretative communities, but also function as the standard by which those communities might themselves be "interpreted".

2. This case study examines the way in which scripture is used in the eucharist section of BEM (which from now on will be referred to as the Lima text) and how this use is viewed by the churches in the earliest stages of reception of the Lima text as evidenced by the official responses.[2] Particular attention is given to the way in which biblical concepts (including terminology) are employed and received in respect of historically divisive understandings on matters such as "sacrifice" and "real presence". The whole study, however, is geared towards identifying hermeneutical principles operative in the BEM process which enable both scholars and churches to transcend their own confessional stances. Consequently, factors other than scripture itself involved in this process are dealt with briefly, in order to identify further issues that may be helpful towards the development of guidelines for ecumenical hermeneutics.

I. THE USE OF SCRIPTURE
IN THE EUCHARIST SECTION OF BEM

1. Direct biblical quotations

3. Unlike the earlier Accra text on the eucharist,[3] the Lima text frequently makes its biblical basis explicit. The opening sentence (E1) declares the eucharist to be a gift to the church from the Lord, a declaration backed up by a lengthy scriptural quotation (1 Cor. 11:23-25). This approach, however, is not a form of "proof-texting" but a very effective use of the historical-critical method. St Paul's record of the oral

tradition of Jesus' words of institution, rather than the synoptic gospels' version of these words, is quoted (although the synoptic parallels are cited), showing a sensitivity on the part of the members of the steering committee which edited the text ultimately adopted at Lima to the fact that the Pauline passage was actually written earlier than the synoptic gospels.

4. The 1 Corinthians 11:23-25 passage is, however, the only lengthy direct quotation in the eucharist section of BEM. In E13, Jesus' words: "This is my body... this is my blood...", are quoted generically, without a specific biblical reference, and in E1 there is a three-word quotation from John 13:1. All other scriptural references in this section of BEM are citations rather than quotations. In addition, the Lima text on the eucharist makes a large number of biblical allusions and draws extensively on biblical concepts and terminology.

2. Biblical citations

5. The editors of the Lima text presuppose a certain amount of biblical literacy on the part of their readers. For example, when Jesus' feeding of the five thousand is mentioned as a sign of the imminent reign of God (E1), the relevant gospel stories are neither quoted nor cited. Similarly, no biblical quotations or references are provided for the allusion in E1 to the "last supper" or to the "post-resurrection meals". The editors, however, do not credit their readers with comprehensive biblical knowledge. For instance, while they assume that their readers would know that the story of the first passover (E1) could be found in Exodus 12, they supply a reference to the meal of the covenant on Mount Sinai (Ex. 24). In the same way, the biblical passages supporting the Christian understanding of the eucharist as "the new paschal meal of the church, the meal of the new covenant, which Christ gave to his disciples, as the *anamnesis* of his death and resurrection..." (E1) are taken for granted, but Revelation 19:9 is cited following the clause "as the anticipation of the supper of the Lamb" which completes the sentence. Presumably, the verse in Revelation is cited merely to direct the readers to a significant passage that mentions "the marriage supper of the Lamb". The impact of the reference, however, may well be taken by the readers as providing a direct biblical warrant for the claims about the eucharist made by the whole sentence, even though most of these claims have nothing to do with the contents of Revelation 19:9.

6. Similarly, the statement that "in accordance with Christ's promise, each baptized member of the body of Christ receives in the eucharist the assurance of the "forgiveness of sins" (E2) is supported with the citation of Matthew 26:28. This biblical text, part of Matthew's account of the

words of institution, while linking the cup with Christ's blood (defined as the "blood of the [new] covenant, which is poured out for many for the forgiveness of sins") does not explicitly confirm each of the claims in the Lima text's statement. All of these claims may be valid, but they do not follow directly from what is said in Matthew 26:28.

7. The same applies to the connection between many of the other statements in the Lima text on the eucharist and the citations from scripture which are appended to those statements. For example, E8 declares: "In thanksgiving and intercession, the church is united with the Son, its great High Priest and Intercessor (Rom. 8:34; Heb. 7:25)." The passages cited clearly identify Christ Jesus as intercessor, and the context of the Hebrews passage refers to Jesus metaphorically as priest. But neither passage explicitly states that the church is united with Christ in thanksgiving and intercession. E20 reads: "The eucharistic celebration demands reconciliation and sharing among all those regarded as brothers and sisters in the one family of God and is a constant challenge in the search for appropriate relationships in social, economic and political life (Matt. 5:23f.; 1 Cor. 10:16f.; 1 Cor. 11:20-22; Gal. 3:28)." The link between the scriptures cited and the eucharistic celebration varies considerably. The context of Matthew 5:23f. is not the eucharist, but the principle of reconciliation prior to common worship is applicable. The corporate nature of eucharistic celebration is certainly emphasized by both passages from 1 Corinthians. Galatians 3:28 obviously stresses the importance of abolishing inappropriate social, economic and political divisions, but the connection between it and eucharistic celebration is not as clear. Presumably, the link is made via the reference to baptism in Galatians 3:27.

8. In the Lima text on the eucharist, therefore, citations from scripture serve as a means of pointing readers to biblical references when the editors cannot take it for granted that the readers will be familiar with the passages which, at least in part, support the particular dimension of the eucharist set forth in the relevant paragraph of BEM. No attempt is made to provide an exhaustive list of references, nor are the passages cited meant to provide the warrant for claims made about the eucharist in the statement to which the citations are appended. The way in which the passages are interpreted and linked to the statement is normally left unexplained but can frequently be discerned by the order in which the passages are listed or juxtaposed.[4]

3. Biblical allusions

9. As already noted,[5] the Lima text on the eucharist draws on the biblical knowledge of its readers by alluding to a large number of biblical

stories and passages to provide the biblical context and a biblical warrant for its multidimensional portrayal of the institution, meaning and celebration of the eucharist. In addition to those mentioned above, this section of the Lima text includes (among others) allusions to the meals of Jesus' earthly ministry (E1, E24); the institution of the eucharist (E13, E13 comm., E14 [cf. E27]); Jesus' crucifixion (E1, E5, E6, E8, E8 comm.); resurrection (E1, E5, E6, E8, E14); promise to be with his own to the end of the world (E13); ascension (E6, E8); the sending of the Holy Spirit (E6); the second advent (E1, E6, E18); and the eternal reign of God (E1, E2, E3, E4, E5, E7, E18, E22 [cf. E27]).

10. As in the case of the use of biblical citations, the precise way in which the biblical stories or passages alluded to are interpreted and linked to the eucharist is normally not spelled out.

4. Biblical concepts

11. Biblical concepts (as contrasted with stories or specific passages) also are important to the Lima text's presentation of the eucharist alluded to in this section of BEM. They include the Trinity (E2, E14, E14 comm.); the "new covenant" (E1, E17); Christians as "the continuing people of God" (E1); the grace of God (E22); creation (E2); new creation (E18, E20, E22, E23); incarnation (E6, E8, E14 [cf. E21); redemption and salvation (E1, E2, E8); justification (E9); reconciliation (E4, E20, E21, E24) and sanctification (E2, E9, E17, E23 [cf. E19, E24, E25]); participation in God's [or Christ's] mission of peace and justice for the world (E20, E21, E22 [cf. E23], E24, E25, E26); and the "communion of saints" (E11 [cf. E27]).

12. The biblical concepts listed above are normally alluded to in the eucharist section of BEM without any detailed explanation or interpretation. However, more care is taken to explain the connection of the eucharist to three other biblical concepts: thanksgiving, memorial and invocation. These concepts, based on Greek terms found in the New Testament, are linked in the Lima text with Father, Christ and Holy Spirit, giving a trinitarian structure to the first part of the text's discussion of the meaning of the eucharist.

5. Biblical terminology

5.1. EUCHARISTIA

13. An essential element of the Lima text's presentation of the meaning of the eucharist is the emphasis on "The Eucharist as Thanksgiving to the Father" (E3-4 sub-heading). "The eucharist", declares BEM, "... is the great thanksgiving to the Father for everything accomplished in creation, redemption and sanctification, for everything accomplished by

God now in the church and the world... [and] for everything that God will accomplish..." (E3). Similarly, according to BEM, "the eucharist is the great sacrifice of praise by which the church speaks on behalf of the whole creation" (E4).

14. The editors of the final draft of this section presumably presupposed (perhaps incorrectly) a widespread liturgical familiarity with the term eucharist and its New Testament Greek roots. Hence, they do not provide New Testament references for its usage. The text does, however, spell out in detail how the "eucharist" functions as a "sacrifice of praise" (E4).

5.2. ANAMNESIS

15. Crucial to understanding BEM's treatment of the eucharist is its presentation of "The Eucharist as *Anamnesis* or Memorial of Christ" (E5-13 sub-heading). According to the Lima text, "the eucharist is the memorial of the crucified and risen Christ" (E5). This is described as "the living and effective sign of his sacrifice, accomplished once and for all on the cross and still operative on behalf of all humankind" (E5). The biblical idea of memorial as applied to the eucharist is then explained as referring to the "present efficacy of God's work when it is celebrated by God's people in a liturgy" (E5). The opening paragraph of BEM's section on the eucharist (E1) had already provided the biblical basis for the use of the word *anamnesis* as it is cited as the word translated by the English "remembrance" in the quotation from 1 Corinthians 11:23-25. It is referred to again in the description of the eucharist as the "meal... which Christ gave to his disciples as the *anamnesis* of his death and resurrection, as the anticipation of the supper of the Lamb" (E1). E7 makes clear that the Lima text understands *anamnesis* and anticipation as mutually inclusive terms rather than as parallel ones.

16. BEM stresses that *anamnesis* is not focused on the past. It is both representation and anticipation. God's work in redemption is not only remembered, but made present, proclaimed and celebrated, and its future completeness prayed for and anticipated (E5-9). Christians, who already participate in the benefits of all that Christ has accomplished (E6), are united to Christ in life, suffering and prayer (E7-11). They are to live lives acceptable to God as servants of reconciliation in the world (E10), nourished by the eucharist (E6, E9, E13), which is the sacrament of Christ's "real presence" (E13 and E13 comm.).

17. The editors of the final text at Lima, and those who adopted it, believed, with great optimism, that explaining the "biblical conception of memorial" (E8 comm. [cf. E5]) – in other words, recapturing the biblical meaning of *anamnesis* – would lead to greater understanding and

convergence on two divisive issues relating to the eucharist: namely "propitiatory sacrifice" and "the real presence". The commentary on E8 explains that the Roman Catholic theology of propitiatory sacrifice does not contradict the unique sacrifice of the cross; rather, that unrepeatable act is "made actual in the eucharist and presented before the Father in the intercession of Christ and of the church for all humanity". The biblical concept of *anamnesis*, it was hoped, should help to clarify the doctrine of propitiatory sacrifice and to eliminate some of the misunderstandings inherent in the use of the term sacrifice.

18. Similarly, the commentary on E13 appears based on the hope that what had been explained about *anamnesis* in E5-13 would lead to a convergence on the understanding that Christ is really present in the eucharist while enabling different traditions to continue to hold varying views regarding the mysterious way in which this presence is linked to the bread and the wine.

5.3. EPIKLESIS

19. Convergence on the "real and unique presence of Christ in the eucharist" (E15 comm.), it was also hoped, should be facilitated by a greater appreciation of "The Eucharist as Invocation of the Spirit" (E14-18 sub-heading). As with *eucharistia* and *anamnesis*, the term *epiklesis* is a biblical one, although its use in the New Testament is normally verbal (for example, see 2 Cor. 1:23). According to BEM: "The Spirit makes the crucified and risen Christ really present to us in the eucharistic meal, fulfilling the promise contained in the words of institution" (E14). "Being assured by Jesus' promise in the words of institution that it will be answered, the church prays to the Father for the gift of the Holy Spirit in order that the eucharistic event may be a reality: the real presence of the crucified and risen Christ..." (E14). And again: "The church... confidently invokes the Spirit, in order that it may be sanctified and renewed... and empowered to fulfill its mission in the world" (E17).

The commentary on E14 stresses that: "There is an intrinsic relationship between the words of institution, Christ's promise, and the *epiklesis*, the invocation of the Spirit, in the liturgy", and expresses the hope that a recovery of an understanding of *epiklesis* as the invocation of the Spirit both on the believing community and on the elements of bread and wine may help the churches to overcome difficulties concerning "a special moment of consecration". The commentary on E15 describes in more detail that some churches have emphasized that the work of the Spirit, along with the words of institution, effect a change whereby "there is no longer just ordinary bread and wine but the body and blood of Christ".

6. Summary

20. The Lima text on the eucharist intentionally and explicitly uses scripture to support components of its presentation of the meaning and celebration of the eucharist. Its method of utilizing scripture is economic rather than expansive. It takes for granted that readers have a basic familiarity with scriptural stories, passages and references. Consequently, it rarely quotes scriptures directly, preferring to point readers to relevant passages by means of biblical citations. Even these are omitted when it may be assumed that readers will not have any difficulties in identifying the intended passages. Biblical allusions abound and biblical concepts and terms (especially when these terms are also rooted in liturgical tradition) are also used and, where deemed necessary, explained.

21. The Lima text's method of using scripture in the eucharist section has four major advantages for an ecumenical convergence document. Firstly, its direct biblical quotations and numerous biblical references and allusions, as well as its biblical terminology, emphasize that the convergence statement on the eucharist achieved after more than fifty years of ecumenical discussions is solidly based on scripture. Secondly, by drawing on the readers' own biblical literacy, it establishes a direct connection between the document and the readers, thus potentially facilitating the process of reception. Thirdly, by providing only minimal explicit interpretation of the biblical passages alluded to or cited, the Lima text enables readers to interpret these passages from within their own context in ways that are compatible with the document's own conclusions. Fourthly, by providing more explicit explanations of the way in which biblical terminology (such as *anamnesis*) is understood in the document, the Lima text, at least theoretically, provides a means by which the biblical concept underlying these terms may be recaptured and serve as the means by which misunderstandings and divisions regarding certain aspects of the eucharist may be overcome.

22. The Lima text's method of using scripture, however, also has some potential disadvantages for an ecumenical convergence document on the eucharist. Some readers may have expected more direct quotations from scripture for the document to be recognized as truly biblically based. Others may have expected their favourite passages on specific issues to have been cited. More importantly, the minimal interpretative comments in respect of citations and allusions means that it is not always immediately clear how specific passages have been interpreted by the scholars who produced BEM and how they arrived at particular conclusions about the eucharist. The hermeneutical principles involved can often be reconstructed, but normally only as a consequence of "reading between the lines".

II. RESPONSES TO THE USE OF SCRIPTURE
IN THE EUCHARIST SECTION OF BEM

23. The official responses from the churches[6] include widespread appreciation of the biblical material contained in the Lima text's section on the eucharist. For example, the response of the Evangelical Church of the River Plate (Argentina) declares: "We express our satisfaction at the enrichment brought to our church by the consideration of all the aspects dealt with in this section, particularly its broad biblical foundation" (V.176).[7]

24. Some responses, while indicating general appreciation, also articulate concerns. The Church of Ireland (Anglican), for example, initially reports: "Much of the strength of Lima seems to us to lie in its summaries of the New Testament evidence. These provide a concrete conspectus of New Testament theology" (I.66). The church continues, however, by saying that it considers much of that which is included in the section on the eucharist "is essentially theological interpretation, not directly based on the evidence of the New Testament" *(ibid.)*.[8]

The Waldensian and Methodist churches in Italy acknowledge "the serious effort that has been made to give a scriptural basis..." (II.245), but raise a number of hermeneutical questions concerning the way in which scripture has been used in the Lima text.[9] The Swiss Protestant Church Federation is disappointed that in the Lima text the Bible still "appears as a collection of timeless pieces of information, whereas it would have been more desirable to meet the biblical authors as partners in ecumenical discussion" (VI.77). The Anglican Church of the Southern Cone criticizes the section on the eucharist for "insufficient application of the biblical guidelines" (I.59), and the Church of Jesus Christ in Madagascar considers that "the scriptural references in all the commentaries in BEM are quite inadequate" (III.188).[10]

25. Some responses point to biblical texts (such as 1 Cor. 11:26) which appear to their churches to have been overlooked[11] or texts which, while cited, could (also) have been cited elsewhere in the section on the eucharist to support or strengthen particular statements.[12] A few statements within the section on the eucharist are considered by some churches to lack biblical foundation.[13] On the whole, however, the biblical quotations, citations, allusions, concepts and terminology which are part and parcel of the Lima text's treatment of the eucharist are warmly welcomed and appreciated by the churches. Specific comments on each of the ways in which BEM utilizes scripture provide some helpful insights towards developing ecumenical hermeneutics.

1. Direct biblical quotations

26. There is no doubt that placing the quotation from 1 Corinthians 11:23-24 almost at the beginning of E1 was largely responsible for setting the "biblical tone" of the Lima text's section on the eucharist and that this, in turn, elicited many of the positive comments from the churches about the biblical foundation of BEM's treatment of the eucharist.

27. The historical-critical approach inherent in quoting 1 Corinthians 11:23-24 rather than the synoptic gospels' accounts of the institution of the eucharist was well received by the churches. The Evangelical Lutheran Church of Hanover, for example, is appreciative of the fact that "the *verba testamenti* traditioned by St Paul are explicitly quoted (1 Cor. 11:23-25)" and comments that "the sentence 'the church receives the eucharist as a gift from the Lord' (§1) clearly summarizes the present result of the exegetic and systematic-theological discussion of the holy communion as being a gift of the Lord" (IV.50).[14] The Evangelical-Lutheran Church of Mecklenburg declares similarly: "We are convinced that we are closest to the origins of the Lord's supper in the tradition presented by Paul in 1 Corinthians" (V.157). The report of this church is pleased that this tradition is cited in E1, but regrets that it is not dealt with adequately thereafter *(ibid.)*.

28. The Waldensian Evangelical Church of the River Plate (Uruguay) concurs with E1's statement that the eucharist is a gift, but interprets 1 Corinthians 11:23-24 differently: "... We think that the passage in 1 Corinthians 11 speaking of Paul receiving something from the Lord does not refer to the sacrament but to the teaching which he now wishes to share with the other believers of his time" (IV.119).

29. That biblical quotations may be interpreted quite differently raises two separate but related issues for ecumenical hermeneutics: authority and applicability. The basic question inherent in the issue of authority is well formulated by the response of the United Protestant Church of Belgium: "What is the authority of the scriptural texts quoted, if different and indeed contrary theologies interpret them by applying their own particular hermeneutical principles?"[15] The basic question inherent in the related issue of applicability is the extent to which a biblical text, which is open to more than one interpretation, may be used as backing for a particular statement. The report from the Religious Society of Friends (Quakers) in Great Britain, for example, states: "... while quotations from the Bible may illuminate a truth for us, we would not use them to prove a truth" (IV.219). It also offers the comment "that occasionally the Lima text shows too little discrimination in the evidential use of scripture" *(ibid.)*.

30. Biblical authority cannot be treated as an abstract concept. It always relates to particular matters of faith or practice in the context of competing authorities. In order to determine whether a particular biblical text is "authoritative", it is crucial to ask: "Authoritative for what?" and "authoritative in what sense when seen alongside other 'authorities' such as traditional formulations of the faith?"[16] The various churches may (and do) give different answers to these questions. Consequently, certain biblical texts may be considered "authoritative" for a particular matter of faith or practice by some churches but not by others because of a different understanding of the meaning of these texts. Even when the same texts are seen to be authoritative for the same matter of faith or practice, the weight given to this authority over and against the weight of other authorities may (and does) vary as the different churches articulate their view of the matter under consideration.

31. Ecumenical hermeneutics, as distinct from (but not incompatible with) confessionally based hermeneutics, needs to take into account (and, indeed, rejoice in) the fact that there may be and often is more than one legitimate interpretation of a specific biblical text in relationship to a particular matter of faith and practice and that a different authoritative weight may be (and often is) given to such a text by different churches.

32. In ecumenical hermeneutics, a scriptural text may be considered as authoritative for a particular matter of faith or practice even if confessional hermeneutics interprets that text variously – as long as those interpretations fall within a range of interpretations shown to be legitimate by generally accepted hermeneutical principles. In other words, the "authoritativeness" of a text is not to be ruled out because the interpretation of that text by one church differs from that of another. Both interpretations may be legitimate and may enrich one another. Moreover, the interplay of the two interpretations may provide a hitherto unrecognized valuable insight which may lead to greater convergence.

33. Similarly, in ecumenical hermeneutics, the applicability of a scriptural text is not to be ruled out even if a specific interpretation, based on confessional hermeneutics, deems that text to be irrelevant to a particular matter of faith or practice. As long as the range of legitimate interpretations of the text includes interpretations which are applicable to the matter under consideration, the text may (and should) be included in an ecumenical understanding of the matter at hand.

34. A major task of ecumenical hermeneutics in respect of the related issues of the authority and applicability of biblical quotations (and other references) is to identify the acceptable range of diverse, yet legitimate, interpretations of particular texts in relationship to specific dimensions of faith and practice such as the eucharist. The Lima text undertook this

task primarily by applying the hermeneutical principles inherent in the historical-critical approach to scripture. This, on the whole, was well received by the churches – or, at least, by those persons responsible for the final draft of the official responses (many of whom had received a theological education based on the historical-critical method). From now on, this task will need to be achieved by using a much wider spectrum of methodologies, such as reader-response theory, narrative theology, the rediscovery of the importance of orality, structural-linguistic analyses and the utilization of a host of other methodological tools including those provided by the major expressions of post-modernism.

2. Biblical citations

35. Because of the paucity of direct biblical quotations in the Lima text's section on the eucharist, the generally positive response to this section's biblical content must have been based largely on the way churches viewed this section's use of biblical citations. The citations, however, raised for some churches two further issues for ecumenical hermeneutics: choice and context – as illustrated by the response of the Waldensian and Methodist Churches in Italy:

> [The] biblical references, at times well chosen but cited without considering the setting in which each of these texts is found in the varying writings and levels of the New Testament, are immersed in a general context which alters and, not infrequently, contradicts their meaning: biblical texts having equal value but found in different New Testament contexts and having different theological value are put side by side; they are thus objectively in an optic which tends towards ecclesiastical synthesis of different and often opposed elements (II.245-46).

36. No explanations are given in the Lima text regarding the choice of a certain biblical citation (or citations) to support a particular statement, nor, in the case of multiple citations, regarding the order in which these citations are listed. In many instances, the reasons behind these choices are obvious, but as they are not spelled out explicitly they are subject to challenge. As already noted,[17] it is not always clear whether the citations are meant to support the whole of the statement or only part of it. Given the potentially wide range of legitimate interpretations of biblical texts, the effectiveness of ecumenical hermeneutics will be enhanced if the specific reasons underlying the choice of biblical citations for specific purposes is made more explicit – even at the expense of brevity.

37. Similarly, it is important in ecumenical hermeneutics to be as clear as possible about the way in which the particular passages cited are

dealt with contextually. The Church of the Brethren (USA) is not alone in expressing concern that the Lima text speaks of eucharist "in a context that is quite different from the context Brethren find in New Testament writings and witnesses" (VI.110).[18] The complaints in some of the responses about "the questionable use of certain Bible citations"[19] could have been averted by more detailed exegetical comments of the type contained in the "Draft Classifications and Comments on Critical Points",[20] but this would have made BEM a longer (and different!) document.

38. The Lima text's use of the two citations in E2 received the most criticism. The Union of Evangelical Free Churches in the GDR (Baptists), for example, reports:

> We do not share the conviction which in §2 is based on Matthew 26:28 and John 6:51-58, that every baptized member of the body of Christ receives in the eucharist the assurance of the forgiveness of sins and the pledge of eternal life. According to our understanding, the assurance of the forgiveness of sins is a pneumatic event through the agency of the risen Lord Jesus Christ... Bread and cup are but the signs of his sacrificed life. John 6:47 belongs unquestionably to John 6:51-58. Here it is without question *faith* in Jesus Christ, and not participation in the eucharist, which is the condition for eternal life (IV. 196).[21]

From a completely different ecclesial tradition, the Roman Catholic Church comments:

> The link between the eucharist and forgiveness of sins is grounded [in BEM] on Matthew 26:28. But the "assurance of the forgiveness of sins" through the eucharist is preconditioned by the state of reconciliation with God in the church... In our understanding the previous reconciliation would take place through the sacrament of penance (VI.18).

39. The way in which biblical citations are understood, therefore, is affected not only by the biblical context from which they arise but also by the ecclesial context in which they are received. Ecumenical hermeneutics must take into account both these contextual dimensions. Particularly challenging in this respect is the search for a way by which "sacramentalist" and "non-sacramentalist" ecclesial communities may enrich each other's understanding of Christian life and worship on the basis of their respective understanding of biblical texts.

3. Biblical allusions

40. The decision by the editors of the final draft of the Lima text to take for granted a great deal of biblical literacy on the part of their intended readers appears to have been a wise one, especially as a means of capturing attention and establishing rapport. The Evangelical

Lutheran Church of Iceland comments that in the section on the eucharist "biblical images are used extensively... [and] their richness draws our attention,... the central issues are always in focus" (IV.62). The Evangelical Lutheran Church in Bavaria notes that "the use of biblical images makes the text appear familiar to many parishioners..." (IV.25). The Moravian Church in America, Southern Province, finds "the constant use of biblical imagery..." to be both helpful and necessary (II.257).[22] This church, like the United Church of Christ [USA] (II.329), however, expresses the view that, in certain instances, the biblical allusions could have been more explicit (II.257).

41. On the whole, the responses from the churches do not disagree with the way in which the Lima text draws on biblical allusions to support its various statements about the eucharist. The main exception is that some churches question the significance, for understanding the eucharist, placed on the meals which Jesus had during his ministry.[23] Other churches, however, see this as "a broadening and deepening of our understanding of communion"[24] and as compatible with the findings of modern exegetics.[25]

42. The overwhelming positive responses by the churches to the extensive use of biblical allusions in the Lima text illustrates the importance of drawing on a common biblical heritage. To facilitate effective ecumenical hermeneutics, care should be taken, however, to make the allusions as explicit as possible. Hermeneutics, including ecumenical hermeneutics, has to do with communication as well as interpretation.

4. Biblical concepts

43. Appreciation is shown in the responses for the way in which general biblical concepts are utilized in the Lima text's section on the eucharist. Occasional criticisms are related to issues of emphasis rather than content. An analysis of the precise way in which the various churches respond to each concept is outside the scope of this paper. Of great significance for this case study in ecumenical hermeneutics, however, is the way in which the churches responded to the Lima text's use of three specific biblical concepts related to three Greek terms (thanksgiving, memorial and invocation) to help overcome old divisions about the meaning and practice of the eucharist.

5. Biblical terminology
5.1. EUCHARISTIA

44. Although the word *eucharistia* is used in the New Testament, many Reformed or Free churches report that for them the term "eucharist" is unfamiliar, or at least less common, than the phrases "the

Lord's supper" or "holy communion".[26] For some the term carries unacceptable overtones or emphases, especially in being associated too closely with "a certain type of communion celebration"[27] and, hence, "tendentious".[28] For others, the term conveys too great a stress on human (rather than divine) activity.[29]

45. A major problem for some Reformed or Free churches with the term eucharist appears to be that although *eucharistia* is a New Testament Greek word, its New Testament usage is not seen as being linked closely to the Lord's supper – at least not to the extent of describing the whole celebration. The Waldensian and Methodist churches in Italy go as far as to say that the term eucharist "is never used in the New Testament in reference to the Lord's supper" (II.249). That the term is seen as having been derived more from liturgical tradition than from the Bible is clear from a comment by the Union of Evangelical Free Churches in the GDR:

> For our free church, the terms "supper", "Lord's supper" and "breaking of bread", which are tied to biblical tradition, stand in the foreground. Usage of the term "eucharist" is not common, although an old, legitimate tradition... stands behind it" (IV.195).

Some Reformed or Free churches, however, report that while the term eucharist is unfamiliar to them, it provides a welcome opportunity for gaining a broader understanding of the sacrament.[30] The American Baptist Churches in the USA, for example, report that they "recognize the biblical validity of understanding this meal in terms of thanksgiving" (III.260) and "particularly appreciate the manner in which the section on 'the eucharist as thanksgiving to the Father' deals with many of the painful divisions among Christians over the idea of 'sacrifice' in connection with the Lord's supper" *(ibid.)*.

5.2. ANAMNESIS

46. As already noted,[31] members of the Faith and Order commission were particularly optimistic that the Lima text's use of *anamnesis* would help to avoid divisive controversy on "sacrifice" and "the real presence" in the eucharist and, indeed, to heal some of these old divisions. On the whole, the responses indicate that the commission's optimism was justified.

47. More so than with the term *eucharistia*, the churches that report unfamiliarity with the term *anamnesis* recognize it as a biblical concept directly related to the Lord's supper, but one that perhaps needed to have been defined with greater clarity or precision.[32] Such a call for greater clarification of the term is, understandably, not included in the responses

of the Roman Catholic Church and the Orthodox churches. The Roman Catholic Church comments that "the presentation of the 'eucharist' as *anamnesis* or memorial of Christ is well done. The biblical concept of memorial is employed in a precise way" (VI.19). Some Orthodox churches[33] and the Church of England,[34] however, call for a closer relationship between *anamnesis* and *epiklesis* than is, at first sight, apparent in the Lima text.

48. Although some churches found the Lima text's use of *anamnesis* too "sweeping",[35] "unduly extended",[36] "concerned with expanding a liturgical term and justifying traditional practice, rather than the use of the word in the biblical sense",[37] many churches found it extremely helpful for broadening their own general understanding of the eucharist.[38] They welcomed its potential for overcoming the divisions of the past.[39] The extent to which churches viewed this potential as having been realized in respect of "sacrifice" and "real presence", however, varied from church to church.

a) Sacrifice

49. Churches agree unanimously that the language of "sacrifice" is appropriate for describing Christ's death on the cross. The main issue at stake, however, is the extent to which the eucharist, as "the memorial of the crucified and risen Christ" (E5), may be viewed as "the sacrament of the unique sacrifice of Christ" (E8) in which Christ's sacrifice is "made actual and presented before the Father in the intercession of Christ and of the church for all humanity" (E8).

50. The Lima text's explanation of *anamnesis* in terms of "representation and anticipation expressed in thanksgiving and intercession" (E8) is viewed by many churches as successfully providing a means of showing that the Roman Catholic and Orthodox positions and those of the Reformed churches on sacrifice are not mutually exclusive.[40] The Presbyterian Church of Wales, for example, sees in the Lima text's use of the word *anamnesis* "a safeguard against mere memorialism on the one hand, and unacceptable sacrificial language on the other and a consequent way forward for further dialogue and understanding" (II.170). The Methodist Church of Southern Africa reports that "the treatment of the sacrament as *anamnesis* or memorial is very helpful and should help us to overcome fears of the 'eucharistic sacrifice'" (II.239). The Federation of the Evangelical Churches in the GDR, similarly, sees the use of *anamnesis* as being "helpful towards finally overcoming the long-standing and passionate controversies about communion as 'atoning sacrifice'" (V.134).

51. That such positive statements are more than rhetoric is evident from the response of the Evangelical Church of the Augsburg Confes-

sion in the Socialist Republic of Romania. This church not only welcomes "the attempt to use the central concept of recollective and anticipatory memorial (*anamnesis*) to settle interconfessional controversies about the sacrificial character of the eucharist" (IV.85). It also reports real "reception" on this issue: "The statements on *anamnesis* prompt us to reappropriate this concept, which in our traditional reflections has been interpreted quite differently" (*ibid.*, 87 [cf. 85]).

52. Other churches declare a willingness to study further the issue of sacrifice in light of the biblical concept of memorial with a view to further convergence.[41]

53. For some, however, the use of *anamnesis* in relationship to "sacrifice" is only partially successful. The Anglican Church of Canada approves of the way in which *anamnesis* is used as a "working term" but reports that some within this church question the treatment of "sacrifice" (II.39).[42] The Presbyterian Church in Canada reports that, for its constituency, E8 commentary is "ambiguous and leaves us wondering whether the eucharist is considered by the drafters of the document as a propitiatory sacrifice or not. The Reformed response would be that it is not" (II.155). According to the American Lutheran Church, "the disproportionate emphasis on the language and theology of representation/anamnesis... tends to emphasize the cultic action of the community over the gift and promise of God in Christ in the sacrament" (II.82).[43]

b) "Real presence"

54. The use of *anamnesis* as an appropriate way to understand the presence of Christ in the eucharist and to overcome past divisions found wide acceptance in the churches. According to the Christian Church (Disciples of Christ): "The rediscovery of the biblical meaning of *anamnesis* in the ecumenical discussion offers a way in which 'real presence' may be widely embraced" (I.117).[44] For some, however, certain significant issues were not resolved by means of this approach.

55. The Russian Orthodox Church's response points out that in that church's view, the Lima text does not take seriously the position of those churches that believe in transubstantiation: "The document recognizes *anamnesis* as the essence of the eucharistic meal, whereas the Orthodox church confesses as the essence of the eucharist the transubstantiation of the holy gifts" (II.8).[45]

Some Lutheran responses, while not calling for transubstantiation, point out that, from their perspective, there is not sufficient emphasis on the presence of Christ in the elements. For example, the Lutheran Church of Australia declares:

We believe that no presentation of the eucharist can be regarded as satisfactory that does not give clear expression to the real presence of the body and blood of Christ (not merely the person of Christ) in the bread and wine of the elements, and to the physical eating and drinking of the body and blood of Christ (not only an eating by faith), including the *manducatio indignorum* (II.91).[46]

56. For other churches, however, the link between the physical presence of the risen Christ with the eucharist is too close in the Lima text's utilization of the concept of *anamnesis*. The Union of Welsh Independents, for example, can only subscribe to the wording of E13 if the sense is symbolic and conveys the view that "the bread and wine are sacraments of the real *spiritual* presence of Christ" rather than permit the possibility of belief in transubstantiation (III.273).

57. The Union of Welsh Independents also raises the question of the lack of relationship between the Lima text's approach and the view of "those whose belief is that Christ's body is glorified in heaven and is not ubiquitously present wherever the bread and wine are laid out for that rite of the eucharist" (*ibid.*, 274).

5.3. EPIKLESIS

58. As with the other terms discussed above, a number of churches report unfamiliarity with "*epiklesis*",[47] some challenging the biblical basis of the way in which the term is used and applied to the work of the Holy Spirit in the Lima text. The Estonian Evangelical Lutheran Church, for example, states: "The great importance of *epiklesis* is not clearly demonstrated; there is also no biblical proof" (IV.43-44).[48]

59. The Baptist Union of Scotland deems the whole idea of *epiklesis* unnecessary: "We question the need to invoke the Spirit. According to our reading of the New Testament he is ever present" (III.238), and the Lutheran Church in Hungary considers *epiklesis* irrelevant to Christian unity (III.129).

60. In general, however, the Lima text's use of *epiklesis* was welcomed, even by those churches for whom the concept was a novel one,[49] especially because it challenged them to expand their understanding of eucharist.[50] The Evangelical Lutheran Church of Iceland, for example, reports: "The Lima statement emphasizes the role of the Holy Spirit in making Christ really present in the eucharist. This emphasis is new to us" (IV.64). Nevertheless, that church goes on to declare: "We want to express a most sincere desire to deal thoroughly with the question[s] which §§14 through 18 raise" (*ibid.*).

61. As noted earlier,[51] the Lima text's sub-section on "The Eucharist as Invocation of the Spirit" utilizes the concept of *epiklesis*, among other things, in order to help resolve two related, previously divisive, issues:

the "real and unique presence of Christ in the eucharist" (E15 comm.)
and "a special moment of consecration" (E14 comm.).

a) "Real and unique presence"

62. Along with the use of *anamnesis*, many churches found the use
of *epiklesis* helpful in gaining a non-divisive way of understanding the
"real presence". The report of the Evangelical Church of the Augsburg
Confession in the Socialist Republic of Romania is illustrative of the
positive reaction by churches that would not normally have used the
term *epiklesis*:

> We welcome the emphasis on the activity of the Holy Spirit, since this makes
> it clear that the church has no control over the gifts of the sacrament but prays
> for the presence of God. In this connection, we are delighted with the empha-
> sis on the real presence of Christ in the Lord's supper. We thereby affirm our
> repudiation of any magical or mechanical view of Christ's presence in the
> eucharist (commentary §14) (IV.86).[52]

The Roman Catholic Church, with its long-standing practice of
invoking the Holy Spirit as part of its eucharistic liturgy, similarly com-
mends the Lima text's use of the concept of *epiklesis* in this sub-section,
as long as this concept is "interpreted in the light of the implication of
the theology of the *epiklesis* of the Spirit, as founded in patristic teaching" (VI.21).

63. A major concern for some Reformed and Free churches, however,
is the inclusion of the adjective "unique" in respect of the presence of
Christ in the eucharist. Even when viewed in connection with the term
epiklesis (or *anamnesis*), a number of churches consider the idea of
"unique presence" unbiblical[53] and definitely problematic if taken in the
sense of superior.[54] For these churches, Christ's presence in the eucharist
may be different in kind but is not inferior to Christ's presence in the
gathered Christian community[55] or in the proclaimed word.[56]

b) "Special moment of consecration"

64. Locating the consecration of the elements within the epikletic
character of the whole eucharist (E16) and as part of the invocation of
the Spirit on the whole community (E17) was a helpful insight to many
churches, diminishing for them even further the fear of the eucharist
being interpreted as a magical rite linked to a specific moment of consecration. The Mar Thoma Syrian Church of Malabar (India), for instance,
welcomes the Lima text's use of *epiklesis* in dealing with this issue:
"This makes relating the moment of consecration with the rest of the
service important" (IV.9).[57]

65. For a few churches, nonetheless, the way in which BEM utilizes *epiklesis* still contains the possibility of encompassing unacceptable interpretations on the matter of consecration. The American Lutheran Church, for example, believes that:

> The statement that the Spirit makes Christ present... runs the risk of removing the mystery of Christ's presence in the sacrament as a whole and rather identifying it with a particular moment in a ritual of consecration (II.82).[58]

This, of course, is exactly the opposite of what the Faith and Order commission had hoped would have been the reaction to this subsection.

66. Some churches saw in the treatment of *epiklesis* hints of transubstantiation,[59] an overemphasis on human activity,[60] or an unacceptable "sacramentarian doctrine of grace".[61]

67. Two issues related to terminology, important for ecumenical hermeneutics, are raised by the churches' responses to the use of "eucharist", *anamnesis* and *epiklesis* in the Lima text: familiarity and neutrality. Lack of familiarity with a term does not seem to be as important as neutrality of meaning for that term. Churches appear to be more willing to adopt unfamiliar terms and have their understandings broadened by the insights inherent in those terms, if the terms do not already carry for them negative overtones or emphases. If these terms can be shown to have a biblical basis, readiness to adopt them may be enhanced, but even "biblical terminology" needs to be shown to be applicable to the matter under discussion. The mere fact that a word occurs in the New Testament is not determinative.

6. Alleged absence of biblical foundation

68. As well as commenting on the way in which scripture or biblical terminology is used in the Lima text's section on the eucharist, a number of churches comment on statements made in the text which are not supported in the text by specific quotations, citations or allusions and which the respondents do not consider to have biblical warrant. Often, the respondents will give a scriptural reference for the alternative view they put forward. Typical is the following comment by the Baptist Union of Scotland:

> We question the statement: "Every Christian receives this gift of salvation through communion in the body and blood of Christ" (2). We do not find this true to the New Testament, where salvation is through faith in response to the gift of God's grace in Jesus Christ (Eph. 2:8-9) (III.237).[62]

Similarly, the Union of Welsh Independents affirms: "There is nothing in the New Testament to justify [the assertion that 'the eucharist embraces all aspects of life' (E20)]" (III.275). The Presbyterian Church of Rwanda comments: "The idea that Christ's presence in the conse-crated elements continues after the celebration [E32] is not biblical" (III.184).[63] The Salvation Army declares in respect of E26:

> We are bound to challenge the totally unscriptural view that "the eucharist brings into the present age a new reality which transforms Christians into the image of Christ". It is the work of the Holy Spirit to create the image of Christ in holiness of life, independent of outward observance (IV.245).

The Presbyterian Church of Wales reports: "We would welcome a record of the textual basis for the eucharist-creation connection in §3..." (II.169).

69. A significant issue for ecumenical hermeneutics arises from all this: comprehensiveness. It appears important, at least to many churches, that all significant statements about matters such as the eucharist be sup-portable by biblical teaching.

70. The need for comprehensiveness is also illustrated by the appeal, on the part of some churches, to biblical material not included in the Lima text. For example, the Church of the Brethren, in referring to that church's celebration of the agape meal ("love feast") and its practice of footwashing, points out that "our common scriptural heritage is richer than the eucharistic discussion in the BEM text" (VI.110).[64]

7. Summary

71. The Lima text's use of scripture in the section on the eucharist was, on the whole, extremely well received and appreciated by the churches. In particular, the text's use of the biblically based terms *anam-nesis* and *epiklesis* was successful in helping churches to deal with pre-viously divisive matters in a constructive manner. Although some churches expressed disagreements with or doubts about the way in which scripture was used in relation to specific paragraphs or statements, the insights these churches provided through their responses are helpful not only for understanding the eucharist but also in terms of "ecumeni-cal hermeneutics".

III. OTHER FACTORS

1. Scripture, Tradition and traditions

72. The responses from the churches show clearly that in evaluating the Lima text's statements on the eucharist, they were influenced to a large extent by the position they took on the relationship between scrip-ture and Tradition. The report on the process and responses to BEM,

published in 1990, contains an excellent analysis of the churches' responses in terms of "Scripture, Tradition and traditions".[65] This analysis need not be repeated here. Suffice it to say that whereas some churches argued in one way or another for the normative authority of scripture in judging the adequacy of the various statements in the Lima text on the eucharist,[66] other churches gave greater weight to the importance of patristic,[67] Reformed[68] and contemporary[69] insights.

73. Ecumenical hermeneutics must provide a way by which the various churches can clarify for themselves the relationship which they see between scripture, Tradition and traditions and the relative weight they give to each.

2. Perspective

74. Commenting from the vantage point of their own particular ecclesial heritage, some churches in their responses declare the Lima text's treatment of the eucharist to be "too Catholic"[70] (or "insufficiently Reformed"[71]), "too patristic",[72] "too sacramentalist",[73] or "too European" (or "too Western") in that insufficient consideration is given to the contemporary contributions of "younger" and "minority" churches.[74]

75. Another issue for ecumenical hermeneutics, therefore, is to help churches to identify the perspective from which they view the perspective of others and to learn to see in those perspectives dimensions of authentic Christian faith and practice.

3. "Ecumenical tradition"

76. The responses to the Lima text on the eucharist (and to BEM as a whole) exhibit some confusion regarding the first question addressed to the churches by the Faith and Order commission:

> The commission would be pleased to know as precisely as possible the extent to which your church can recognize in this text the faith of the church through the ages (p.x).

Many churches consider the question ambiguous; respondents are often uncertain as to whether "the faith of the church through the ages" is intended to be taken as historically descriptive or theologically normative. Consequently, some churches reformulate the question in terms of "historic faith"[75] whereas others reformulate it in terms of "the faith of the original church, as we find this faith testified in the New Testament".[76] The Church of England understands the question to refer to "the apostolic faith of the universal church: that is that faith which is 'uniquely revealed in the holy scriptures and set forth in the catholic creeds, which faith the church is called upon to proclaim afresh in each generation'..." (III.31). In this understanding, which reflects accurately the way in which the Faith and Order commission intended the phrase to be understood, "apostolic faith" is not restricted to the "apostolic age" of the New Testament but incorporates "apostolic faith" "through the ages" including the "present age".

77. Issues important for ecumenical hermeneutics inherent in this are: continuity and discontinuity. Granted that not all expressions of faith are authentically "apostolic" and that some churches (for example, those of the Reformation) frequently stress the importance of discontinuity as a means of calling the church back to authentic apostolic faith, there exists also that apostolic faith which is signified by "the continuity of the Christian faith which manifests itself in more than one way in the lives of the different churches".[77] As well as taking account of the way in which apostolic faith has been revealed and recorded in scripture, the development of an effective ecumenical hermeneutic must take account of this "common Christian Tradition" and produce criteria by which to identify and interpret it correctly while, at the same time, enabling this "common Christian Tradition" to inform and re-evaluate the individual churches' traditions which, as mentioned above, have often developed justifiably as a result of historic discontinuity.

78. As Max Thurian has pointed out clearly in his introduction to volume 1 of the responses: "The fruit of a common 'reading' of holy scripture and of the great Tradition interpretative of the word of God, by the churches" is what may rightly be called an "ecumenical tradition".[78] The Faith and Order commission's question, quoted above, asked the churches to identify the extent to which they recognized in the Lima text this "ecumenical tradition". That this was not universally understood illustrates the need for ecumenical hermeneutics to incorporate pedagogical dimensions which communicate clearly that churches are no longer merely in dialogue with scripture and their own tradition but also with an "ecumenical tradition".

79. Moreover, the responses to the Lima text, even of those churches that did not fully understand the process in which they were asked to participate, have clarified and shaped the "ecumenical tradition" so that it has become more clearly defined and more readily identifiable. Consequently, it should be easier for ecumenical hermeneutics to find ways of enabling churches to recognize further expressions of the apostolic faith in the shared "ecumenical tradition" and in the faith and practice of other churches.

4. Language

80. One of the obstacles to seeing new, but authentic, expressions of the apostolic faith in the life and witness of other churches or in the

formulations of "ecumenical tradition", such as the Lima text, is language.

81. The official responses indicate that some churches found the language of BEM unfamiliar,[79] too patristic,[80] too sacramentalist,[81] too culturally biased in favour of the West[82] – as viewed from their own particular perspective.[83] Some also considered the language to be too patriarchal,[84] too dogmatic,[85] too complex, especially for lay people,[86] and even "too Christian".[87]

82. A major concern for some respondents is what they deem to be ambiguous language.[88] This is especially problematic when it is not clear to them whether the language is intended to be taken literally or symbolically[89] (as, for example, in respect of the word "sign"[90]), descriptively or prescriptively.[91]

83. Some churches also accuse BEM of containing a "convergence of *words*" rather than a "convergence of thought"[92] by the way it sometimes juxtaposes contradictory, or not fully synthesized concepts, "cleverly written" to produce a false impression of convergence,[93] but which may, in fact, be counterproductive to "authentic convergence".[94]

84. Irrespective of the legitimacy (or otherwise) of these criticisms, the need for precision of language is of paramount importance in ecumenical hermeneutics.

5. Summary

85. Factors other than the use and interpretation of scripture are involved in ecumenical hermeneutics. A particular interpretative community's understanding of the relationship between scripture, Tradition and traditions determines its perspective and its openness to being enriched (and potentially changed) by expressions of faith and practice other than its own, seen not only in the life and witness of other churches but in an "ecumenical tradition" which may or may not coincide fully with any one historic or contemporary expression of the apostolic faith. The task of ecumenical hermeneutics in this regard is to facilitate appropriate interpretation and communication, including clarification of the language used in this process.

CONCLUSION

86. The Lima text on the eucharist appears to have been most successful in helping churches move towards ecumenical convergence in its use of the biblical concept of *anamnesis* to formulate statements which, while dealing with the previously divisive matters of "sacrifice" and

"real presence", showed how the different views on these matters were within the range of appropriate interpretations of common apostolic faith as contained within "ecumenical tradition".

87. Somewhat less successful was the Lima text's use of the term *epiklesis* to deal also with the matter of "real presence", especially in the sense of "unique presence", and with the matter of conflicting views about a "special moment of consecration". A significant amount of progress towards further convergence on these matters, nevertheless, is evidenced by the responses of a number of churches.

88. Convergence on other aspects of Christian understandings about the eucharist was achieved whenever those churches which place a high degree of emphasis on the normative authority of scripture could readily identify with the biblical basis of the statements about the eucharist contained in the Lima text, or whenever those churches which place a high degree of emphasis on the importance of Tradition or traditions could recognize the Tradition or traditions in the formulations.

89. Convergence was never facilitated whenever churches considered the statements about the eucharist to be lacking in biblical basis and/or not rooted in authentic Tradition or traditions. However, whenever churches understood the concept of "ecumenical tradition", this greatly affected, in a positive way, their willingness to accept concepts and formulations about the eucharist, even if these were not part of their own confessional heritage or expressed in language other than that with which they were familiar.

90. Any suspicion that language, even allegedly biblically based language, was used ambiguously in order to give the appearance of convergence, rather than expressing genuine convergence, ruled out the possibility of the particular statement or paragraph being a vehicle for helping churches gain new insights.

91. The Lima text's use of scripture and the churches' response to that use raise ten major issues which may be helpful for developing guidelines for ecumenical hermeneutics:

a) The goal of ecumenical hermeneutics is not to achieve uniformity of interpretation of biblical texts. Nor is it the task of ecumenical hermeneutics to establish criteria by which some texts may be deemed more "authoritative" than others. Biblical texts can carry a range of legitimate interpretations in relationship to specific matters of faith and practice. This range of meanings can and does enrich Christian understanding of the particular matters under consideration. Ecumenical hermeneutics must, however, play a role in helping to delineate the acceptable limits of the range of legitimate interpretations of biblical texts in connection with specific matters of faith and practice. This includes identifying ways in which particular interpretations of texts are applicable to the matter under consideration and encouraging the use of methodologies other than the historical-critical approach to expand the range of interpretations.

b) In respect of biblical citations, even more so than with direct biblical quotations, ecumenical hermeneutics must help readers to establish the applicability of the texts cited to the matter at hand. Reasons why particular texts are chosen and how these texts are dealt with contextually need to be articulated clearly.

c) Biblical allusions appeal to a shared biblical heritage and establish rapport with readers but have a greater potential for miscommunication than direct quotations or even citations. Ecumenical hermeneutics needs to ensure that the intended point of the allusion is conveyed as explicitly as possible.

d) Biblical concepts and terminology are effective facilitators of convergence. Ecumenical hermeneutics, however, must provide the means by which these concepts or terms are explained carefully and accurately, taking account of the way in which these concepts and terms have been used both in scripture and in the Tradition or traditions of the church.

e) In respect of biblical terminology, lack of familiarity does not appear to be as great a problem for ecumenical hermeneutics as terminology that has negative connotations for some churches. In both cases, ecumenical hermeneutics needs to develop ways of showing that the terms carry meanings which are both legitimate and helpful for convergence.

f) In light of the comments by some churches that they found certain of the statements on the eucharist in the Lima text not to be biblically based or that they were aware of biblical material which would have contributed to the Lima text's discussion of the eucharist, it is important for ecumenical hermeneutics to develop safeguards against insufficiently broad-based presentations and discussions.

g) Ecumenical hermeneutics must also provide the means by which churches may clarify for themselves the relationship which they see between scripture, Tradition and traditions and the relative weight they give to each in their interpretation of both the biblical material and the continuing expressions of "apostolic faith".

h) Similarly, ecumenical hermeneutics must develop ways of enabling churches to identify the perspectives from which they interpret scripture, Tradition and traditions.

i) Perhaps most importantly, ecumenical hermeneutics must provide ways by which to help churches engage meaningfully the reality of "the ecumenical tradition" as another factor to take into consideration along with scripture and their own ecclesial tradition.

j) Ecumenical hermeneutics must take into account issues of communication as well as interpretation and formulate criteria by which language may be used as precisely and unambiguously as possible in ecumenical dialogues and texts.

NOTES

¹ Faith and Order Paper no. 111, Geneva, WCC, 1982.

² Max Thurian, ed., *Churches respond to BEM*, vols I-VI, Faith and Order Papers nos 129, 132, 135, 137, 143, 144, Geneva, WCC, 1986-88.

³ *One Baptism, One Eucharist and a Mutually Recognized Ministry*, Faith and Order Paper no. 73, Geneva, WCC, 1975, pp.18-28.

⁴ See also the way in which Rom. 12: 1 and 1 Pet. 2: 5 are used in E10 and 1 Cor. 11:26 and Matt. 26:29 are used in E22.

⁵ See §5 above.

⁶ These are cited below by name of church and volume and page of Thurian, *Churches Respond to BEM*, vols I-VI.

⁷ Cf. North Elbian Evangelical Lutheran Church, I.40; Anglican Church of Canada, II.38; Congregational Union of Scotland, II.313; Mission Covenant Church of Sweden, II.315; Church of England, III.42; Church of the Province of Southern Africa, III.102; Evangelical-Lutheran Church of Denmark, III.110; Evangelical Lutheran Church in Oldenburg, IV.76; Evangelical-Reformed Church of North-West Germany, IV.95; Evangelical-Methodist Church: Central Conference in the GDR, IV.170; Evangelical-Methodist Church: Central Conference in the FRG, IV.176; Federation of the Evangelical Church in the GDR, V.121; Church of Lippe, VI.70.

⁸ Cf. Netherlands Reformed Church and Reformed Churches in the Netherlands, IV.105.

⁹ Cf. Baptist Union of Scotland, III.237; Evangelical Lutheran Church in Bavaria, IV.26.

¹⁰ It seems clear from the context that the Church of Jesus Christ in Madagascar is referring here to an insufficient number of biblical citations in the text of BEM as a whole.

¹¹ E.g., Church of Ireland (Anglican), I.66.

¹² E.g., Roman Catholic Church, V.18 (on John 6: 52-56).

¹³ See § 68 below.

¹⁴ Cf. the Evangelical Lutheran Church of Denmark, III.110. Interestingly, the Evangelical Church of Westphalia reports that the biblical texts quoted and cited in E1 are the criteria for its understanding of communion (IV.141), but then (inadvertently?) reverses the order of the quotations and citations as given in E1 by placing the gospel parallels ahead of 1 Cor. 11: 22-25 (*ibid.*).

¹⁵ The Baptist Union of Scotland, for example, reports: "We do not... accept that the words 'This is my blood, this is my body' can be taken literally..." (III.236). The Roman Catholic Church, on the other hand, reports that transubstantiation is, for Catholics, a central mystery of faith which needs to be stated unambiguously (VI.22).

¹⁶ See §72 below.

¹⁷ See §§5-8 above.

¹⁸ Cf. the United Protestant Church of Belgium's comment: "Scriptural data will be exegetically understandable only from their setting in life (*Sitz im Leben*) of the church. This is a prerequisite for their ultimate theological interpretations and for living them out in liturgy" (III.173).

¹⁹ Reformed Church of Alsace and Lorraine, III.166.

²⁰ *Baptism, Eucharist and Ministry 1982-1990: Report on the Process and Responses*, Faith and Order Paper no. 149, Geneva, WCC, 1990, pp.112-20.

²¹ Cf. The Salvation Army, IV.243.

²² Cf. United Church of Christ [USA], II.329.

²³ Church of Iceland (Anglican), I.62; Lutheran Church of Australia, II.90; Presbyterian Church in Canada, II.155; Presbyterian Church of Wales, II.169; Seventh-day Adventists, II.341; Moravian Church in Jamaica, V.170.

²⁴ Churches of Christ in Australia, II.269; Church of England, III.42; Evangelical Lutheran Church of Denmark, III.110; Evangelical Church of Westphalia, IV.142; cf. United German Mennonite Congregation, VI.127.

25 Evangelical Lutheran Church of Bavaria, IV.31; cf. Evangelical Church of the Augsburg Confession in the Socialist Republic of Romania, IV.85.
26 Church of Scotland (Reformed), I.95; Evangelical Lutheran Church of Denmark, III.111; Baptist Union of Scotland, III.243; Moravian Church in Great Britain and Ireland, III.286; Waldensian Evangelical Church of the River Plate (Uruguay), IV.121; Burma Baptist Convention, IV.187; Evangelical Lutheran Church in Brunswick (FRG), VI.47.
27 United Methodist Church, Central and Southern Europe, II.204; cf. Anglican Church of Australia, II.34; American Lutheran Church, II.82; Presbyterian Church in Ireland, III.211; Uniting Church in Australia, IV.158; Evangelical Church of Westphalia, IV.143.
28 Evangelical Church of Kurhessen-Waldeck (FRG), V.55.
29 Lutheran Church in Hungary, III.129; Lutheran Church-Missouri Synod, III.135; Evangelical-Methodist Church: Central Conference in the GDR, IV.170; Evangelical Methodist Church: Central Conference in the FRG, IV.178.
30 Church of Sweden, II.131; Presbyterian Church in Canada, II.154; Presbyterian Church in Wales, II.171; Evangelical-Reformed Church of North-West Germany, IV.95; Evangelical Church of Westphalia, IV.142-143; cf. Christian Church (Disciples of Christ), I.113.
31 See §§17-18 above.
32 Lutheran Church-Missouri Synod, III.136; United Protestant Church of Belgium, III.171; Evangelical-Methodist Church: Central Conference in the FRG, IV.176-177; Burma Baptist Convention, IV.188; Old Catholic Church of Switzerland, V.11, 12.
33 E.g., Bulgarian Orthodox Church, II.18; Russian Orthodox Church, III.7.
34 Church of England, III.43.
35 Presbyterian Church in Ireland, III.212.
36 Union of Welsh Independents, III.272; cf. Burma Baptist Convention, IV.188.
37 Baptist Union of Scotland, III.238.
38 E.g., Christian Church (Disciples of Christ), I.113; Church of Norway, II.113, 114; Churches of Christ in Australia, II.270; American Baptist Churches in the USA, III.260; Church of the Brethren (USA), VI.109.
39 E.g., Moravian Church in America, Southern Province, II.257; Evangelical Church of Czech Brethren, IV.113; Union of Evangelical Free Churches in the GDR, IV.195; Evangelical Lutheran Church in the Netherlands, V.20-21.
40 E.g., Ecumenical Council of Churches in Czechoslovakia, II.295-296.
41 Church in Wales, III.84; Evangelical Lutheran Church of Iceland, IV.63; cf. United Church of Christ in Japan, II.289.
42 Cf. European Continental Province of the Moravian Church, VI. 119; Evangelical Church of the Rhineland (FRG), V.79.
43 Cf. Church of England, III.43; Independent Evangelical Lutheran Church (FRG and West Berlin), VI.55.
44 Cf. Church in Wales, III.91; Presbyterian Church (USA), III.195; Mar Thoma Syrian Church of Malabar (India), IV.9; Evangelical Church of the River Plate (Argentina), V.177.
45 Cf. Roman Catholic Church, VI.21, 22.
46 Cf. Church of Norway, II.115; Evangelical Lutheran Church of Finland, III.122-123.
47 E.g., Evangelical-Lutheran Church of Denmark, III.111; Evangelical-Lutheran Church of Finland, III.121.
48 Cf. Anglican Church of Australia, II.34; Anglican Church of Canada, II.43; Union of Evangelical Free Churches in the GDR (Baptists), IV.197.
49 E.g., Evangelical Church in Hesse and Nassau, IV.134; Evangelical Church of Czech Brethren, IV.114.
50 E.g., Church of Norway, II.113, 114; Church of England, III.44-45; Swiss Protestant Church Federation, VI.81, 83.
51 See §19 above.
52 Cf. Baptist Union of Sweden, IV.207; Evangelical Church of the River Plate (Argentina), V.176.
53 Presbyterian Church of Wales, II.169; Evangelical Lutheran Church in Oldenburg, IV.77.
54 Methodist Church [UK], II.233; Union of Welsh Independents, III.273.
55 E.g., Methodist Church [UK], II.233; The Salvation Army, IV.244.
56 E.g., Presbyterian Church in Korea, II.162; Methodist Church [UK], II.233; Evangelical Church of the Augsburg Confession of Alsace and Lorraine, III.153; Baptist Union of Denmark, III.249; The Salvation Army, IV.243.
57 Cf. Church of the Province of New Zealand, II.66; Mission Covenant Church of Sweden, II.319.
58 Cf. Church of Norway, II.115; Lutheran Church-Missouri Synod, III.136-137; Evangelical Lutheran Church of Hanover, IV.52; Evangelical Lutheran Church in Oldenburg, IV.77; Evangelical Church of Westphalia, IV.144; Evangelical Church of Kurhessen-Waldeck (FRG), V.99.

[59]Union of Welsh Independents, III.274; Evangelical Church of the Rhineland (FRG), V.78-79; cf. Federation of the Evangelical Churches in the GDR, V.135.

[60] Evangelical-Lutheran Church of Finland, III.122; Independent Evangelical Lutheran Church (FRG and West Berlin), VI.55.

[61] Baptist Union of Scotland, III.239.

[62] Cf. similar statements in *ibid.*, 238, 239.

[63] Cf. Presbyterian Church in Ireland, III.214.

[64] Cf. Seventh-day Adventists, II.343; Salvation Army, IV.242.

[65] *Baptism, Eucharist and Ministry 1982-1990*, pp.132-35.

[66] E.g., Waldensian and Methodist Churches in Italy, II.247; Standing Council of the Lutheran and Reformed Churches of France, III.143, 144; Presbyterian Church in Ireland, III.214; American Baptist Churches in the USA, III.257; Evangelical Church of the Augsburg Confession (Austria), IV.18; Independent Evangelical Lutheran Church (FRG and West Berlin), VI.50, 51-52, 54.

[67] E.g., Bulgarian Orthodox Church, II.17; Finnish Orthodox Church, II.25; Inter-Orthodox Symposium, I.123; Ecumenical Patriarch of Constantinople, IV.3.

[68] E.g., Church of Scotland (Reformed), I.98; Presbyterian Church in Canada, II.152; Evangelical-Reformed Church of North-West Germany, IV.94.

[69] E.g., Religious Society of Friends (Quakers) in Great Britain, IV.219; The Salvation Army, IV.231.

[70] E.g., American Lutheran Church, II.81; United Church of Canada, II.284; Presbyterian Church in Ireland, III.211; Union of Welsh Independents, III.271; Evangelical Methodist Church: Central Conference in the GDR, IV.168.

[71] E.g., Presbyterian Churches of Wales, II.169; United Methodist Church, Central and Southern Europe, II.200-201; Evangelical Lutheran Church in Bavaria, IV.24; The Salvation Army, IV.234.

[72] E.g., American Lutheran Church, II.81; Waldensian Evangelical Church of the River Plate (Uruguay), IV.125-126.

[73] E.g., United Methodist Church, Central and Southern Europe, II.201; Waldensian and Methodist Churches in Italy, II.246; Baptist Union of Scotland, III.239; Baptist Union of Sweden, IV.206.

[74] E.g., United Church of Christ in Japan, II.290; Melanesian Council of Churches, V.180.

[75] E.g., Anglican Church of Canada, II.38; Presbyterian Church (USA), III.195; Moravian Church in Great Britain and Ireland, III.284; Church of Ceylon, IV.15.

[76] Mission Covenant Church of Sweden, II.316; cf. American Baptist Churches, III.258-259; Evangelical Lutheran Church of Hanover (FRG), IV.47.

[77] Evangelical Lutheran Church of Iceland, IV.58.

[78] Thurian, *Churches Respond to BEM*, I.4.

[79] E.g., Finnish Orthodox Church, II.25; Standing Council of the Lutheran and Reformed Churches of France, III.143; Presbyterian Church in Ireland, III.221; Old Catholic Church of Switzerland, V.11; see also §§44-45, 47, 58 above.

[80] E.g., United Church of Christ [USA], II.327; Evangelical Church of the Augsburg Confession of Alsace and Lorraine, III.146.

[81] E.g., The Salvation Army, IV.234.

[82] E.g., Methodist Church of New Zealand, I.78-79; United Church of Canada, II.285.

[83] See also §§74-75 above.

[84] E.g., United Methodist Church [USA], II.197-198; United Church of Canada, II.285.

[85] E.g., Union of Evangelical Free Churches in the GDR (Baptists), IV.191.

[86] Methodist Church of Southern Africa, II.236; Waldensian Evangelical Church of the River Plate [Uruguay], IV.118; The Salvation Army, IV.245-246; United German Mennonite Congregations, VI.125.

[87] Religious Society of Friends (Quakers) in Great Britain, IV.219.

[88] E.g., Lutheran Church of Australia, II.90, 91; Presbyterian Church in Canada, II.153; United Church of Christ [USA], II.327; Baptist Union of Denmark, III.249; Independent Evangelical Lutheran Church (FRG and West Berlin), VI.55.

[89] E.g., Baptist Union of Great Britain and Ireland, I.75; Church of Scotland (Reformed), I.97; Remonstrant Brotherhood, II.305; Lutheran Church-Missouri Synod, III.137; Union of Welsh Independents, III.273.

[90] E.g., Bulgarian Orthodox Church, II.18; Church of Norway, II.115; Seventh-day Adventists, II.343; Evangelical-Lutheran Church of Finland, III.122; The Salvation Army, IV.254.

[91] E.g., American Lutheran Church, II.80.

[92] Union of Welsh Independents, III.273.

[93] Anglican Church of the Southern Cone, I.54-55; cf. Baptist Union of Great Britain and Ireland, I.75; Baptist Union of Denmark, III.249; Evangelical Lutheran Church in Bavaria, IV.25; Evangelical Methodist Church: Central Conference in the FRG, IV.172.

[94] Presbyterian Church in Canada, II.153; cf. Presbyterian Church in Ireland, III.221.

Hermeneutics and Ecumenical Dialogue:
BEM and Its Responses on "Apostolicity"

WILLIAM HENN

I. INTRODUCTION

Hermeneutics is a complicated topic. At first glance, it may seem that it need not be so. Werner Jeanrond opens his study of theological hermeneutics with the words:

> By "hermeneutics" we mean *the theory of interpretation*. The word contains a reference to Hermes, the messenger of the gods in Greek mythology. Hermes' task was to explain to humans the decisions and plans of their gods. Thus, he bridged the gap between the divine and the human realm. Similarly, hermeneutics is concerned with examining the relationship between two realms, the realms of a text or a work of art on the one hand, and the people who wish to understand it on the other.[1]

Thus, hermeneutics examines the way a subject may be said to understand a text or a work of art. Within this basic framework, hermeneutics challenges the subject to be "faithful" to that which he or she is interpreting:

> All interpretations of literary works which wish to be called "adequate" (in terms of how they understand the texts) must be faithful to the texts themselves and not to any extra-textual authority, such as "I understand Samuel Beckett's texts better because I am his cousin or because I am studying at Trinity College Dublin where Beckett himself was once a student".[2]

An important aspect of such fidelity is what might be called the "negative" step of self-scrutiny on the part of the subject, who seeks to eliminate prejudices that could mar the adequacy of his or her interpretation: "We may wish to know what strategies could help us to make sure that our listening is true listening and not a distorted or ideological listening."[3]

Here, then, is a rather simple framework for understanding hermeneutics. Hermeneutics explores the way a subject adequately understands an object, emphasizing the need for faithful attention to the object and distortion-eliminating self-scrutiny on the part of the subject.

Yet as Jeanrond, along with many others, laboriously details, hermeneutics has not remained so simple. The theory of interpretation of texts or of works of art has provided occasion for the elaboration of the impressive epistemological and metaphysical constructions associated with names such as Schleiermacher, Dilthey, Heidegger, Gadamer, Habermas and Ricoeur. These more philosophical hermeneutical theories have been integrated into biblical exegesis and theology by Barth, Bultmann, Fuchs, Ebeling, Tracy and others.[4]

The prospect that the sophisticated theories of these writers could be of immediate use to ecumenism is probably somewhat remote. To be sure, divided Christians very likely can benefit from many of the insights of people such as Heidegger or Ricoeur. But progress in healing divisions about very specific questions such as Christ's presence in the eucharist or the structure of church ministry will probably not be resolved by the common acceptance of this or that hermeneutical theory. What is more likely to contribute to ecumenical progress is the more simple conception of hermeneutics which urges subjects to be *attentive* and *self-critical*. These two basic hermeneutical "principles" can be applied directly in the course of ecumenical dialogue or in such an exercise as that envisioned for this essay: the consideration of the responses to the statement on *Baptism, Eucharist and Ministry* (BEM) about apostolicity.

Before beginning that task, one final point should be drawn from Jeanrond's study. He adds that, in addition to the normal considerations that enter into the interpretation of texts, the interpretation of *biblical* texts by Christians introduces some unique questions.

> Since it is the very nature of the Christian church to reflect upon God's self-disclosure as witnessed by the biblical texts, these texts have always held a prominent and normative status in the Christian community. This status, however, makes the hermeneutical problem even more acute since it points to two related questions, namely the question of adequate criteria for biblical interpretation and the question of who has the competence and authority to validate such criteria as well as any particular act of interpretation in terms of such a set of accepted criteria.[5]

Thus, because of the "normative status" of biblical texts for the Christian community, the hermeneutical problem is even more important, and questions of "criteria" and of "validating authority" must be addressed. These comments obviously add the consideration of two additional questions to the simple two-principle framework we have just extrapolated from Jeanrond's book.[6] But since it is true that questions of "criteria" and "authority" are present in various degrees in the responses to BEM on apostolicity, some attention will be paid to these questions as well in our analysis of those responses.

What follows now, in Part II, is a rather lengthy account of the responses to BEM concerning the precise theme of apostolicity.[7] If hermeneutics requires "being faithful to the texts themselves", as the

quotation from Jeanrond above indicates, then it is of paramount importance to listen extensively to the responses before beginning any kind of
analysis. Part III, then, will seek to apply to the responses the following
hermeneutical principles which have emerged in this introduction:
1) that accurate interpretation is faithfully attentive to the texts themselves;
2) that accurate interpretation avoids ideological distortions by means
   of self-scrutiny; and
3) that interpretations which concern the identity of the Christian community should address questions of criteria and authority.

II. SURVEY OF RESPONSES TO BEM ON APOSTOLICITY

None of the responses includes a comprehensive statement about the
terms "apostle" and "apostolicity", from either an exegetical or a theological point of view. Rather, they comment about BEM's use of these
terms. Therefore, to best benefit from the following analysis of the
responses, readers would be well advised to take a few minutes to re-
familiarize themselves with the ministry section of BEM, especially
paragraphs 34-38 and commentaries 34 and 36, which deal most directly
with the theme of apostolicity.

A. Responses by national or regional communities which can be grouped along church-family lines[8]

1. Anglican responses on apostolicity

> *Responses cited: Church of Ireland (I.6-69); Scottish Episcopal
> Church (II.48-56); Church of England (III.30-79); Church in Wales
> (III.80-95); Church of Ceylon (IV.14-16).*

The Anglican responses to BEM's presentation of apostolicity show
general agreement in appreciating:
a) the contextualization of ministerial succession within the broader
   theme of the apostolicity of the church as a whole;
b) the presentation of ordained ministry as exercising a valuable role in
   fostering apostolicity in faith; and
c) the understanding of orderly transmission in ministry as a powerful
   sign of apostolic continuity.[9]
The Church of England notes that both scripture and the authority of
church practice during the early centuries provide the basis upon which
some developments "became settled into a more universal pattern of

ministry". Such reliance on both scripture and the authority of the early centuries "would command the support of most Anglicans" (England III.51-52).

As one might expect, all of the Anglican responses tend to place a special importance on the value of episcopal succession in expressing the apostolicity of the church. A range of opinion appears, however, concerning the "normativity" of episcopal succession. In response to its question "to what extent should this early history be normative", the Church of England (III.52) seems to go no further than to state that "some Anglicans would wish to make stronger claims than the Lima text is able to make". The Church of Ireland (I.69) states: "Apostolic succession is probably the most important issue, and some churches need to recover episcopal ordination as its outward sign", adopting a more affirmative position than BEM M53b, which only states that some churches "may need to recover the sign of the episcopal succession". More clearly affirmative of the normative character of episcopal succession would seem to be the response of the Church of Ceylon (IV.16), stating that "however difficult it may seem,... the varying church traditions have to accept and hold together" the two points of view that the church as a whole is apostolic and that "the orderly transmission of the ordained ministry is a powerful expression of the continuity of the church throughout history".

Two other responses, on the other hand, would appear to lessen the insistence on normativity. The Scottish Episcopal Church (II.51) places the whole question within the context of "comprehensiveness": a united church's doctrine and practice should be broad enough to enable Christians of diverse views to live together; it should not ask any church to repudiate its past; it should enable present forms of episcopacy to be fashioned in light of current experience and it should allow for a range of interpretations of episcopacy. The Church in Wales (III.86) challenges the non-episcopal churches to indicate how they will put into practice BEM's recognition of the value of episcopacy. At the same time, it challenges itself to recognize the apostolicity of non-episcopal churches (for example, it speaks of the need of the Church in Wales to consider viewing "the Methodist celebration of communion [as] a valid sacrament"). Such a consideration would suggest that, at least with regard to considering sacraments as "valid", episcopal succession would not be normative.

2. Baptist responses on apostolicity

Responses cited: Baptist Union of Great Britain and Ireland (I.70-77); Baptist Union of Scotland (III.230-45); Baptist Union of Denmark (III.246-53); American Baptist Churches in the USA (III.257-

63); Burma Baptist Convention (IV.184-90); Union of Evangelical Free Churches in the German Democratic Republic [Baptists] (IV.191-99); Baptist Union of Sweden (IV.200-13).

The Baptist responses tended to be rather short with regard to the precise topic of apostolicity. Two specific themes in BEM were widely appreciated: the consideration of apostolicity as a characteristic applying to the church as a whole (Great Britain and Ireland I.72; Scotland III.241; Denmark III.252; American III.262; Sweden IV.210) and the recognition that the New Testament does not single out any one pattern of ministry as normative (Scotland III.242; American III.262; Burma IV.188). With regard to the first, not only did several responses mention that the way in which paragraph 34 of the Ministry section of BEM nicely elaborates the global nature of the church's apostolic continuity, but the Burma Baptist Convention (IV.188-89) went so far as to say that now in ecumenical dialogue "the question of 'apostolic succession' has been replaced by that of 'succession in the apostolic tradition'". In the view of this church, such a move represents a more balanced approach to apostolicity.

The more critical comments about BEM's presentation of apostolicity come from three communities which identify themselves as not belonging to the World Council of Churches. The Baptist Union of Scotland (III.240-41) states that too much of what BEM affirms about apostolic succession in ministry is assumed and not proven. Moreover, too much emphasis is given to the apostles (Scotland III.240; German Democratic Republic IV.199). The Baptist Union of Sweden (IV.210-11) notes that not only is it true that ministerial succession has occurred legitimately in other forms than that of episcopal succession but also that communities which have more successfully preserved the apostolic tradition have been called heretical and persecuted by those who have preserved "apostolic succession". Finally, these respondents point out what they consider to be some inconsistencies in BEM. If the New Testament in fact does not require any one form of ministry, why does BEM urge communities to accept the threefold form (Scotland III.241)? Or again, if apostolicity is really to be understood as a characteristic of the church as a whole so that those communities which do not practise episcopal succession are rightly understood to be apostolic, then why is such importance given to ministerial structure and why should such communities adopt episcopal structure (Scotland III.241; German Democratic Republic IV.199)?

3. Brethren responses on apostolicity

Responses cited: Evangelical Church of Czech Brethren (IV.110-17); Church of the Brethren USA (VI.104-14).

These two responses have distinctive tones. The Czech response several times records that it is glad about one or another aspect of BEM, while the USA response speaks of joy but also of "deep concern" and of the pain of ecumenical dialogue, adding: "We are often alienated by the language and sacramental ontology which characterizes BEM." Scripture is clearly a prominent criterion for these communities in considering apostolicity. The Czech response states that, for Brethren, the sign of apostolic succession is adherence to scripture and the early Christian creeds (Czech IV.116). Another comment (Czech IV.110) also notes that BEM needs greater clarity on the relative authority of scripture and tradition. Both communities are pleased that BEM acknowledges the diversity and flexibility of ministry in the New Testament (Czech IV.115; USA VI.111), although the USA response registers its disappointment that BEM did not proceed to apply such New Testament data to the question of "patterns of ministry relative to changed and changing circumstances".

There is an appreciation for the attempt to solve the problem between episcopal and non-episcopal communities by recourse to the distinction between continuity in the apostolic tradition, on the one hand, and apostolic succession of ministry, on the other (Czech IV.116). Moreover, it is good that BEM presents ministerial succession as only a sign, and not a guarantee (Czech IV.116), although the Church of the Brethren USA (VI.111) has serious reservations regarding whether episcopal succession is truly a sign of church continuity and unity. Ministry structured in a hierarchy tends to become episcopal monarchy, and so the Reformation idea of a local college of laity at the level of the congregation is indispensable for the renewal of those communities without such a structure (Czech IV.117). Perhaps here also fits the suggestion that BEM needs a stronger emphasis upon the priesthood of all believers (USA VI.110).

Finally, a very interesting comment comes from the Czech Church of the Brethren (IV.115), when it states:

> We are thankful that in the interest of convergence the document omitted mention of some elements which have divided and do divide Christians: the hierarchical arrangement of ordained ministries, papal primacy, the essentiality of apostolic succession for the validity of the sacraments, and the definition of ordination as a sacrament.

This comment raises the question of whether BEM may have omitted relevant issues which are part of the discussion of apostolicity.

4. Disciples of Christ responses on apostolicity

Responses cited: Christian Church [Disciples of Christ] (I.110-21); Christian Church [Disciples of Christ], Canada (III.264-67).

The Disciples of Christ responses concerning apostolicity are very modest and conciliatory, professing a need and a willingness to consider the various aspects of this topic in greater detail. The shorter Canadian response simply registers its overall agreement with much in BEM, adding that the precise section about apostolic succession challenges them to reflect upon the ways in which their community exhibits apostolicity. The longer response makes four points regarding apostolicity. First, it states that the historical background of the Disciples predisposes them to "react against any view which defined apostolic succession through bishops as the only valid expression of guarding continuity of the faith". Secondly, it appreciates BEM's wide understanding of the continuity of the church as a whole within apostolic tradition by means of teaching, preaching and witness. Third, it notes that Disciples are growing more appreciative of the importance of the ministry of oversight and of the role of the laying-on of hands in ordination. Finally, it expresses the hope that present patterns of ministry might all be recognized as "differing forms of continuity".

5. The Religious Society of Friends (Quakers) on apostolicity

Responses: Quakers of Netherlands (III.297-99); Canadian Yearly Meeting, Religious Society of Friends (III.300-302); Religious Society of Friends (Quakers) in Great Britain (IV.214-29).

These responses unanimously indicate that BEM, with its emphasis upon sacraments, doctrines and hierarchy, is quite foreign to the thinking and practice of the Religious Society of Friends. These communities approach BEM as "humble learners" (Great Britain IV.214), with an openness to self-examination, since differences in doctrine and practice can be opportunities for growth and for enriching spiritual experience (Canada). But, feeling somewhat "excluded from the current draft of BEM", the Friends emphasize that unity is fundamentally spiritual, an inner unity rooted in love and in the presence of the Holy Spirit. The Christian community should be widely diverse, and that should not be seen as scandalous or sinful (Great Britain IV.218).

Only the Religious Society of Friends (Quakers) in Great Britain (IV.222) supplies any comments specifically about apostolicity. They note that BEM assumes "that the twelve are the apostles and that the apostles are the authority for ordained leadership". Quakers cannot make such assumptions, especially since, in addition to the apostles, there were many other witnesses, including women, to the life, death and resurrection of Jesus. Moreover, the New Testament presents a wide variety of ministries. True apostolicity is not to be found in the restoration of ancient systems, but rather in living according to the same Spirit as the apostles lived.

6. *Lutheran responses on apostolicity*

> *Responses quoted: North Elbian Evangelical Lutheran Church (I.39-53); American Lutheran Church (II.79-84); Lutheran Church of Australia (II.85-98); Church of Norway (II.105-22); Church of Sweden (II.123-40); Evangelical-Lutheran Church of Denmark (III.106-15); Evangelical-Lutheran Church of Finland (III.116-27); Lutheran Church in Hungary (III.128-30); Lutheran Church-Missouri Synod (III.131-41); Evangelical Lutheran Church in Bavaria-FRG (IV.21-41); Estonian Evangelical Lutheran Church (IV.42-46); Evangelical Lutheran Church of Hanover-FRG (IV.47-56); Evangelical Lutheran Church of Iceland (IV.57-72); Evangelical Lutheran Church in Oldenburg-FRG (IV.73-80); Evangelical Church of the Augsburg Confession in the Socialist Republic of Romania (IV.81-92); Evangelical Lutheran Church in Brunswick-FRG (VI.44-49); Independent Evangelical Lutheran Church-FRG and West Berlin (VI.50-57).*

These Lutheran responses, by and large, seem to fit together into a rather homogeneous whole. Even methodologically, many churches express their intention to reply by following the same three steps of (1) affirming the points of BEM with which they agree; (2) indicating statements which challenge them to reconsider their own doctrine or practice; and (3) pointing out statements which they find questionable or unacceptable (Finland III.116; Bavaria IV.21; Hanover IV.47; Romania IV.81; FRG and West Berlin VI.50). The first and third of these steps – that is, of affirming points with which they agree and of pointing out statements which they find unacceptable – seem to predominate when the responses consider the precise topic of apostolicity.

On the whole, there is a strong affirmation of the importance of apostolicity within the Lutheran understanding of the church (North Elbian I.49; American II.83; Denmark III.106; Hungary III.130; Estonia IV.45; Brunswick VI.48). This apostolicity is usually thought of in terms similar to those used by the Evangelical Lutheran Church of Bavaria-FRG (II.39) when it speaks of apostolicity as the *successio evangelii*. The apostolicity of the church means that the faith, life and ministry of the church "are based upon and measured by the gospel" (North Elbian I.49; see also American II.83). What is essential to apostolicity is teaching and proclamation which are in harmony with the message of the apostles (Sweden II.138-39; Norway III.121; Missouri III.140; Hanover IV.52-53; Iceland IV.68).

Because of this, Lutheran responses rather forcefully endorse BEM for speaking first of apostolic tradition and of the apostolicity of the church as a whole before turning to the topic of ministerial succession (Australia II.97-98; Norway II.117-118; Denmark III.114; Finland III.123; Missouri III.140; Estonia IV.44-45; Iceland IV.67; Romania IV.89).[10] While many communities are pleased with the distinction between these two ways of speaking of apostolicity and with the priority given to fidelity to the gospel as the fundamental criterion of apostolicity, nevertheless, apostolicity of ministry is by no means of negligible importance for most of the Lutheran churches. The ministry is said to be "instituted by God" or "by Christ" and necessary for unity (North Elbian I.48 and 53) and to "depend on Christ" (Iceland IV.66). Succession in ministry serves the continuity of the church (Missouri III.140); some transmission of ordained ministry is "necessary" (Australia II.97-98). Moreover, while the role of the apostles was unique (Sweden II.135; Finland III.123; Hanover IV.54), nevertheless something of the apostolic ministry is said to be continued in the ordained ministry (Sweden II.135; Iceland IV.66); ordained ministry is derived from the ministry of the apostles (Brunswick VI.48).

But to these affirmations of the importance of ministerial succession several nuances must be added. Some responses emphasize that ministerial structure is not "of the very substance" of the church (Estonia IV.45) and that, for the Lutheran tradition, structure is in principle *adiaphora*, that is, not prescribed or foundational (American II.83). The American Lutheran Church (II.83) explains this by means of a distinction between "function" and "structure". The variety of ministries present in the New Testament shows that what is truly primary for the church is the function of ministering; the structures which this function takes are contingent. Perhaps such a nuance is also reflected in the statement of the Evangelical Lutheran Church of Iceland (IV.68) when it asserts that an unbroken succession in the transmission of ministry is necessary for the church's apostolicity, but not a succession precisely of bishops.

Another nuance about the way ministerial succession serves apostolicity which is very significant for Lutheran churches is contained in BEM's statement that, while such succession is a valuable, helpful sign of continuity, it should never be understood as a "guarantee" or as "indispensable" (Australia II.97-98; Norway II.121; Sweden II.138-39; Finland III.124; Hungary III.129). Especially underlined is the fear that too much emphasis on the "indispensability" of ministerial succession could run the risk of diminishing the attention which should be given to the fundamental importance of doctrine as a measure of apostolicity (Norway II.121; see also Bavaria IV.39). In this regard, a number of churches, in contrast with the view of the Church of Iceland expressed above, explicitly reject the idea that there is an unbroken chain of continuity in the transmission of ministerial responsibility from the time of the apostles (North Elbian I.49; Norway II.121; Denmark III.114). The Evangelical Lutheran Church of Australia (II.97-98) adds that the reality of apostolic succession is present in those churches which do not practise the historical episcopal succession. When understood as a sign which is neither indispensable to nor a guarantee of apostolic continuity, a number of churches express either their appreciation of the threefold ministry and of episcopacy as they already practise it within their own communities (Iceland IV.69-70) or, among those who do not presently have such a form of ministry, their willingness to adopt it (North Elbian I.49; Australia II.98; Denmark III.114).

Also, in this context of commenting upon the transmission of ministry, several responses address the question of the validity or the legitimacy of ministry. The Church of Norway, which does have an episcopal structure, states:

> We cannot see that the validity of ministerial acts performed by ordained persons are dependent on being able to trace back to the first apostles a formal succession of the laying-on of hands. The question of a church's apostolicity, and thereby the validity of its ministry, depends rather on the extent to which it has preserved the apostolic witness to Christ and apostolic teaching. Its validity does not depend on whether or not it has maintained an episcopate within the framework of apostolic succession. We are, against this background, pleased that the Lima document specifically states in §37: "In churches which practise the succession through the episcopate, it is increasingly recognized that continuity in apostolic faith, worship and mission has been preserved in churches which have not retained the form of historic episcopate" (II.121).

Some of these latter churches, on the other hand, are "deeply affronted when the full legitimacy of [their] ministry is denied" (North Elbian I.49) and "take exception to the normative status" accorded to the threefold ministry, especially since other ministerial structures have functioned just as well (American II.84). Other responses provide a rationale for this position. The Holy Spirit works directly through word and sacrament to create faith (Finland III.124); thus the Reformation understanding of continuity by means of word and sacrament contradicts the view that ministerial succession is indispensable (Estonia IV.45).

Perhaps the criticism most forcefully made by Lutherans of BEM's treatment of apostolicity concerns the respective roles of scripture and tradition as criteria for indicating the structure of church ministry. Some claim that scripture was not given decisive weight, as, for example, when the Lutheran Church of Australia (II.97) states that a wide variety of ministerial forms is present in the New Testament and asks why the full range of these ministries was not explored in BEM.[11] The Evangelical Lutheran Church in Oldenburg (IV.78) states that BEM's view of ministry is unbiblical on two accounts: it makes ministry constitutive for the life of the church in a way that the New Testament does not and it relinquishes the diversity which one finds there. The Lutheran Church in Hungary (III.129) simply states that it cannot accept the threefold pattern of ministry because it is not in scripture. Others speak against the use of tradition as a criterion for discerning ministerial structure (Missouri III.132 and 140; Oldenburg IV, passim). The threefold pattern cannot be seen as *iure divino* (Denmark III.114), for it is merely the result of an historical development during the first several centuries (Hanover IV.55; Brunswick VI.48). These comments all seem to call for a more decisive role for scripture and a less decisive role for historical developments or tradition in questions of determining ministerial structure.

Finally, several responses explicitly list their own criteria on the basis of which they evaluate questions of faith and order. The Lutheran Church of Australia (II.90) lists reference to scripture, Lutheran confessional documents (the Augsburg Confession), Lutheran theology and spirituality as the regular criteria for such discernment (see also Independent Evangelical Lutheran Church of FRG and West Berlin VI.50-51). The Lutheran Church-Missouri Synod (III.132) simply states: "We believe that the ultimate criterion for the church's faith is the inerrant scriptures, always viewed in the light of the gospel of Jesus Christ." The Evangelical Church of Finland cites as a major difficulty in responding to BEM the fact that "apostolicity" means quite different things to different communities and that there are no agreed-upon meaning or criteria for determining precisely what is "apostolic" and what is not (III.125; also Missouri III.133). This leads the Lutheran Church-Missouri Synod (III.132) to refer to the "unclear hermeneutical basis" of BEM.

7. Methodist responses on apostolicity

Responses cited: United Methodist Church-USA (II.177-99); United Methodist Church, Central and Southern Europe (II.200-209); Methodist Church-UK (II.210-29); Methodist Church of Southern Africa (II.236-44); Evangelical-Methodist Church: Central Conference in the German Democratic Republic (IV.167-72); Evangelical-Methodist Church: Central Conference in the Federal Republic of Germany and West Berlin (IV.173-82).

Many Methodist responses register agreement and satisfaction with the distinction in BEM between, on the one hand, continuity in the apostolic tradition by means of the various elements mentioned in paragraph 34 of the Ministry section and, on the other, continuity by means of succession in the transmission of ordained ministry. These responses highlight the fact that such a distinction allows one to conceive the church's apostolicity primarily as a characteristic of the community as a whole, and not to understand it as primarily limited to one group within the church (Central and Southern Europe II.208; South Africa II.242-43; German Democratic Republic IV.171; Federal Republic of Germany IV.180). This distinction provides a basis for asserting that no community has neglected its task of maintaining apostolicity (Central and Southern Europe II.208; German Democratic Republic IV.171) and, moreover, that there are many ways of accomplishing this task (United Kingdom II.226; Federal Republic of Germany IV.180). Indeed, the Methodist Church-UK (II.226-27) states that episcopal succession is only one way of maintaining continuity, a goal which has been accomplished equally well in non-episcopal communities. With regard to apostolicity, the important question is *whether* a community has maintained continuity with the apostolic community; *how* it has done so may be left open to a wide variety of ways (Central and Southern Europe II.208).

These general considerations about apostolicity provide the context for the Methodist responses concerning the episcopacy. The Methodist Church-USA is by far the largest of those Methodist churches which responded to BEM.[12] It modestly notes that it has not reflected at length precisely on the meaning of the episcopacy, as distinct from its exercise, and that it tends to designate those who exercise this function by the term "elder" (II.195). Because of this, the Methodist Church-USA sees the need for much more dialogue before reconciliation can be achieved in this matter of the relation between apostolicity and episcopacy.

The positions of the other respondents is more determined. Episcopacy has not been historically shown to be the ministerial form that all should adopt, nor is the view convincing that this is the form which will best serve Christian unity (Central and Southern Europe II.208; see also Federal Republic of Germany IV.181). Episcopacy is not normative for church order (United Kingdom II.226) nor can one identify apostolic continuity with episcopal succession (South Africa II.242-43). Therefore, recognition of ministry cannot be made to depend upon episcopal succession (Central and Southern Europe II.208). Some note that they would not accept the interpretation that their adoption of episcopacy made up for some "lack" in their present order or that their present order is in some way "invalid" (United Kingdom II.226; South Africa II.242-43).

To these misgivings concerning the necessity of episcopacy should be added the comments in a somewhat different direction that welcome

BEM's recognition of the necessity of the function of *episkope*, understood as having manifold forms (Federal Republic of Germany IV.181). Moreover, some acknowledge that the orderly transmission of ministerial responsibility is a powerful sign of continuity (South Africa II.242-43), especially when one is careful not to equate orderly transmission with the threefold structure of bishop-presbyter-deacon (United Kingdom II.227). In fact, because of its implication of hierarchical dominance of one order over another, the threefold order is spoken of as a "perversion" since, according to the New Testament, all ministerial functions are equal (Federal Republic of Germany IV.181).

There is some willingness to adopt the episcopal or threefold structure for the sake of promoting greater unity with other churches (United Kingdom II.226), but with the proviso that this structure be understood only as a sign, not as a guarantee of apostolicity (United Kingdom II.227; see also Federal Republic of Germany IV.182). But others counter that unity should be found in faith and discipleship, not in structure (German Democratic Republic IV.172). Some wonder if there is not a basic inconsistency in BEM when it calls upon episcopal churches to recognize the apostolic content of the ministry of non-episcopal churches but does not demand that they acknowledge the "validity" of such ministry (United Kingdom II.227). Or again, is it consistent to recognize the apostolicity of a community as a whole on the basis of its continuity in the apostolic tradition and nevertheless ask that community to adopt episcopal succession for the sake of apostolic continuity (German Democratic Republic IV.172)? Finally, the Methodist Church in South Africa (II.243) challenges the episcopal churches truly to recognize the apostolicity of those communities which are not episcopal.

8. Moravian responses concerning apostolicity

Responses cited: Moravian Church in America, Southern Province (II.255-59); Moravian Church in America, Northern Province (II.260-63); Moravian Church in Great Britain and Ireland (III.284-88); Moravian Church in Jamaica (V.169-72); European Continental Province of the Moravian Church (VI.115-23).

The Moravian responses are unanimous in pointing out their tradition that doctrinal statements of any kind, and therefore also about the apostolicity of the church or of ministry, suffer from a certain insufficiency and precariousness. Several communities state explicitly that, as a matter of principle, they generally refrain from making doctrinal statements (America, Northern Province II.260; Great Britain and Ireland III.284-85; European Continental VI.116). What is most important is not doctrine but rather to live the faith (America, Northern Province II.262). The ultimate source and rule of faith is the Bible (Great Britain and Ireland III.284-85). Moravians can accept BEM as an expression of the apostolic faith, but add that this acceptance must be understood within their overall view that definitive doctrinal statements are impossible (America, Northern Province II.262; Great Britain and Ireland III.284-85).

That being said, three of the responses add some specific points relevant to the topic of apostolicity. Two emphasize that they do not understand succession in ministry as any type of mechanical process (America, Southern Province II.257-58; Great Britain and Ireland III.286), the latter of these noting that the threefold structure is the form which in fact is practised in their own community. The European Continental Province (VI.120) provides the most extensive Moravian reflection when, after pointing out that it has deliberately refrained from developing a detailed theory of ministry, it adds that it does understand itself as practising an orderly transmission of ministry since 1467 and that this transmission is viewed as a connecting link with the ancient church. However, it is not understood "as an episcopal succession (by divine ordinance) in the Roman Catholic sense". Seeing no essential differentiation within ordained ministry, Moravians "can also recognize ministries and ordination in churches with no episcopal tradition".

9. Orthodox responses on apostolicity

Responses quoted: Russian Orthodox Church (II.5-12); Bulgarian Orthodox Church (II.13-23); Finnish Orthodox Church (II.24-29); Romanian Orthodox Church (III.4-14); Orthodox Church in America (III.15-25); Ecumenical Patriarchate of Constantinople (IV.1-6).

Not all of the Orthodox responses took up the question of apostolicity, but the comments of those that did may be summarized under three headings: (1) the meaning and importance of "apostolicity", (2) the necessity of episcopal succession for apostolicity, and (3) miscellaneous critical comments.

First of all, the very word "apostolic" is understood almost always in reference to the faith and practice of the *early* church (Russia II.5; Bulgaria II.15). More specifically, the "apostolic tradition" is preserved and witnessed by the church in its teaching, in conciliar experience, in liturgical-sacramental devotion and in the gracious holiness of the life and teaching of its martyrs, confessors, fathers and doctors (Russia II.10; see also America III.19 on the liturgy). The Orthodox place a strong emphasis upon faithfulness or loyalty to the early church (Russia II.10; Bulgaria II.13). As the Bulgarian Orthodox Church (II.14) states: "... the teaching of the early church and the embodiment of the apostolic tradition in that church's practice ought to be taken as a model and norm in the mutual efforts for closer relations and unity, and... all innovations contrary to that model and norm ought to be rejected."

Secondly, the Orthodox are unanimous in insisting that episcopal succession is an "inextricably" "necessary", "essential" and "constitutive" "prerequisite" for the apostolicity of the church in its fullest sense (the words in quotation marks are used variously on the following pages: Russia II.10; Bulgaria II.14; Finland II.28; Romania III.11; America III.21). Frequently a reason given in explanation of this necessity is the "origin of the priesthood" in Christ, who bestows it upon the apostles (Bulgaria II.21 and 23; Finland II.28). The Orthodox Church in America (III.21) notes as a positive point that BEM does assert the church's dependence on the triune God and on Jesus Christ with regard to ministry. In contrast, the Romanian Orthodox Church (III.11) points out that BEM's recommendation that churches "avoid attributing their particular forms of the ordained ministry directly to the will and institution of Jesus Christ (comm. 11)... denies directly the belief of the churches with the firm conscience that the structures of ordained ministry are wanted and instituted by Christ himself". Bulgaria (II.23) also criticizes BEM for downplaying the institution of ministry by Christ. This notion of institution also appears to provide the context for the insistence upon the transmission of ministry by means of a line of succession in the laying-on of hands. Here the Russian Orthodox Church (II.9) points out that BEM neglects to speak of the transmission of grace which occurs in ministerial succession, and the Bulgarian Orthodox Church (II.21-22) emphasizes the importance of the unbrokenness of the line of transmission. This succession is further considered as necessary for the celebration of the eucharist (Russia II.10; Bulgaria II.19) and as essential to considering as "valid" (Bulgaria II.22-23) or to "recognizing" (Ecumenical Patriarchate IV.3) the sacraments of other churches. Finally, under this second heading concerning the necessity of episcopal succession for the apostolicity of the church, the Orthodox raise a question about the distinction which BEM proposes between apostolic tradition, on the one hand, and episcopal succession, on the other. These churches vary somewhat as to whether they consider this distinction to be useful or clear or valid. (For example, Romania III.10 and America III.21 seem to find the distinction acceptable and useful, even if perhaps a bit ambiguous; Bulgaria II.22-23, on the other hand, seems to reject such a distinction because it divides what cannot and should not be divided.) But regardless of such differences, the Orthodox seem to be unanimous in affirming that one cannot separate episcopal succession from continuity in apostolic tradition.

Finally, several critical comments about BEM appear which do not fit precisely under the previous two categories. The Finnish Orthodox Church (II.28-29) faults BEM for not clearly enough expressing "the unanimity concerning episcopacy and its nature, which prevailed in the patristic period and in the undivided church even after that and which still prevails between the Roman Catholic and Orthodox Church – except in the case of the papacy". The Romanian Orthodox Church (III.11) finds an inconsistency in BEM when, on the one hand, it affirms apostolic succession through the episcopate (comm. 34) and, on the other hand, it asks for the recognition of apostolic succession of the churches which have not retained or do not have episcopal succession (M37). Finally, the Orthodox Church in America (III.21) questions the way in which BEM speaks of the historical development of the episcopacy, almost as if such a development could be seen as a mere historical contingency:

> As in regard to the development of the threefold ministry, we would see an "inner logic" at work here, and not simply "the particular historical circumstances of the growing church in the early centuries" referred to in the Lima statement. Can it really be possible that those charged with *episkope* in the church, and thereby primarily responsible for "the orderly transmission of the ordained ministry", as well as the continuity of the church's essential faith and her necessary structures of communion, came to this position through fortuitous historical circumstances? We think not.

10. Reformed-Presbyterian responses on apostolicity

Responses quoted: United Reformed Church in the United Kingdom (I.101-109); Reformed Church in America (II.141-51); Presbyterian Church in Canada (II.152-59); Presbyterian Church of Korea (II.160-64); Presbyterian Church of Wales (II.165-74); Reformed Church of Alsace and Lorraine (III.165-67); Presbyterian Church of Rwanda (III.183-85); Presbyterian Church USA (III.189-205); Presbyterian Church in Ireland (III.206-21); Cumberland Presbyterian Church (III.222-26); Evangelical-Reformed Church of North-West Germany (IV.93-99); Netherlands Reformed Church and Reformed Churches in the Netherlands (IV.100-109); Reformed Church in Hungary (V.161-64).

These responses register appreciation that BEM reflects the way in which the New Testament relates the apostles to ministry. They also acknowledge that BEM presents apostolicity as entailing a continuity considerably broader than simply continuity in ministry (Presbyterian-Ireland III.216 and 218; Presbyterian-Korea II.164). A number of churches also concur with BEM's statement that ministry and its transmission has an important role to play in serving apostolic continuity (Presbyterian-USA III.199 and 203; Evangelical Reformed-North-West Germany IV.98; Reformed-Hungary V.163; Netherlands Reformed and Reformed Churches in the Netherlands IV.104), although some explicitly mention that ministerial succession must always be seen as subordinate to continuity in apostolic preaching (Presbyterian-Rwanda III.184). Thus some of these communities seem to place more importance upon the role of ministerial continuity for apostolicity than do others.

This group of responses posed several rather serious challenges to what BEM says about apostolicity.

Use of scripture. First of all, some see BEM as failing to ground its proposals about ministerial apostolicity in the message of scripture. BEM does not mention the exegetical difficulties in distinguishing the roles of *episkopoi* and *presbyteroi* in the New Testament (Evangelical Reformed-North-West Germany IV.98; Presbyterian-Wales II.172). Moreover, the threefold pattern that BEM proposes as a model for ministry "can find little foundation in the New Testament" (Presbyterian-Ireland III.217 and Evangelical Reformed-North-West Germany IV.98). As a general principle, it seems that BEM does not give primacy to the New Testament in providing criteria for ministry (Presbyterian-Ireland III.215 and 218-21; Reformed-Alsace and Lorraine III.165-66; Presbyterian-Rwanda III.185). One church states that, according to scripture, ministry is "not a constitutive element of the church" and that a rich variety of ministries is the New Testament model; one should not reduce this richness to the one threefold model of bishop-presbyter-deacon (Reformed-Alsace and Lorraine III.166).

Role of Tradition and history. In a closely related theme, several communities question BEM's use of tradition or of history. The United Reformed Church in the United Kingdom (I.104-105) notes that more work needs to be done concerning the criteria on the basis of which some historical developments are taken to be the work of the Holy Spirit and others not. Might not the Spirit be seen in the break-up of the threefold pattern of ministry during the 16th century, they ask. The Presbyterian Church USA (III.200-201) raises the same question with regard to the ordination of women: might not this recent development be seen as an effect of the Holy Spirit and as such "a faithful expression of the apostolic tradition"? Both of these communities state that the present needs of the mission of Christ's church, and not only models from the past, must also be considered as criteria for determining the ministerial structures appropriate for today (United Reformed-United Kingdom I.108; Presbyterian-USA III.204). Finally, the Netherlands Reformed Church and Reformed Churches in the Netherlands (IV.107-108) state that

BEM's attempt to mediate "between the historical episcopate on the one hand and the rejection of any structural connection with tradition on the other" fails, in part, because it attempts to give a normative status to what is merely one historical development (the threefold ministry).

Questions about episcopacy and recognition. Several churches in this group are of the opinion that BEM contains a bias in favour of a "Catholic" over against a "Reformed" view of ministry (Presbyterian-Ireland III.215 and 220-21 and Presbyterian-Canada II.158). They think also that BEM assigns a certain superiority to the threefold or episcopal order (Presbyterian-Ireland III.219) and that BEM makes no mention of the biblically based ministerial structure found in the Calvinist tradition (Reformed-Hungary V.163).[13] If episcopacy is seen *only* as a sign of apostolicity, and not a guarantee, and if the episcopal churches truly recognize the apostolicity of the non-episcopal churches, why then should these latter be asked to change their present ministerial structure and to begin to have bishops (Presbyterian-Wales II.173)? Perhaps the recognition of non-episcopal ministry by episcopal churches cannot really be counted upon (Presbyterian-Rwanda III.184-85).[14] Moreover, how can Reformed churches adopt the episcopal form of ministry without ipso facto throwing "the existing continuity with apostolic faith, worship and mission into question" (United Reformed-United Kingdom I.108; see also Reformed-America II.149). Some churches here wonder if the proposals of BEM are not in effect a surreptitious way of affirming "apostolic succession" (Presbyterian-Ireland III.218-19; Cumberland Presbyterian III.225).[15] Finally, there is a certain hesitancy that, in promoting the episcopacy, BEM is in fact promoting an historical form of ministry which tended to concentrate authority in the hands of the bishop (Evangelical Reformed-North-West Germany IV.98) and which is "hierarchical" (Reformed-Hungary V.163; Netherlands Reformed and Reformed Churches in the Netherlands IV.108).

11. Waldensian responses on apostolicity

Waldensian and Methodist Churches in Italy (II.245-54); Waldensian Evangelical Church of the River Plate-Uruguay (IV.118-27).

The Waldensian responses find BEM to contain a clerical and sacramental tone that is foreign to the gospel (Italy II.245) and a technical language more suited to specialists than ordinary Christians (Plate IV.118-19). With regard to the precise issue of apostolicity, both responses welcome the distinction between continuity in the apostolic tradition by the church as a whole, on the one hand, and apostolic succession in ministry, on the other (Italy II.251; Plate IV.123). However, the way in which BEM suggests a link between continuity in apostolic tradition and succession in ministry is criticized by these churches, each in a different way.

The Italian Waldensian response (II.251-52) criticizes BEM for paying too little attention to the role of the Holy Spirit. Because BEM does not take with full seriousness the fact that the Holy Spirit maintains the church in apostolic continuity, it requests communities without episcopal structure to adopt this structure. If BEM were really consistent about the role of the Holy Spirit, it would instead ask those communities with episcopal structure to question themselves as to why they attribute so much importance to bishops.

The response from the Waldensian Evangelical Church of the River Plate (IV.123) acknowledges that the Holy Spirit is mentioned in BEM in connection with apostolic continuity. But the fact that non-episcopal churches are asked to adopt an episcopal form shows that, in reality, BEM makes apostolicity depend more on ministerial structure than on evangelical purity or the life of the community. It is not a matter of agreement among the churches that ministry plays such a decisive role. This community explicitly disagrees that churches should accept a form of ministry so as to feel more identified with the church of the apostles (Plate IV.124-25) and, moreover, believes that BEM's focus upon ministerial structure, particularly upon the episcopacy, betrays a bias towards a hierarchical vision of the church which is not promising for the future (Plate IV.126).

B. Responses by individual worldwide communities

12. *Roman Catholic comments on apostolicity (VI.1-40)*

The Roman Catholic response addresses the theme of apostolicity directly in two places: in an opening section which speaks about the need for further ecumenical dialogue about the meaning of "apostolic tradition" (VI.7-8) and in its commentary on paragraphs 34-38 of BEM's Ministry section, which deals with "Succession in the Apostolic Tradition" (VI.32-33).

Regarding "apostolic tradition", the response notes that "according to Catholic teaching sacred Tradition and sacred scripture make up a single sacred deposit of the word of God which is entrusted to the church" (VI.7). This Word, which finds its fullest expression in Jesus himself, is entrusted by Christ to the apostles who hand it on to their successors so that, "enlightened by the Spirit of truth, they may faithfully preserve, expound and spread it abroad by their preaching" (VI.8). In light of this, Roman Catholics hold that there must be a clear distinction "between the apostolic tradition, which obliges us because it is rooted in Revelation, and the various traditions which may develop in local churches" (VI.8). It is by adhering to the word of God as found in both scripture and Tradition that the church remains apostolic, "faithful to the teaching of the apostles and to the gospel of Christ" (VI.8).

Regarding paragraphs 34-38 of BEM's ministry section, the Roman Catholic response seems able to be summarized in three points. First, it sees advantages in the way in which BEM relates the apostolicity of the church and apostolic tradition, on the one side, and the orderly transmission of ordained ministry and episcopal succession, on the other (VI.32). Such an approach has the advantage of setting the problem in a wide ecclesiological context and of enhancing the mutual comprehension of practices which may seem unacceptable when isolated from such a context. Second, the Roman Catholic response judges legitimate the presentation of succession in ministry as one of the several ways in which the church permanently remains in continuity with the church of the apostles. A criticism is made, however, of the lack of integration between these ways, as if the BEM text were content simply to list and juxtapose elements of continuity without showing how they function within the totality or how they relate among themselves. Third, the response comments on BEM's statement that episcopal succession is "a sign, though not a guarantee of the continuity and unity of the church". Roman Catholics agree that it is a sign, but ask for further clarity about the nature of this sign. The earlier Accra document's use of the expression "effective sign" better indicated the unique role of episcopal succession in the catholic understanding of the church.[16] The response continues:

> This is immediately related to the meaning which the ministry of the bishop has in a Catholic ecclesiology: it is more than a function of oversight next to other functions and ministries. In his very personal ministry, the bishop represents the local church entrusted to him. He is its qualified spokesperson in the communion of the churches. At the same time he is the first representative of Jesus in the community. By his ordination to the episcopacy he is commissioned to exercise leadership in the community, to teach with authority and to judge. All other ministries are linked to his and function in relationship to it. Thus his ministry is a sacramental sign of integration and a focus of communion. Through the episcopal succession, the bishop embodies and actualizes both catholicity in time, i.e., the continuity of the church across the generations, as well as the communion lived in each generation. The actual community is thus linked up through a personal sign with the apostolic origins, its teaching and way of living (33).

In light of this, the response concludes that one can rightly think of episcopal succession even as a "guarantee" of apostolic continuity, understanding it as an "expression of Christ's faithfulness to the church until the end of time".

13. The Salvation Army on apostolicity (IV.230-57)

The response of the Salvation Army to BEM is characterized by a "painful awareness" and sense of "regret and concern that the sincerely held views of non-sacramentalist Christians are ignored in this document" (IV.234 and 230). Taking the text of BEM literally may arouse fears regarding the exclusion of these Christians from this fellowship of churches [the WCC?] by the implied denial of the validity of their views (IV.254). Is the Toronto statement of 1950 ("The Church, the Churches and the World Council of Churches") still in force, which welcomes the participation of all communities irrespective of their ecclesiological views (IV.232)?

Salvationists distinguish between "apostolic faith" and "apostolic tradition" (IV.254), finding highly dubious BEM's elevation of the latter to the same status as the former (IV.231). One should be sceptical also about "the elevation to near scriptural authority" of any tradition, since the same history is interpreted quite differently by different readers (IV.234). Pages 250-51 focus upon the precise issue of "Succession in the Apostolic Tradition", commenting respectively upon BEM's two subdivisions "Apostolic Tradition in the Church" and "Succession of the Apostolic Ministry". Under the first of these, the response presents a succinct description of apostolicity:

> Apostleship in Salvation Army terms means being sent by God in the power of the Spirit according to the scriptures. Historical continuity alone does not guarantee apostolicity, and can be used to exclude some branches of the Christian family. Nevertheless, we agree with what this paragraph [§34] says about the church, except for specific "sacramental" references.

The response goes on to say that succession in fidelity to the gospel and in service is more important to succession in ministry. The Salvation Army shows its "concern for 'orderly transmission'" in that it "imposes on its officers and soldiers alike the necessity to adhere to its established doctrines as the only authorized basis for its teaching and practice". These doctrines are based upon the scriptures and upon the Nicene and Apostles' Creeds.

Regarding "Succession of the Apostolic Ministry", the response notes:

> We do not see the preservation of the apostolic faith as being determined by any mystical transmission from one ordained minister to another, but by faithfulness to the word of God and an openness to the Holy Spirit on the part of

each successive generation of Christians. This we regard as the "orderly trans-mission" of apostolic faith.

Salvationists do not deny that the episcopal structure can be an effec-tive means for the preservation of the gospel among those communities which have such a form of ministry. But they insist that the spiritual character and authority of the leader is more important than any office or title which he or she may hold. Finally, the response identifies as the Sal-vation Army's own position BEM's statement in paragraph 37 that con-tinuity in apostolic faith, worship and mission as well as the reality and function of episcopal ministry have been preserved in churches which have not retained the form of the historic episcopate.

14. Seventh-day Adventist response on apostolicity (II.337-48)

The section of this response which directly treats the topic of apos-tolicity can be found on page 347. The relevant text begins with the fol-lowing words: "Adventists, being non-sacramental in the strict sense, have difficulty in appreciating the full force of the theological-sacra-mental reasons for episcopacy." What follows is a series of questions that need to be answered if one is to give a reasonable evaluation of BEM's proposals about apostolicity. Is the structure of ministry divinely ordained or merely an historical accident? Are the ministerial structures within the church permanent or can they change? What precisely does it mean to state that episcopal succession is a "sign" of apostolic continu-ity? Is it "merely a sign" or is the word "sign" to be "taken in a strictly sacramental sense of an efficacious action graced by the Spirit", in which case "then apostolic succession is indeed a need in the church"? Without a more direct response to these questions, the Adventist response finds BEM's presentation unconvincing.

Moreover, the Adventists stress the fundamental importance of apos-tolicity in faith. If faith is the essential criterion of apostolicity, then there would appear to be no valid reason to insist upon the episcopacy as a sign of apostolicity. If one already believes with the faith of the apostles, what is to be added by reception of the sign of episcopal ordination? Or, on the other hand, would anyone claim that episcopal ordination auto-matically made its recipient faithful to the apostolic faith? Moreover, "... if one has the substance but lacks the sign, would not insistence on reception of the sign as a *sine qua non* of union be placing church order above the gospel?"

In summary, the Adventist response finds BEM's presentation of apostolicity to be too sacramental and too influenced by Orthodox, Anglican and Roman Catholic thought (II.348). But its difficulty with this lies precisely in the fact that the Adventists find it, at least as it is expressed in BEM, to be based upon unestablished presuppositions or inconsistencies.

C. Responses by united churches

15. United churches' responses about apostolicity

> *Responses cited: Church of North India (II.69-73); Church of South India (II.74-78); United Church of Christ-USA (II.324-36); United Protestant Church of Belgium (III.168-82); Union of Welsh Independents (III.268-83); Evangelical Church in Hesse and Nassau-FRG (IV.128-36); Evangelical Church of Westphalia-FRG (IV.137-53); Uniting Church in Australia (IV.154-65); Evangelical Church of the Rhineland-FRG (V.69-93); Evangelical Church of Kurhessen-Waldeck-FRG (V.94-118); Federation of the Evangelical Churches in the German Democratic Republic (V.119-60); Evangelical Church of the Congo (V.165-68); Evangelical Church of the River Plate-Argentina (V.175-78); Evangelical Church in Berlin-Brandenburg-West Berlin (VI.58-67); Swiss Protestant Church Federation (VI.75-87).*

The responses considered here come from churches which represent the coming together of several of the ecclesial traditions we have already encountered. Obviously, the respective sensibilities or perspectives of these united communities should not be supposed, in an overly simplistic way, to be homogeneous with each other. Nevertheless, they do have in common the fact that they have undergone the experience of "uniting" and, as such, their being placed together here is not altogether inappropriate.[17]

These communities would agree that the church must live in continuity with the apostles (Westphalia IV.146) and that ordained ministry has a role in serving such continuity (Westphalia IV.146; German Democratic Republic V.143; Berlin-Brandenburg VI.67). But they understand apostolicity primarily as fidelity to the scriptures (German Democratic Republic V.143; Congo V.167). For this reason, there is a generally positive evaluation of BEM's distinction between the continuity of the church as a whole within the apostolic tradition, on the one hand, and apostolic succession in ordained ministry, on the other (North India II.73; South India II.78; Belgium III.177 [the distinction marks "progress" in ecumenical dialogue]; Westphalia IV.146; Baden V.54; German Democratic Republic V.143 ["a great gain"]; Berlin-Brandenburg VI.67).

Many note that scripture itself, which is the source and criterion for church witness and service (Berlin-Brandenburg VI.67), contains a variety of forms of ministry (Westphalia IV.152; Australia IV.163; Rhineland V.89; German Democratic Republic V.143; Congo V.167). Because this is so, it is unbiblical to insist on only one form (Belgium III.176; Wales III.280). Indeed BEM suffers from not being sufficiently biblical in its presentation of ministry (Plate V.178); scripture has yielded too readily to tradition (Belgium III.168). The Evangelical Church of Baden (V.55) attempts what may be called a Reformation reading of the unfolding development of ministry, stating that during the middle ages the early church linkage of ordination and visitation was broken in such a way that "ordination to the pastoral ministry was overshadowed by an ordination to the sacrificial priesthood" (see also the Swiss Protestant Church Federation VI.79 on the "discontinuities" within the transmission of ministry over the ages). The response of the Evangelical Church of Baden continues:

> The Reformers called special attention to the ministry of word and sacrament, reunited the ministry of the ordinator with that of the visitator and thus returned to a correct understanding of the episcopal commission. In view of the variety of forms of episcopal ministry in the different churches and in their history, it is not possible to speak of the historical form of episcopal ministry. Thus we cannot recognize that the Roman Catholic Church, or any other church, has preserved that form, or even could have been able to preserve it. Therefore a "mutual recognition of ministries" (§§51-55) has to be based on the acceptance that just like other churches our Protestant churches have also practised the public ministry of word and sacrament through obligation and obedience (V.55).

In a similar way, the Federation of Evangelical Churches in the German Democratic Republic (V.137-38) points out that while the ministry entrusted with preaching the gospel and administering the sacraments derives from a divine commission, the historically developed forms of ministry must be measured against this commission. No particular form of ministry can be traced back directly to an act of institution on the part of Jesus Christ and, therefore, a variety of forms can be recognized as legitimate expressions of "obedience to the church's Lord". The United Protestant Church of Belgium (III.181) also affirms that Jesus himself founded no form of ministry (nor, they add, did he found a church). Regarding the apostles, some see a relation between ordained ministry and the choosing and sending of the apostles (Baden V.51), while others stress the uniqueness of the role of the apostles (Belgium III.175; USA II.327) and the danger that speaking of the ministry as founded on the apostles may obscure its essential dependence upon Christ (USA II.327).

These reflections about scripture and about the historical development of forms of ministry lead several of the united churches to attribute to the church a rather ample freedom in structuring the ministry (Belgium III.177; Westphalia IV.147) and to deny that any particular form of ministry can be called "constitutive" (Belgium III.175; Westphalia IV.147 and 152). Many of the forms that have developed over the centuries may be considered as "valid" (Westphalia IV.148; German Democratic Republic V.138; Congo V.168). The most important condition for apostolic continuity in ministry is the permanent presence and activity of the Holy Spirit (Belgium III.174; Rhineland V.91; Congo V.168).

Several communities very forcefully add that any acceptance on their part either of the sign of episcopal succession or of the text of BEM about ministry must in no way be interpreted as an admission that their present ministry can be considered as "not legitimate" or "invalid" (Belgium III.180; German Democratic Republic V.143). These sentiments are also connected with the recurrent questioning of the way in which BEM promotes the episcopacy as a sign or focus or service to church unity. A number of responses bluntly state that they simply do not admit such to be the case (Belgium III.176; Wales III.282; Baden V.56; Rhineland V.91). That specifically episcopal succession could be necessary for apostolic continuity is "problematical" (Plate V.177; see also North India II.73; South India II.78; Rhineland V.91; Kurhessen-Waldeck V.98 and German Democratic Republic V.143). Several responses state that BEM contains a prejudice in favour of the episcopal model of ministry as found in the Roman Catholic and Orthodox churches (Belgium III.178-181; Wales III.281; Baden V.56; Rhineland V.84) and that, of the three ministerial models mentioned in earlier Faith and Order discussions (episcopal, presbyterial, congregational), BEM appears to give little or no attention to the latter two (Belgium III.179; Westphalia IV.152; Baden V.56). Why is not a more critical self-examination requested of communities with episcopal succession, several responses ask (Wales III.281; Rhineland V.92). The episcopal ministry is especially in need of challenge because of the clerical, ontological and hierarchical (in the sense of fostering inequality within the church) form and manner of exercise which it has taken in the course of history (USA II.327; Belgium III.174-75 and 177-78; Hesse and Nassau-FRG IV.135 and Westphalia IV.148).

Finally, some communities express an openness to accepting the episcopal form of ministry as a sign of apostolic continuity, although they add that, in agreement with BEM, they could not consider this form in any way as a "guarantee" of such continuity (North India II.73; South India II.78; Australia IV.165; Baden V.54; Rhineland V.91; Berlin-Bran-

denburg VI.67). Others simply state that they "cannot accept the hierarchical form bishop-presbyter-deacon" (Westphalia IV.148). Two
responses see an inconsistency in BEM's apparent acceptance of the
apostolicity of non-episcopal ministry, on the one hand, and its request
that such churches nevertheless adopt episcopal ministry, on the other
hand (Belgium III.177; Wales III.281).

III. HERMENEUTICAL EVALUATION
OF THE RESPONSES TO BEM ABOUT APOSTOLICITY

Now I will attempt to bring the three hermeneutical principles which
were singled out in Part I to bear upon the material presented in Part II.

A. Accurate interpretation is faithfully attentive to the texts themselves

If one poses the simple question, "how attentive were the various
churches in interpreting the text of BEM?", one immediately notices that
the responses did more than merely seek to *understand* the statement
proposed by the Faith and Order commission. In fact, the churches were
asked not only to understand but also to make a *judgment*, to determine
"the extent to which your church can recognize in this text the faith of
the Church through the ages". Instead of the usual "hermeneutical circle" comprised of interpreter and text, a third factor was introduced: "the
faith of the church through the ages". The churches were to compare
BEM with this faith and to judge the degree of correspondence between
the two.[18] This means that, if hermeneutics principally concerns the task
of understanding, an ecumenical process like that of responding to the
text of BEM will need to go beyond the properly hermeneutical task and
enter the further realm of judging whether a particular statement is sufficient to serve as a common expression of what Christians believe to be
the faith of the church through the ages. To understand is one thing; to
judge is quite another. Were one to use the word hermeneutics in reference to both of these tasks without being attentive to this difference, it
could lead to considerable confusion.

That being said, it is nevertheless appropriate to ask: How attentively
did the various churches listen to the text of BEM? Did they accurately
"understand" it? A good guide to answering this question is chapter IV,
"Draft Clarifications and Comments on Critical Points", of *Baptism,
Eucharist and Ministry 1982-1990: Report on the Process and
Responses*.[19] This *Report*, which gave the Faith and Order commission

the opportunity to respond to some of the points within the various responses, notes that criticisms of BEM at times reflect an accurate reading of the text and rightly suggest that the text of BEM should be changed. For example, several responses objected to the ambiguity of BEM in referring to a ministry of *episkope* either as *a* focus or as *the* focus of unity for the Christian community. The *Report* admits that the responses were correct in noticing such ambiguity and says that in the text of BEM the indefinite article should have been used in all instances.[20] At times, on the other hand, the *Report* criticizes the responses for not attending carefully enough to the text of BEM, as when some express fear of a "confusion between the unique priesthood of Christ and the priestly service of the ordained ministry in its intercessory task". To this the *Report* responds: "Such a confusion cannot in any way be seen in BEM."[21] At times a criticism of BEM is answered by means of stating more explicitly what is left implicit in the actual text of BEM. Thus, to those who criticize M8 (which states that ordained ministry "is constitutive for the life and witness of the church") for attributing to the ministry something which is due only to Christ and his word and sacrament, the *Report* replies:

> It is Christ's continuing presence in word and sacrament, through the Holy Spirit, which is constitutive for the church. This implies, however, that for the sake of the ongoing life and mission of the church there must be persons, called by God, sent by Christ, assisted by the Holy Spirit and recognized by the people of God, to preach the word, to celebrate the sacraments, to bring together and guide the Christian community in faith, hope and love (cf. M13). In terms of this service of Christ and of the community the ordained ministry is therefore constitutive.[22]

Here the *Report* has obviously accepted the premise of the criticism – that Christ's continuing presence in word and sacrament through the Holy Spirit is constitutive for the church – and has simply related the ordained ministry to these constitutive factors. In general, the *Report*'s "Clarifications and Comments on the Ministry Text" suggest that the report writers found the text of BEM to be well understood and that therefore the criticisms made of BEM did, in fact, call for correction or for further clarification.

What about the specific theme of apostolicity? Here at least two issues are relevant to our present question. The first concerns the distinction between the church's continuity as a whole in the apostolic tradition, on the one hand, and succession in the apostolic ministry, on the other.[23] The second concerns the word "validity".

As our survey in Part II has shown, most churches were pleased with the distinction between the apostolicity of the church as a whole in the apostolic tradition and succession in apostolic ministry. The hesitancy on the part of several responses seemed directed not precisely to the point that the church is apostolic in more ways than only by means of succession in ministry, but rather to the fact that this distinction could suggest a separation between continuity with apostolic tradition and ministerial succession.[24] Some applauded the distinction as providing a basis for greater understanding between divided Christian communities, even as they added that the organic unity of the various factors bringing about apostolicity must not be forgotten.[25] Most other communities seemed to welcome this distinction without any hesitation whatever.

Obviously this distinction is part of a trajectory that has emerged in a number of ecumenical dialogues over the past thirty years. The discussion has tried to mediate between two sharply distinct and opposed positions that would identify the apostolicity of the church either exclusively with apostolicity within an unbroken chain of ministerial ordination by bishops, on the one hand, or exclusively with apostolicity in the faith of the church of the apostles, on the other. Whether any community ever made such an exclusive identification is a question that need not be addressed here. Probably most communities believed that both some form of ministerial succession as well as some degree of fidelity to apostolic faith were indispensable to full apostolicity. Nevertheless, it is reasonable to state that Roman Catholics, Orthodox, Old Catholics and usually Anglicans believed episcopal succession to be necessary for authentic, genuine apostolicity. Most Lutherans, Reformed, Presbyterians, Baptists, Methodists and other pre- and post-Reformation Protestant communities believed fidelity to the gospel, and not ministerial succession, to be necessary for authentic, genuine apostolicity.

This background has had an impact upon the way in which the various communities "hear" and interpret what BEM is saying. The distinction between global apostolicity, on the one hand, and ministerial apostolicity, on the other, is not unacceptable to those who believe that episcopal succession is necessary, because this distinction does not in itself deny such necessity. It can be interpreted as simply stating that, in addition to episcopal succession, other factors also enter into a complete description of the apostolicity of the church. Thus the distinction does not require one to abandon the view that episcopal succession is necessary. Presumably these churches would acknowledge some level of apostolicity in communities which enjoy various elements of apostolicity but not episcopal succession. However, they would not be able to recognize in such communities apostolicity in its fullest sense.

On the other hand, communities without episcopal succession seem to understand this distinction as implying that apostolicity does not require such ministerial succession. Our survey showed that a repeated theme among these communities is a rather forceful rejection of the necessity of episcopal succession, and this usually on the grounds that such a necessity does not seem to be mandated in scripture[26] or that the mere historical development to which it may owe its origin cannot be normative for the church.[27] The distinction which sees ministerial succession as only one of the many means by which the church is apostolic thus is interpreted by these communities as implying that such succession is not strictly speaking necessary or, in that sense, constitutive of apostolicity and that communities without it are apostolic in the fullest sense of that term. Most of these communities would agree with BEM, however, that such ministerial succession is a valuable or powerful "sign", though not "guarantee", of apostolicity[28] and some who do not have the threefold structure of ministry even express a willingness to adopt it, if it is understood only as a sign.[29]

There appears to be at least one additional position that modifies these two to some degree: the view that some form of transmission of ministerial responsibility and some form of oversight is not just one element but is actually necessary for apostolicity, but that this necessary transmission and form is not that which came to be embodied in the historic episcopate.[30] This view would seem to be congenial to any community that placed a high priority on orderly transmission, but which did not recognize any essential differentiation within ordained ministry, any "hierarchy" between the various forms of ordained ministry.[31]

Here then we have a distinction presented by BEM which is more or less accepted by most respondents to the document but which, at least in one specific aspect – that of the necessity of episcopal or of ministerial succession – is understood quite differently. Those who believe episcopal succession to be necessary and those who do not both find that the distinction in no way alters their conviction. Indeed for the latter, the distinction seems to confirm their view. The lack of agreement in the way the various communities interpret the significance of this distinction explains why communities on both sides of the episcopacy question charge BEM with inconsistency.[32] Those without episcopal succession charge that if BEM truly accepts the full apostolicity of the non-episcopal churches, it is inconsistent to insist that those communities adopt the episcopal form of ministry.[33] Moreover, they ask, would not such a change imply a lack in the current ministerial practice of these communities, a point which they simply cannot accept? On the other side, some found it inconsistent that BEM places such a high regard on the value of succession in the threefold form of ministry as a sign of continuity with the church of the apostles and yet at the same time asks for the recognition of the apostolicity of those churches which lack this sign.

What can one conclude from these points? Certainly the distinction between continuity in apostolic tradition, on the one hand, and succession in apostolic ministry, on the other, has allowed divided communities to appreciate the importance which apostolicity has for each of them as well as the various ways in which communities identify their own apostolicity and that of others. Moreover, the responses suggest important questions that could be pursued and could lead to greater convergence in this area of apostolicity. If one can distinguish a plurality of factors that comprise apostolicity, are they related to one another and, if so, in what way? Would it be appropriate to speak of degrees of apostolicity corresponding to presence and configuration of the various elements in any given community? Are any specific elements absolutely necessary to the church's apostolicity or would the presence of any or of a sufficient number of elements qualify a community as fully apostolic?

A briefer comment under this heading can be made about the word "validity". In M38, BEM states that churches "cannot accept any suggestion that the ministry exercised in their own tradition should be invalid until the moment that it enters into an existing line of episcopal succession". As our survey above indicated, this note resonated well with many communities.[34] At the same time, several responses made specific mention of their belief in an essential bond between ordination within the episcopal succession, on the one hand, and recognition of the validity of the celebration of the sacraments, on the other.[35]

In this apparent conflict, one cannot help but wonder what precisely is meant by the words "valid" and "invalid" when used by BEM and by the apparently disagreeing communities. Might it not be the case that the word "valid" in BEM's statement and in the responses of many communities who do not see episcopal succession as a necessary component of full apostolicity means something like "authentic" or "an effective vehicle of the proclamation of the word and the celebration of the sacraments" or "an instrument of the Holy Spirit"? For those who see episcopal succession as necessary for full apostolicity it might mean as well "being in the line of ordination through episcopal succession". When the latter group has concerns about the "validity" of a particular ministry, perhaps it does not thereby intend to call into question its effectiveness in serving the holiness of the people to whom it ministers. It would seem that the ecumenical discussion of ministry needs to take into more explicit consideration the variety of meanings suggested by the word "validity".

B. Accurate interpretation avoids ideological distortions by means of self-scrutiny

This principle of ecumenical hermeneutics can perhaps be captured in the phrase Hegel uses in the introduction to his *Phenomenology of Spirit* when he speaks of the overcoming of "natural consciousness" as travelling along "a highway of despair".[36] Hermeneutics lays bare the danger that one's interpretation can be distorted by presuppositions or ideological commitments. If the protection against such distortion is self-scrutiny and if we are dealing with issues which are existentially very engaging because they are tied up with one's faith, then such self-scrutiny can be very much like Hegel's "highway of despair" or, more biblically, like Malachi's "refining fire" (3:2).

With regard to the responses to BEM, it should be noted that many communities adopted a methodology that included an element of self-scrutiny. Not only did these communities try to evaluate BEM in light of the faith of the church through the ages, they also noted points that challenged them to reconsider their own doctrine or practice. This methodology was especially strong among the Protestant communities, but can be seen to one degree or another in most of the responses.

At the same time, it is important to note that the responses to BEM are reactions to a text which, as such, cannot defend itself and challenge the comments made in the responses.[37] Probably the element of self-scrutiny would most effectively be fostered if the responses to BEM could be placed in dialogue with one another. Such a procedure would lead communities quite naturally to scrutinize their responses, examining whether the positions they espouse are truly demanded by faith or rather may in some way be derived from self-serving presuppositions.

A few examples could illustrate this point. Some churches state that Christ himself instituted the ordained ministry and that, therefore, the unbroken transmission of ministry through ordination by bishops is a necessary aspect of apostolicity.[38] Other churches state that Christ did not institute any specific ministerial structures and that one cannot therefore impose such structures as a requirement for apostolicity today.[39] A confrontation of these views could invite those who have stated that Christ instituted the ordained ministry to examine whether they have taken into sufficient consideration the complexities involved in proving historical affirmations from the biblical texts, as well as the apparent difficulty in reconciling an institution of ordained ministry by Christ with the seemingly fluid form of ministry in the New Testament. Might not the affirmation of divine institution be self-serving and simply validate the status quo, shielding those who make it from truly accepting the need to reform the ministry? In a similar way, those who claim that Jesus did not institute any specific ministerial structures could be invited to examine whether they have given sufficient consideration to the possibility that institution may be considered as a complex historical process. It need not be discounted simply if one cannot prove historically one precise moment of institution. Indeed, a degree of fluidity in ministerial structures could have been part of the process of institution, begun by Jesus in the selection and commissioning of certain of his disciples and brought to completion in the course of time under the influence of the Holy Spirit. Might not the denial of divine institution be self-serving and simply validate the status quo, a way of giving oneself permission to reject that ministerial structure which was recognized so early and which universally characterized church order for such a long time?

Another issue which could invite self-scrutiny concerns the need for or even possibility of an "unbroken" transmission of ordained ministry.[40] Those who insist on an "unbroken" handing on of ministerial power and authority might ask themselves why it would be impossible or unlikely for Christ and the Holy Spirit to continually provide all the divine assistance needed to render the ministry fully apostolic and effective. Could not such continual accompanying make an unbroken line of ministerial succession unnecessary? On the other side, those who find the unbroken transmission of ministerial authority untenable seem to do so for various reasons. Some doubt that such a series could be historically verifiable. Is it not naive to suppose that there have not been any gaps in this history? Others may fear that such a view of ministerial transmission reflects a doctrine of justification by works. Does it not make God's salvific activity in the church dependent upon a human activity – the orderly transmission of ministry? Those who hold such views might be invited to consider whether historical *verification* is truly decisive for this issue. Every human being is in fact part of a continuous line of generation, even though most people cannot trace back that line very far. Moreover, why may not God have freely determined to order the church in such a way that ministry would be empowered and authorized by means of unbroken succession of ordination from the time of the apostles? What would prevent God from choosing to employ tangible, sacramental means for maintaining the church in fidelity to the apostolic community, in which case it would hardly make sense to say that such means condition or limit God's freedom in acting to save human beings?

Many other examples which invite self-scrutiny could be gleaned from the responses to BEM. For those communities that say that apostolicity is to be understood only in terms of fidelity to the gospel or to the scriptures or to the faith of the apostles or to the presence of the Holy Spirit, one may pose the question: why should it not be attributed to all of these, and to the unbroken succession of ordained ministry as well? For those communities who insist on the threefold pattern of bishop-presbyter-deacon, one may pose the question: why is precisely this structure necessary, especially since there are many other factors which make for apostolicity and those who claim that the threefold form is necessary themselves acknowledge the legitimacy of ministerial development over the course of time? Why then could not other legitimate forms emerge? The three questions posed by the Seventh-day Adventist response could provide an occasion for careful self-scrutiny by all the churches, whatever their respective positions. Is ministerial structure divinely ordained or merely the result of historical accident? Are ministerial structures within the church permanent or can and do they change? What precisely does it mean to state that ministerial succession is a "sign" of apostolic continuity? If one does not remain content merely with attempting to answer these questions but proceeds to scrutinize the reasons behind one's answer as well as to ask if there are potentially self-serving or ideological motivations entwined with these reasons, then one will have gone far in doing all that is possible to avoid distorted or ideological interpretations of the apostolicity of the church.

This step of self-scrutiny could also include making a deliberate attempt to explain one's position in a way that takes into account the objections and questions of Christians who hold opposed points of view. This requires careful listening to the other so as to accurately understand the objection as well as an attempt to correct oneself in light of the objection or to rephrase one's position in such a way that it becomes clear that there is really no conflict between the two points of view after all. Of course, all of this self-scrutiny and effort to speak with the theological concerns of the other in mind does not preclude the possibility that, in the end, there may still remain irreconcilable differences which are sincerely held and which are not considered by oneself or even by both dialogue partners to be distorted or ideological interpretations of God's will for the church. In that case one probably has little recourse except that most excellent one, of praying for further enlightenment by the Holy Spirit. But these reflections about self-scrutiny have suggested ways in which the positions presented in the responses could be the point of departure for further dialogue on some significant questions. Perhaps this could be especially important for communities which have not had many other occasions than the BEM process in which to engage in ecumenical dialogue, for example, at the bilateral level.

C. Interpretations which concern the identity of the Christian community should address questions of criteria and authority

What criteria and what authority are relevant to the discernment of the identity of the Christian community? Earlier we noted the complexity this question introduces into the hermeneutical task.[41] Immediately some issues need to be clarified.

For example, is "authority" meant primarily to indicate living persons who currently hold some position in the church or does it also include figures from the past (fathers, doctors and saints), events (liturgy, councils) and documents (official teachings, canons)? Is "reason" an authority that contributes to the discernment of Christian identity?[42] If authority is understood in a broad sense to include many or all of these meanings, then does it differ from what is meant by the word "criteria"? Has the church ever compiled a complete or partial list of the criteria which are relevant to discerning Christian identity? Who would be competent "officially" to confirm such a list? Are there a limited number of evident criteria that every reasonable Christian or community would acknowledge as appropriate for discerning Christian identity? How do the elements that go into an adequate description of Christian identity furnish those necessary and sufficient conditions for the unity which the churches engaged in the ecumenical movement are seeking in obedience to the will of Christ? Any one of these questions could probably spark a lively discussion among theologians and believers.

The respondents to BEM do not enter into these rather complex issues but simply presuppose that they do know the relevant criteria and move straightaway to an evaluation of BEM's statements about apostolicity on the basis of such knowledge. What are the criteria or authorities used by the communities responding to BEM? The *Report* on the BEM process provides a very helpful analysis, in which all of the responses are said to base their argumentation on one of "six different combinations and correlations between the three elements of scripture, Tradition and traditions".[43] The six are:

a) Scripture is the only authority for the life and faith of the church.
b) Together with the priority of scripture, the Tradition of the "early" church is accepted as authoritative.
c) Additional statements of faith are accepted together with the priority of scripture and ancient creeds.
d) Together with scripture and Tradition a teaching office of the church, authoritatively interpreting scripture and Tradition, is affirmed.
e) A fifth group emphasizes the place of reason as a valid criterion for the shaping of an authentic and living faith.
f) The "faith of the church through the ages" is synonymous with the

dynamic understanding of "Tradition" which was expressed at the Faith and Order conference in Montreal (1963).[44]

The *Report* admits that there is "a certain artificiality about the delineation of six categories for they are not necessarily mutually exclusive".[45] While it is helpful to differentiate these various positions, it may be too great an understatement simply to acknowledge that "they are not necessarily mutually exclusive". For example, with the omission of the word "only" from the first statement, a community such as the Roman Catholic Church would probably associate itself with *all* of these categories and, indeed, would not want to be seen as excluding any of them. Probably most communities would find themselves in a similar situation, that is, not satisfied to be identified exclusively with only one of these categories. This makes one wonder whether the real difficulty concerning criteria may not ultimately remain the word "only" as it appears in the first of the configurations presented above. Even when one differentiates six or seven different emphases regarding criteria, one is still inevitably drawn back to the fundamental question of the normative authority of scripture or Tradition. What authority is acknowledged respectively to scripture and Tradition in the responses to BEM regarding apostolicity?[46]

Scripture. The responses to BEM suggest that some Christian communities ultimately accept only scripture as the *determining* criterion for the apostolicity of the church as regards faith and ministerial structure. Thus quite a few responses gratefully applaud BEM for stating that the New Testament exhibits a certain fluidity regarding ministry, not determining its precise structures or forms of transmission. These responses appear to interpret this affirmation as implying that any further post-New Testament determination of structure would be in some way contrary to the ministerial fluidity of the New Testament and even, in that sense, "unbiblical". Thus these views seem to imply that a more fixed determination of ministerial forms and their transmission in the post-New Testament period is either unwarranted by scripture, since scripture itself does not already make such determinations, or in contradiction to scripture, since it would make "determined" what scripture leaves fluid.

But what here seems to be rather compelling reasoning should be challenged to acknowledge its hidden premise. This argument presupposes that, in what it states about ministry, scripture intends to bind the Christian community in such a way that any subsequent determination of ministerial structure and transmission – which would be more fixed than the fluid state of ministry which one finds in the New Testament – is unwarranted and even in contradiction to scripture. But this hidden premise is itself neither self-evident nor can it be explicitly found in scripture.[47]

Obviously it is possible that some post-New Testament determinations concerning matters of faith or order can be unwarranted by or in contradiction with scripture. Already the letters of Paul and John contain warnings about deviations in Christian doctrine and practice. The struggle against the various heresies in the early centuries was occasioned precisely by post-New Testament determinations of faith and order which contradicted how the community interpreted the scriptures.[48] But such deviant determinations do not exhaust the possibilities of post-biblical developments. A good example which probably would enjoy wide acceptance is the determination concerning Christian faith which was made at the council of Nicea in 325. The use that this council made of the expression "of the same nature" in describing the relation of the Son to the Father, an expression which had not already been explicitly determined in the scripture, was not thereby a contradiction of the scripture or a subordination of the word of God to human invention. To be sure it intended to make normative an expression which was not normative in the New Testament, but it did so precisely in order to submit faithfully to the New Testament. Within the precise context of the questions posed by Arianism, it would have been disobedience to and contradiction of the word of God *not* to have spoken of the Son as "of the same nature" as the Father.

A similar "fidelity" to the scriptures, in the form of an action which determines or settles a matter about which the scriptures themselves provide much guidance but about which they intended neither to say everything nor to restrict the community from discerning the need for some normative determination in the future, can also apply to other issues as well. With regard to the role of ministerial structure and its transmission within the overall apostolic continuity of the church, the mere fact that the New Testament may not be proven to have determined the particulars of the structure and transmission of ministry does not lead logically to the conclusion that any ulterior determination of this structure and transmission is either unfaithful or contradictory to the scripture. On the contrary, that the church, from so early and for so long and so firmly, saw orderly transmission within a particular ministerial structure as an essential and normative characteristic of its apostolicity suggests as a possible and even more plausible interpretation that, in this case, the church discerned that these ulterior determinations were the logical application of what the scripture does say about apostolicity and ministry. A critical appraisal of the principle that "only" scripture can serve as the norm and criterion for ministerial structure and transmission thus suggests that issues such as those noted in the previous four paragraphs be taken up again for common consideration in the hope of greater convergence.

Tradition. While I just now have attempted to call into question a scripture-only understanding of the criteria for discerning Christian identity as applied to the question of ministerial structure and transmission, there is also a serious challenge which should be addressed to those who positively utilize "tradition" in their understanding of such criteria. Here too, there is an "only" which can be rationally troubling. Some responses to BEM's presentation of apostolicity state that only the ministerial structures and forms of transmission which can be traced back to the early church can and should serve as the model today for the re-establishment of unity among divided Christian communities.[49] Some further state that there is an essential difference between "apostolic" tradition, on the one hand, and the various traditions within specific Christian communities, on the other. Only that tradition which expresses the revealed Word of God and thus the will of God for the church can be called "apostolic".[50]

These points immediately call to mind Montreal's discussion of scripture, Tradition and traditions, with its affirmation that the many ways of believing or acting which may be called "traditions" cannot be simply identified with the "Tradition", which is the gospel as handed down from age to age under the guidance of the Holy Spirit. Traditions are more or less faithful embodiments of the Tradition. This position of Montreal would seem to be quite consonant with the point made by those responses to BEM which embraced tradition as a criterion for identifying the faith of the church through the ages: only some traditions can serve as the model and can be called apostolic. These alone are said to be normative.

This raises the legitimate question: which ones are part of this "only"? Have those communities which claim that, along with scripture, Tradition is normative for the discernment of the church's faith and order provided any convincing criteria for evaluating Tradition? Is mere "age" a convincing or even practicable criterion for discerning Tradition within the tradition? If an undeniable and absolutely essential premise for considering the tradition as a vehicle of revelation and therefore as normative for church faith and life is the belief that the Holy Spirit is guiding the church through history, then what reason would one have for maintaining that, at least as regards its precisely normative implications, such guidance at some point in history seems to have ceased? If Tradition may be described accurately, although not exhaustively, as the handing on of the gospel in history, in the historical development of the Christian community over the course of time, why should only ancient developments be normative? As some responses to BEM on apostolicity have challenged, why might not a presbyterial or synodal structure be discerned to be normative for the church today, even if these only came into particular relief at the time of the Reformation?

Moreover, the question of differentiating between traditions would seem to be more than just a question of measuring their age. Are there perhaps elements within ancient tradition which are not "apostolic" and therefore not binding upon the church today? Is it not at least possible that some prejudices or practices, even relatively old ones, may need to be "abandoned" precisely so that the church can be more faithfully apostolic? Thus the appeal to Ttradition, understood in the sense that only some aspects of the Tradition are apostolic and normative, also contains a hidden premise, in this case the premise that it is possible to distinguish with relative certainty between the various traditions so as to identify the ones which are truly apostolic and distinguish them from those which are not. While it does not seem that there is any logical inconsistency in affirming this premise, those who hold it can rightly be asked to provide credible criteria on the basis of which such distinguishing between traditions is carried out. This may prove to be a very difficult task indeed.[51] A critical appraisal of the principle that only some traditions are apostolic and binding thus suggests that issues such as those noted in the previous four paragraphs be taken up again for common consideration in the hope of greater convergence.

Thus, this third heading dealing with criteria and authority has examined the way in which the responses to BEM base their positions about ministerial structure and its transmission upon scripture and Tradition. Both forms of recourse appear to contain hidden premises: on the one hand, that scripture intends to preclude any further normative determination of ministry and, on the other, that there are criteria for uncovering those issues of faith and order which tradition determines in a normative way. These issues need to be taken up quite explicitly by the various communities engaged in dialogue, if there is to be realistic hope for greater convergence about questions of criteria and authority.

CONCLUSION

This study has sought, first, to individuate a few general and rather simple hermeneutical principles (Part I), to synthesize what the published responses to BEM say about apostolicity (Part II) and to apply the principles of Part I to the material uncovered in Part II (Part III). It is left to the reader to judge whether the foregoing has been helpful in illuminating the way in which hermeneutics can be ecumenically fruitful.[52]

However, after this rather long study, it would not be out of place to attempt a reply to the question that appeared on the front page of the July 1995 Faith and Order *Information Letter*, which was meant to capture the purpose of the present study: "How were these terms [apostle/apostolicity as... developed in *Baptism, Eucharist and Ministry*] used in respect of the biblical materials, and secondly what was the hermeneutic which enabled people to move from their confessional positions to a more inclusive use of these terms?"

It can be said that none of the responses to BEM gives a detailed presentation of biblical materials relevant to the words "apostle" and "apostolicity". This is so for two reasons. First of all, even the longest of the responses are relatively short (40 pages in the Thurian version we have been using) and are faced with the task of addressing many topics concerning not only ministry, but also baptism and eucharist. Therefore, at most they can devote only one or two pages of the ministerial sections of their responses to the precise topic of apostolicity. Such space allows no response to state in any detail its overall approach to biblical interpretation or to indicate the precise way that it interprets either the biblical terminology or the scriptural passages which are relevant to the topic of apostolicity.

Secondly, the responses are governed by the controlling condition that they are replying to what BEM says about apostolicity. BEM itself seems to base its assertions upon some of the general findings of the historical critical method. A possible example of this could be the opening sentence of M19: "The New Testament does not describe a single pattern of ministry which might serve as a blueprint or continuing norm for all future ministry in the church", a statement which reflects the kind of historically conscious analysis of New Testament material common to many contemporary exegetes. BEM does not draw upon the New Testament in the fashion of stringing together "proof texts". This is evident by the relative paucity of actual citations. In the block of 55 paragraphs and 14 commentaries which BEM devotes to ministry, a mere 31 references to biblical texts appear within parentheses and only a few actual quotations of the biblical text are provided.

More often BEM employs biblical support by means of broad general statements such as: "In the New Testament the term 'apostle' is variously employed" (comm. 9); "The New Testament says very little about the ordering of the eucharist" (comm. 14); "The New Testament never uses the term 'priesthood' or 'priest' (*hiereus*) to designate the ordained ministry or the ordained minister" (comm. 17) and "The original New Testament terms for ordination tend to be simple and descriptive" (comm. 40).

In the specific section entitled "Succession in the Apostolic Tradition" (§§34-38 and comm. 34 and 36), there is very little reference to
scripture, although the biblical evidence which runs throughout the ministry section is relevant to this section and it would not have made sense
to repeat all of it again in these precise paragraphs.

The responses seem to judge BEM's biblical interpretation positively. There is no sharp criticism that BEM has mishandled the scriptures while, on the other hand, there are a good number of compliments
affirming that BEM has done well to point out this or that piece of relevant biblical evidence. The only strong criticism concerning BEM's use
of the Bible came from those responses which wanted BEM to limit its
discernment of ministerial structure and transmission to that which is
found in the Bible and who objected that BEM allowed tradition to have
a determining voice at times, a role which these critics would not themselves admit, at least with regard to these ministerial issues.[53]

This then is the way in which BEM uses the biblical materials with
regard to the terms apostle and apostolicity. It quotes the scripture rather
selectively and judiciously, mainly utilizing a number of general conclusions about these terms which would find wide acceptance among
exegetes who employ the historical critical hermeneutical techniques in
their study of the Bible.

"What was the hermeneutic which enabled people to move from their
confessional positions to a more inclusive use of these terms?" Neither
BEM nor any of the responses to BEM explicitly identifies its own
"hermeneutic". However, if what has just been said is true, it is clear
that, as far as biblical hermeneutics are concerned, most respondents to
BEM appreciated its prudent use of widely acknowledged findings of
contemporary biblical exegesis, all the while avoiding biblical interpretations which may be more idiosyncratic or speculative. Thus one can
conclude that BEM's interpretation of the Bible with regard to apos-
tle/apostolicity, while quite modest and in no way intending to be
exhaustive, nevertheless was convincing both to the faith and to the
intelligence of those who read it.

Of course, both BEM and its respondents were concerned not only
with interpreting the Bible (thus employing a *biblical* hermeneutic) but
also with discerning the "faith of the church through the ages". How did
they interpret this faith? Here again, neither BEM nor the responses
identify their respective "hermeneutics", as would be the case, for example, were any of the texts to state something like: "We now intend to
interpret the faith of the church through the ages following the principles
outlined by Gadamer or Ricoeur." However, the methodology followed
by most of the responses of (a) *attending* to BEM and to the scriptures

and the Tradition, so as to delineate statements of BEM which could either be affirmed or denied as expressing the faith of the church through the ages, and (b) *scrutinizing their own positions*, though this step was perhaps less thoroughly pursued, suggests that most communities did try to incorporate the fundamental hermeneutical principle: "Be attentive and avoid ideological distortions."

Both of these "hermeneutics" – recourse to widely held and reasonably convincing conclusions of biblical exegesis and use of a general method of attention and self-criticism – have allowed communities "to move from their confessional positions to a more inclusive use" of the language of apostolicity. There is today much common awareness that all communities, even if perhaps in varying degrees and with varying meanings, prize the church's characteristic of apostolicity and believe that the church is and must be apostolic. Also there seems to be a rather wide acceptance that the church's apostolicity includes many elements. These two points would seem to render possible even now a higher degree of mutual recognition of apostolicity on the part of communities, even though they may not yet have arrived at full communion in faith, life and witness.

At the same time, the responses to BEM indicate what may well be the most striking difference concerning apostolicity which still divides Christian communities from one another: the relation of episcopal succession to apostolicity. The *Report* notes:

> ... a considerable number of responses from Reformation and Free churches remain unpersuaded by the arguments in favour of episcopal succession as an important element in apostolic tradition.... For many on both sides of the issue the question of episcopal succession remains the most difficult problem for further dialogue on ministry. Behind this issue lie significant ecclesiological questions. It can, therefore, only be tackled in the framework of a broader, more intensified discussion on ecclesiology in Faith and Order.[54]

One wonders whether this issue may not ultimately concern the degree to which the church may be considered an organic reality and the very "bodiliness" included in the Christian understanding of the economy of salvation. These are anthropological and sacramental questions.

However the ecclesiological discussion may go, the *Report*'s final statement that "only" the framework of a more intensified discussion of ecclesiology will be able to tackle this question needs perhaps a word of nuance. The present study, especially in the questions which Part III has addressed to all dialogue partners, has tried to show that the hermeneutics of attention and self-scrutiny can also play an important role in tackling this difficult question and, hopefully, in helping divided Christians to arrive one day at full communion in their faith concerning the apostolicity of the church.

NOTES

¹ Werner G. Jeanrond, *Theological Hermeneutics: Development and Significance*, New York, Crossroad, 1991, p.1.
² *Ibid.*, p.82.
³ *Ibid.*, p.63, commenting on Heidegger's approach to hermeneutics.
⁴ These names I have drawn from the survey presented in chs 3 and 6 of Jeanrond's book; one can also consult the select bibliography he presents in *ibid.*, pp.207-12. But even this impressive grouping of ponderous hermeneutical thinkers barely begins to introduce the extensive list of authors who have published works on hermeneutics. This is especially evident when one recalls the extensive development of biblical hermeneutics in the past century, with its many distinct forms of criticism and interpretation. In fact, until rather recently, most articles devoted to the topic "hermeneutics" in theological reference works limited the discussion almost entirely to theories of biblical interpretation. This suggests that the application of hermeneutics to theology as such or, even more, to the specific field of ecumenism is a relatively recent phenomenon.
⁵ *Ibid.*, p.10. Jeanrond's entire last chapter, "The Development of Theological Hermeneutics (III): Hermeneutics and Christian Identity," pp.159-82, with notes on 202-206, is an attempt to deal with the question of how interpretation relates to Christian identity. In my view, this last chapter rapidly and without enough careful documentation gives interpretations of church history and of the contemporary available options among Christian theologians, which result in a rather unappreciative and deprecatory view of the role of ministerial authorities as well as an overly optimistic trust in the abilities of "critical hermeneutics" to help Christians live with plurality and ambiguity yet retain their identity. In general this is a fine book which makes good points against ideology. Ironically, it ends with what, from my point of view, appears to be a somewhat ideological final chapter.
⁶ Questions of criteria and authority raise complex issues in relation to hermeneutics. For example, although in theory they need not do so, authority and community identity in practice could get in the way of the effort to understand biblical texts with "scientific" objectivity. At the same time, however, most contemporary Christians, along with much of the witness of the early centuries of church history, would maintain that the full meaning of the scriptures is not accessible except within that particular perceptivity characteristic of the community of believers. Those who have written about the precise theme of "ecumenical hermeneutics" tend to address questions of criteria and authority; see Robert Kress, "Leise treten: An Irenic Ecumenical Hermeneutic", *Theological Studies*, 44, 1983, pp.407-37; and Anton Houtepen's two articles: "'Ökumenische Hermeneutik,' Auf der Suche nach Kriterien der Kohärenz im Christentum", in *Ökumenische Rundschau*, 39, 1990, pp.279-96, and "The Faith of the Church through the Ages: Ecumenism and Hermeneutics", in *Centro pro Unione Bulletin*, 44, fall 1993, pp.3-15.
⁷ I am referring to the responses published in the six volumes edited by Max Thurian, entitled *Churches Respond to BEM* I-VI (Geneva, WCC Publications, 1986-88). Hereafter the response of any particular church will be referred to by giving the name of the church, followed by Roman and Arabic numerals, the former indicating the volume and the latter the pages in the Thurian collection. These volumes contain 142 responses. Irmgard Kindt-Siegwalt, "Evaluating the Churches' Responses to *Baptism, Eucharist and Ministry*," *Midstream*, 25, 1989, pp.238-48, mentions that, at the time of her article (a year after the final volume of *Churches Respond to BEM*), there were some 170 responses from the 312 member churches of the WCC and from other churches, thus 28 more than those printed in the *Churches Respond* series. Our present study is limited to the 142 texts available in the Thurian volumes.
⁸ Since there are so many responses (142) and of such variety in length and intention, I have opted to divide them along family lines and to cite only those more elaborate ones which, in addition to simply registering agreement or disagreement, also provide a developed theological argument. I am aware that there are dangers – and precisely hermeneutical ones – in grouping responses together in this way. However, the alternative would be to treat each of the 142 responses individually, which would simply be too cumbersome. On the difficulty of giving "a balanced evaluation" of the responses to BEM because of their own "imbalance of quantity and quality" see Anton Houtepen, "Towards an Ecumenical Vision of the Church: The Ecclesiology in the Responses to BEM", in *One in Christ*, 25, 1989, pp.217-37 at p.226, note 7. Under each family heading, I will begin by listing the complete title of each of the communities cited in that section, along with the volume and page numbers where its response can be found in the Thurian collection.
⁹ The full titles of the Anglican churches referred to in this section will be shortened to the names of the countries or regions with which each is identified. The three points which I have listed

here are affirmed in: Ireland I.68-69; Scotland II.51; England III.50-51 and 55-57; and Wales III.93. I will use a similar form of abbreviation throughout the analysis of the responses. Only those churches listed under the particular family heading will be cited within parentheses in each particular section.

[10] A dissenting voice from this endorsement is that of the Independent Evangelical Lutheran Church of the FRG and West Berlin (VI.57), which suspects that the distinction between global apostolicity and ministerial apostolicity tends, in fact, to conceal what may really be fundamental differences between the churches.

[11] In contrast, some responses understand BEM as explicitly recognizing the ministerial variety present in the New Testament (Romania IV.89; Brunswick VI.48) and praise it for that fact.

[12] This community lists its membership as 9.8 million, while the other nine Methodist churches responding to BEM, taken together, add up to 1.3 million.

[13] In contrast, the Evangelical-Reformed Church of North-West Germany (IV.98) notes that it has no difficulty with the fact that BEM promotes the threefold structure and that this structure can be found within the Reformation tradition as well.

[14] The Presbyterian Church in Canada (II.157) phrases this issue in a way suggesting that it is fundamentally a matter of common courtesy: "... our position is that the sacraments and ministry of other churches are valid. We recognize the baptism, eucharist and ministry of sister churches to be authentic. We would humbly invite them to do the same for us!"

[15] With a somewhat different nuance, the Netherlands Reformed Church and Reformed Churches in the Netherlands (IV.104) state that one need not "speak disparagingly about the apostolic succession" but that one should not "make the legitimacy of office dependent on an unbroken chain of ministries that should be historically provable."

[16] *One Baptism, One Eucharist and a Mutually Recognized Ministry*, Faith and Order Paper no. 73, Geneva, WCC, 1975.

[17] Obviously some of the responses presented earlier in the text come from churches which are united, such as the United Methodist Church-USA or the United Reformed Church in the United Kingdom. Wherever a "united" church seems identifiable primarily with one particular confessional family, I treated it in the section devoted to that family.

[18] Is a kind of epistemology of "correspondence" presupposed by the BEM process? Better, does not the way in which communities responded show that they are convinced (1) that there is a "faith of the church through the ages" which they can and do know, and (2) that they are capable of judging the extent to which an ecumenical text corresponds to that faith? If the BEM process has uncovered the fact that Christians from many different communities share such a common confidence, it has already achieved something of no little importance. It would mean that the ecumenical community does not accept the hermeneutical relativism which Anton Houtepen associates with the position of Gadamer; see A. Houtepen, "The Faith of the Church through the Ages: Ecumenism and Hermeneutics," pp.12-13, and "'Ökumenische Hermeneutik': Auf der Suche nach Kriterien der Kohärenz im Christentum," p.288. Similar criticisms of Gadamer are presented in Jeanrond, pp.67-75. See also H.G. Stobbe, *Hermeneutik: ein ökumenisches Problem. Eine Kritik der katholischen Gadamer-Rezeption*, Zürich, 1981.

[19] Faith and Order Paper no. 149, pp.107-30, Geneva, WCC Publications, 1990.

[20] *Report*, p.122.

[21] *Report*, p.123.

[22] *Report*, p.121.

[23] Many of the groups presented above in Part II mentioned this distinction: Anglican, Baptist, Brethren, Disciples, Lutheran, Methodist, Orthodox, Reformed-Presbyterian, Waldensian, Roman Catholic, Salvation Army and United.

[24] So the Orthodox and Roman Catholic responses.

[25] So the Roman Catholic response.

[26] So some of the Lutheran and the United responses. Many communities (Baptist, Brethren, Friends, Lutherans, Reformed-Presbyterian and United) state that the New Testament supplies no one pattern for ministry.

[27] So some of the Reformed-Presbyterian responses.

[28] So the Anglican, Brethren, Lutheran and Methodist responses. The Roman Catholic response states that, understood with the proper nuance, even the language of "guarantee" could be used in relation to ministerial succession.

[29] So some of the Lutheran, Methodist and United responses.

[30] See the Moravian response; the same idea seems to underlie the criticisms of emphasizing precisely "episcopal" succession in several of the United responses.

[31] Some Reformed-Presbyterian communities criticize BEM's biblical component for not stating that the New Testament does not distinguish sharply between *episkopoi* and *presbyteroi*. A good

number of responses criticize the "hierarchical" tone of the threefold ministry: Brethren, Methodist, Reformed-Presbyterian, Waldensian and United.

[32] So some of the responses in the following groups: Baptist, Methodist, Orthodox, Reformed-Presbyterian and United.

[33] The *Report*, p.125, responds that BEM is not fairly criticized on this point: "... the proposal to accept the threefold pattern for the sake of unity was not formulated in M22 in terms of an indispensable condition, but rather as a means to this end."

[34] So some of the Lutheran, Methodist, Reformed-Presbyterian and United responses.

[35] See the Orthodox responses above.

[36] G.W.F. Hegel, *The Phenomenology of Mind*, trans. J.B. Baillie, New York, Harper Torchbooks, 1967, p.135.

[37] Jeanrond, 7: "... the text is a somewhat weaker partner which, for instance, is unable to defend itself against violations of its integrity by ideological readers."

[38] So the Orthodox and Roman Catholic responses.

[39] See for example, some of the United responses above.

[40] See above, the Lutheran, Moravian, Orthodox and Roman Catholic responses, which raise this issue.

[41] See above, note 6. Perhaps here it should be added that, to the extent that hermeneutics, properly so called, is to be understood precisely as the reflection upon the conditions for the accurate interpretation of texts, works of art and so forth, it does not enjoy, on its own, the competence which must be engaged in order to discern Christian identity. This identity is lived by Christians. The criteria by which it is discerned falls within the competence of those who are Christians, especially when taken together as the community of the church as a whole. This discernment would not fall within the expertise of those who may be very knowledgeable about hermeneutics but who are not committed believers and members of the church.

[42] These kinds of authorities, as well as an interesting reflection about a "hierarchy" among authorities, can be found in the Denver report (1971) of the Methodist-Roman Catholic conversations; printed in Harding Meyer and Lukas Vischer, ed., *Growth in Agreement*, New York, Paulist, and Geneva, WCC, 1984, pp.330-36.

[43] *Report*, p.132. This list is quite similar to that presented by Anton Houtepen in his Centro Pro Unione talk of 1993, entitled "The Faith of the Church through the Ages: Ecumenism and Hermeneutics", pp.8-11. Unlike the *Report*, Houtepen's list very helpfully provides extensive documentation indicating where these criteriological configurations can be found in the actual responses to BEM.

[44] These six are found in *Report*, pp.133-35. Houtepen, instead, lists seven ways in which the responses to BEM describe "the faith of the church through the ages": (a) as synonymous with the dynamic idea of Tradition according to Montreal; (b) as "apostolic faith", i.e. the faith of the eye-witnesses and their direct successors in the constitutive period of the church (150-787 C.E.); (c) as the apostolic faith attested in the scriptures, especially the New Testament; (d) as "faith according to the scriptures" which was explicated also by later confessions of faith and catechisms; (e) as the apostolic faith which was received in one particular tradition and mediated through the authoritative teaching of that tradition; (f) as the faith which is taking shape in the *fides qua creditur*, the cloud of witnesses whose personal testimony is essentially pluriform, guided by the Holy Spirit and not tied to fixed formulae of the past; and (g) not "as" any particular formulation but simply with an "awareness of the hermeneutical problems involved in the formulation" of the "faith of the church through the ages". See Houtepen, "The Faith of the Church through the Ages: Ecumenism and Hermeneutics", pp.8-11.

[45] *Report*, p.132.

[46] It is not my intention in the following paragraphs to take a particular position regarding ways in which communities employ scripture or tradition as criteria. Rather my intention is only to supply questions which could be used to scrutinize the use of these criteria. I do not presuppose that convincing answers cannot be given to these questions. However, it does seem to me that one of the greatest benefits hermeneutics could offer to ecumenical dialogue would be to help Christians submit their own interpretations to vigorous examination.

[47] Another way of saying the same thing would be to affirm that God intended the New Testament to be the determinative statement of all Christian faith and order. In that case, any determination of faith or order that is not explicitly already determined in the New Testament would be therefore contrary to the will of God. But the New Testament itself does not make this claim. It does not present the will of God as excluding all subsequent determinations of faith and order which are not already determined in scripture.

[48] Many heresies from the early centuries claimed to be based upon scripture. This led the church of the patristic era to view "scripture alone" as insufficient for maintaining the unity of faith of

the Christian community. Appeal to tradition could also be a ploy of those proposing false doctrines, as in the case of many Gnostics who found support in oral tradition. In the face of these uses of scripture and tradition by those whose teachings were eventually discerned as heretical, the church maintained its identity by recourse to the faith and order of those principal apostolic churches which could show their line of succession back to the apostles. Even this principle, however, underwent some modification after the beginning of the 4th century, when the proponents of heretical views were at times the bishops of some of the oldest and most prestigious churches. I have tried to sketch out some of this story in my presentation of the patristic contribution to understanding faith and its unity. See William Henn, *One Faith: Biblical and Patristic Contributions toward Understanding Unity in Faith,* Mahwah, NJ, Paulist, 1995, pp.87-191.

[49] So the Orthodox response.

[50] So the Roman Catholic response.

[51] An introduction to some of the difficulties encountered in providing a convincing justification for distinctions between various traditions is Gerald O'Collins, "Finding the Tradition within the Traditions", ch. VIII of his *Fundamental Theology,* London, Darton, Longman & Todd, 1981, pp.208-24.

[52] Above in note 6, I have referred to the works on ecumenical hermeneutics by Robert Kress ("Leise treten: An Irenic Ecumenical Hermeneutic") and Anton Houtepen ("'Ökumenische Hermeneutik,' Auf der Suche nach Kriterien der Kohärenz im Christentum" and "The Faith of the Church through the Ages: Ecumenism and Hermeneutics"). These are very stimulating studies. Kress argues for a third way between requiring full agreement on all divisive issues of faith and order or simply acquiescing in such division. Instead we should differentiate between three classes of issues which may be divisive among Christians. These classes are named "creed", "theology" and "spirituality". All issues which are discerned to belong to the category "creed" must be held in common by all. Issues falling under the other two categories are "optional" with regard to Christian unity; wide diversity would be possible on these without detriment to unity. Houtepen's position contains many points but seems to have at its core the suggestion that the medieval approach to biblical interpretation captured in the phrase *littera gesta docet, quid credas allegoria, moralis quid agas, quo tendas anagogia,* referring to the literal, significative, moral and eschatological senses of scripture, could help divided Christians to fashion a "hermeneutical community", whose unity would be based more broadly upon all four senses. These manifold senses are contained in BEM's description of apostolicity in M34, claims Houtepen, but instead of drawing consequences from the wide approval given to this particular paragraph, churches preferred to focus on specific issues which they cannot accept, such as the threefold structure of ministry or the ordination of women. Houtepen's conclusion: the literal sense has conquered and communities have not appreciated the extent of their agreement, as reflected, for example, in their common appreciation of M34 ("Ökumenische Hermeneutik", p.285). Both of these approaches offer distinctive and stimulating contributions to reflection about ecumenical hermeneutics. In particular they seem to argue that hermeneutics can be precisely "ecumenical" by helping to explain legitimate differences between communities, differences which full communion need not and even should not exclude.

There always will and even must be legitimate diversities in Christian faith and practice if the church is really to be "catholic". It is undeniable that hermeneutics can help uncover the rationale for such diversities. But it also could assist communities or individuals whose positions directly conflict to try to overcome the contradictions between their positions. That is the approach I have focused upon in this paper, especially by advocating the value and use of greater attentiveness and self-scrutiny.

[53] Criticisms of this sort can be found above among the Lutheran and Reformed-Presbyterian responses. Of course, this kind of criticism is not the same as criticizing BEM for improperly interpreting the scriptures.

[54] *Report,* p.128.

"Scripture, Tradition and traditions": A Reflection on the Studies of This Issue in the 1960s

MARTIN CRESSEY

In the recent work on ecumenical hermeneutics, the chief focus of attention in the 1960s studies has been the report of the Montreal Faith and Order conference of 1963 on "Scripture, Tradition and traditions",[1] and within that text paragraph 45:

> In our present situation, we wish to reconsider the problem of scripture and Tradition, or rather that of Tradition and scripture. And therefore we wish to propose the following statement as a fruitful way of reformulating the question. Our starting-point is that we are all living in a tradition which goes back to our Lord and has its roots in the Old Testament, and are all indebted to that tradition inasmuch as we have received the revealed truth, the gospel, through its being transmitted from one generation to another. Thus we can say that we exist as Christians by the Tradition of the gospel (the paradosis of the kerygma) testified in scripture, transmitted in and by the church through the power of the Holy Spirit. Tradition taken in this sense is actualized in the preaching of the word, in the administration of sacraments and worship, in Christian teaching and theology, and in mission and witness to Christ by the lives of the members of the church.[2]

The Montreal report, however, must be set in the context of several other documents. Before 1963 there was the work of two separate sections of the Faith and Order theological commission on "Tradition and traditions", one in North America and one in Europe. Their report is the basis for the Montreal section work. After Montreal, Faith and Order continued in the field with studies of biblical hermeneutics, biblical authority and the relation of the Old and New Testaments. At the same time the Second Vatican Council was engaged in a considerable struggle over what became the text *Dei Verbum*.[3] In particular, the council leaders had to reach agreement on the question whether Tradition is still to be regarded as extending at its source beyond the written scriptures – in other words, the problem of the material completeness of scripture.

Commentaries on the Vatican text, such as those by Cardinal Joseph Ratzinger, and volumes such as Yves Congar's *Tradition and Traditions*, need to be considered when studying the Montreal discussion. Furthermore, the fuller entry of Orthodox theologians into Faith and Order work at Montreal enabled them to help their Western colleagues to relate Orthodox teaching on Tradition to the 1960s debate.[4]

This paper seeks to do two limited things. First it tries to summarize the advances and the perplexities of the 1960s. At the close of that round of debate, it will be argued, claims about new agreements at Montreal should be treated with caution. Therefore, secondly, this paper will look at chief questions from the 1960s and try to focus them for our present discussion on ecumenical hermeneutics.

It must first be observed that the distinctions used in the Montreal text between Tradition (capital "T"), tradition (with a small "t") and traditions (plural) are not at all easy to maintain. Paragrah 45, quoted above, has small "t" twice in the third sentence but is reproduced with capital "T" at those places in an earlier draft from 1996 of the ecumenical hermeneutics text.[5] In paragraphs 45 and 48 of Montreal there are sentences beginning with the word "Tradition" with the consequence that the rules of typography make the references ambiguous in terms of the desired distinctions.

Setting aside such drafting problems, there are admissions in the Montreal text itself that the distinctions do not solve central problems. Paragraph 48 lists questions about how to distinguish between traditions embodying the true Tradition and merely human traditions. Paragraph 53 lists – but without deciding between – a range of varied hermeneutical principles as proposed keys for the understanding of what is said in scripture. Paragraphs 57 and 58 draw out the difference between the understanding of Tradition most characteristically present in Orthodox theology and another understanding that regards Tradition as "expressed with different degrees of fidelity in various historically conditioned forms, namely the traditions". In that view Tradition is nowhere separately existent. Even those who followed up the Montreal work did not derive a clear view from it. We can find James Barr writing in *The Ecumenical Review* that, according to Montreal, "the genuine Tradition is scripture, rightly interpreted".[6] Yet such a statement seems to be well out of line with the Montreal text, which says that Tradition has as its content "God's revelation and self-giving in Christ, present in the life of the church"[7] or is "substantially the same as the revelation in Christ and the preaching of the word, entrusted to the church which is sustained in being by it.[8]

One emerges from reading through the Montreal text several times with a sense that "Tradition with a capital 'T'" is like "Gospel with a capital 'G'"; it refers to the formal concept of that which God intends shall be made known and be embodied in the continuing life of the church without it being possible so to specify Tradition as to be of any great help in enabling Christian agreement in faith. The first advance at Montreal was in recognizing the formal character of the concept and in definitely refusing to identify it with any particular confessional or cultural tradition. This enabled the second advance, which was that the Protestant representatives broke away from their inherited suspicion of any concept of tradition.

For this latter step forward the preparatory work of the North American section of the Theological Commission on "Tradition and traditions" was particularly important. In a position paper "Overcoming History by History"[9] Jaroslav Pelikan argued (1) that the American churches' experience showed how they had preserved the very traditions they had left in Europe; (2) that in the ante-Nicene church "there was simply no way of imagining possible conflict between the Christian scripture and the Christian tradition – and, therefore, no necessity to choose between them";[10] and (3) that "the relativization of tradition, begun by the Reformers when they declared that church councils can err and have erred, forces reconsideration of those traditions which, for both religious and political reasons, the Reformers felt themselves bound to retain".[11] Pelikan did not conclude from all this that theological historiography supports total scepticism (though some members of the commission did!); rather he saw the way opening for what became the Montreal convergence.

A positively cautious account of the Montreal achievement is confirmed by examining the wider context of studies in the 1960s. On the one hand, Orthodox theologians were beginning to share with others their understanding of the Tradition as a mystery, a reality not to be tied down by definition. John Meyendorff, for instance, writes:

> There cannot be, therefore, any question about "two sources" of revelation. It is not in fact a formal dictation of certain formally definable truths to the human mind. Revelation in Jesus Christ is a new fellowship between God and man, established once and for all. It is a participation of man in divine life. Scripture does not create the participation; it witnesses, in a final and complete form, to the acts of God which realized it. In order to be fully understood, the Bible requires the reality of the fellowship which exists in the church. Tradition is the sacramental continuity in history of the communion of saints; in a way, it is the church itself.[12]

This approach echoes that of Georges Florovsky in *Bible, Church, Tradition: An Eastern Orthodox View*.[13] However, Florovsky emphasized:

> I am going to preach and to commend to all whom I may be called to address the message of salvation, as it has been handed down to me by an uninterrupted Tradition of the church universal. I would not isolate myself in my own age. In other words, I am going to preach "the doctrines of the creed".[14]

In a way similar to Pelikan and Meyendorff, the Second Vatican Council, while retaining a distinction between scripture and Tradition, moved away from earlier formulations involving reference to "two sources". The council, however, carefully used a different (and rare) Latin word, *scaturigo*, instead of *fons*, to declare that "sacred Tradition and scripture... both flow from the same divine well-spring". The council leaders declined to affirm the material completeness of scripture and instead declared that "the church's certainty about all that is revealed is not drawn from holy scripture alone; both scripture and Tradition are to be accepted and honoured with like devotion and reverence". Yet this was a formulation regarded with reserve by some Catholic commentators; it was remarked that "the function of Tradition is seen here as making certain of the truth, i.e. it belongs in the formal and gnoseological sphere – and in fact, this is the sphere in which the significance of Tradition is to be sought"; indeed, "The post-apostolic age discovered the 'scriptural character' of the New Testament at a time when Christian doctrine threatened to be more and more dissolved by wildly proliferating traditions."[15] The long discussion and careful decision-making over drafts of *Dei Verbum* indicates that there is opportunity for a broadly stated ecumenical hermeneutic to which the Roman Catholic Church could assent.

What then are the focusing questions to which the 1960s discussions can lead us as we seek to give direction to the current study of ecumenical hermeneutics?

I suggest three – but I have to point out that they do not necessarily lead in the same direction.

To read the preparatory papers and the succeeding Faith and Order studies on either side of the Montreal text itself is to realize how central is the contention that no tradition (small "t") is to be identified with the Tradition (capital "T") while the Tradition exists only in and through authentic traditions. The tension between this view and the Orthodox understanding or the Vatican II reverence for *sacra traditio* is concealed by the diplomatic drafting at Montreal. It takes a drafter sometimes to see what one's predecessors were up to! So my first question is whether current study sufficiently takes account of the possibility that authentic traditions are not those which pass some criterial tests based on our perception of the Tradition but rather a family of ways of responding to Jesus Christ which are as diverse as the units in a family of meanings whose extremities are indeed poles apart. If that is so, what does it mean for ecumenism? In a recent discussion in class at Columbia Theological Seminary, Georgia, USA, where as a visiting scholar I researched and wrote this paper, it was argued that the globalization of theology is a threat to the contextualization of theologies. On that view, if the family of meanings is to find full expression in its many contexts, there must be a moratorium on seeking one global formulation for the Tradition as a basis of visible unity.

It is my own nervousness about the direction pointed by my first question that leads me to my second. Suppose we take as a starting point John Meyendorff's view that "Tradition is the sacramental continuity in history of the communion of saints; in a way, it is the church itself". The study on ecclesiology then becomes even more vital for Faith and Order. But it cannot be approached as a primarily intellectual exercise; it will depend for any real progress on a deepened entry into the actual life of the church, wherever that life is (here I struggle for the right word) "sensed", "experienced", "discerned". The calls from Orthodox churches to exercise patience and not rush into decisions and policies for an activist WCC will have to be taken with a new seriousness.

So, thirdly, the Montreal debate may push us to the discussion of a teaching magisterium for the church, of a ministry of unity. Such a discussion will have to go beyond the present stage of discussion about *episkope*-episcopacy (as seen in *Episkopé and Episcopacy and the Quest for Visible Unity: Two Consultations*,[16] the report of meetings at Strasbourg and Crêt-Bérard).The need for further development is twofold. Re-reading Vatican II texts and some Orthodox volumes has made me aware that in Strasbourg and Crêt-Bérard the participants did not hear clearly enough the claim that episcopacy has the *charisma veritatis*; it is a claim some of us find very difficult to accept but it must be examined in the context also of ecumenical hermeneutics. Is the bishop by God's call the Christian hermeneut? In addition, in our work on hermeneutics we backed away from discussion of primacy, just as it was becoming relevant!

I myself think, despite my nervousness, that the first line of thought of my three is the one that is consistent with my Reformed theology – but it also threatens my hopes for visible unity. So how can I be a "United" "Reformed" churchman?

Some help I have found. The first help came from Eduard Schweizer through a reference supplied to me by Charles Cousar of Columbia Seminary. Schweizer[17] discusses the credal formulae in 1 Corinthians 15:3-5 and 1 Timothy 3:16. In his opinion, the unity between these two creeds is obvious. Jesus Christ is the subject of every verb. The church is interested in what he did, or rather what God did in him. And yet one creed speaks in a Jewish environment to the question raised by that situation and in historical patterns of thought. The other addresses a different context in which humankind articulates its situation in cosmological categories. Encouraged by our discussion at Bossey, I summarize and rest my case on the basis of Schweizer's remark about the two credal formulae; amid all the confusion, "Jesus Christ is the subject of every (changing) verb".

A second source of help came from a quite distinct part of my reading in the United States. I was pursuing an interest in how local churches in the Atlanta area respond to the diversity of the population and communities. In a book about the experience of Oakhurst Presbyterian Church in Decatur[18] I found this descriptive paragraph, which strikes me as giving, from the story of a white suburban congregation that determined to become diverse as its surrounding community changed, a positive parable for what ecumenical hermeneutics is about:

We affirm diversity not because we want to win points for being inclusive but because we believe that this diversity is a buffer against human arrogance. We believe that God has given us diversity to remind us that our particular history is both important and limiting. We must know our own stories of who we are and how we came to be. Without a sense of that story, we have no roots. In our distrust of diversity, in seeing diversity as a problem, we have come to believe that our story is the story. By emphasizing the gift of diversity, we lift up the sense that our story is only part of the story. The whole story is to be found in looking not only at our own experience but in considering the validity of the experiences of others. This approach does not lead to relativism, as so many... seem to believe. This approach leads to a rich and deep sense of what it means to be human and created in the image of God.

NOTES

[1] *The Fourth World Conference on Faith and Order: The Report from Montreal 1963*, Patrick C. Rodger and Lukas Vischer, eds, Faith and Order Paper no. 42, London, SCM Press, 1964, pp.50-61.
[2] *Ibid.*, pp.51-52.
[3] *Constitutio Dogmatica de Divina Revelatione*, Sessio VIII, 18 Nov. 1965.
[4] Cf. John Meyendorff, *Living Tradition*, New York, St Vladimir's Press, 1978.
[5] See *Minutes of the Meeting of the Faith and Order Board, 8-15 January 1997*, Abbaye de Fontgombault, France, Faith and Order Paper no. 178, Geneva, WCC, 1997, p.79.
[6] *The Ecumenical Review*, vol. 21, no. 2, 1969, p.135.
[7] §46.
[8] §48.
[9] *The Old and the New in the Church*, Minneapolis, Augsburg, 1961, for the WCC, pp.36ff.
[10] *Ibid.*, p.39.
[11] *Ibid.*, p.41.
[12] *Living Tradition*, p.16.
[13] Belmont, Nordland, 1972.
[14] Page 11.
[15] Ratzinger and Grillmeier, in *Commentary on the Documents of Vatican II*, vol. III, New York, Herder & Herder, 1969, pp.195 and 232.
[16] Geneva, WCC, 1999.
[17] *Neotestamentica*, Zurich, Zwingli, 1963, pp.127-29.
[18] Nibs Stroupe and Inez Fleming, *While We Run This Race: Confronting the Power of Racism in a Southern Church*, Maryknoll, Orbis, 1995, p.160.

Tradition Revisited

NICHOLAS LOSSKY

Scripture, Tradition and traditions have been mainstays in the Faith and Order discussion for a long time. Yet, in study as in teaching, it is necessary to take up the same questions again and again, to recall what has been done and, it is hoped, to shed new light on aspects presumed to be already fully understood and remembered. New studies often require a return to issues which, in theory at least, have been assimilated by those engaged in work oriented towards the future. If the fourth world conference on Faith and Order, held in Montreal in 1963, clarified the distinction and the link between Scripture and Tradition, questions nevertheless constantly arise especially about the nature of the latter. Consequently, to examine the notion once again is perhaps not altogether superfluous.

In spite of all that has been written and said, some still think of scripture and Tradition as two sources of revelation. The result is that they either accept this duality or reject Tradition (which comes to the same thing: both approaches stem from the Reformation-Counter-Reformation conflicts). Others equate Tradition and traditions. In spite of exposure to a variety of Christians through a common study of history and theology, too many people still believe that so long as "they" (anyone who is not "we") do not confess the apostolic faith in exactly the same terms as we do, do not celebrate exactly as we do, do not fast exactly as we do, we cannot pray with them, for prayer with "heretics" is forbidden by ancient canons. Concerning this latter identification of traditions (with a small "t") with Tradition (with a capital "T"), it seems appropriate to point out something about those who gather together in the name of Christ, who are seeking to recover the unity of Christians through a rediscovery of our common roots, which are Jesus Christ the Son of the Father, and his Holy Spirit. It is not possible to regard these "others" as heretics. The said canons cannot apply in these cases. Heretics are those who have consciously cut themselves off from the communion of the church in the name of false doctrines and are not seeking to restore this communion in a movement towards those they regard as "enemies".

The point concerning the identification of traditions with Tradition should be viewed (once more) in the light of the providential historical "accident" of the Russian emigration and exile after 1917. If many émigrés thought that they would soon return to Russia to rule it and that therefore their Orthodoxy should be preserved intact as in a ghetto, the best among them understood that their exile, their uprooting from a "traditional" Orthodox soil and context, was a divine invitation to ask questions. The first question concerned the relation between Orthodoxy and Russian culture (and consequently with every culture). This is how they discovered that Orthodoxy could exist in *any* culture, provided a serious distinction is made between what is fundamental and what is secondary (what Richard Hooker liked to call the "adiaphora"). This discovery led to the most essential question of all: if Orthodoxy is not to be identified with one particular culture, what is the true nature of Orthodoxy? The best answer was given by a most distinguished representative of this group of exiles, Father Sergius Bulgakov, in his book *Orthodoxy* (1935).[1] The first sentence may sound triumphalistic: "Orthodoxy is the Church of Christ on earth." But the second sentence quite clearly addresses all Christians and is a distinct call to enter the ecumenical movement: "The Church of Christ is not an institution; it is a new life in Christ moved by the Holy Spirit." One may add: to the glory of the Father. With such a definition of Orthodoxy, it should be impossible to substitute "traditions" for *Tradition*.

This however is not enough. Too often, Tradition is understood by many, including many Orthodox, as a mere remembrance of things expressed before in scriptural or patristic writings and in decisions – particularly conciliar decisions and definitions. No doubt, these are important and should not be disregarded or discarded. Yet, such a narrow conception of Tradition runs the risk of leading to what might be termed a "repetitive" form of orthodox Christianity: it is sufficient to recite the creeds, to quote what has been written by the fathers, to celebrate liturgical services as they have reached us, all this indiscriminately, in a spirit of obedience understood as a passive form of reception. The same principle may of course be applied to the scriptures. Such an attitude to Tradition tends first of all to deny the existence of history, to deny the fact that every moment presents new challenges, a new context in which "Jesus Christ, the same yesterday and today and for ever" (Heb. 13:8) is to be confessed. In such a view, history ceased to develop at some point in the past and the point in the past will vary from one theologian, or one community, to another.

The recognition of the existence of history, which implies for instance that those whom we call the fathers spoke of the Mystery to *their* time (but in such a way that their invitation to contemplate the fullness of the Mystery transcended their time and became an invitation for all times), should not in any way lead us to a conception of a "dogmatic development". We must pay very serious attention to what Metropolitan John of Pergamon (Zizioulas) said about history in a remarkable lecture about apostolic succession, delivered in Rome in November 1995.[2] He reminds us of the essential fact that for Christians, history has its roots in the *eschaton,* in the fullness of Christ of which a Christian community has at least a foretaste each time the eucharist is celebrated. This means that the accomplishment of this meeting of history with the *eschaton* is the work of the Holy Spirit who actualizes the reality of Christ in the eucharist.

Already in the early 1950s, Vladimir Lossky, writing on "Tradition and traditions",[3] foreshadowed Metropolitan John's view when he said: "It is not a further dogmatic development that will suppress St Paul's knowledge 'in part' (1 Cor. 13:12) but the *eschatological actualization* of the *fullness* in which Christians, here and now, dimly but with certainty, know the mysteries of Revelation" (my italics). J.-M. R. Tillard, in his most valuable book on the local church,[4] also speaks, in a detailed study of the Epistle to Diognetus, of the condition of Christians who live fully in history but at the same time are citizens of the *eschatological* heavenly Jerusalem. Again, it is through *communion* actualized by the Holy Spirit.

The main thrust of Lossky's essay on Tradition[5] is that Tradition cannot possibly be understood in a static way. In order to grasp its true nature, it may be necessary to *distinguish* it from scripture but, as so often with Lossky, to distinguish is not to separate or to oppose (he coined the phrase "distinction-identité" which he uses in different theological contexts[6]). This distinction leads him to describe Tradition not as the *content* of revelation but as the ecclesial capacity of *receiving* revelation. This capacity is nothing less than the gift of the Holy Spirit, received by the apostles at Pentecost and given to every Christian community and every member of the community in baptism-confirmation-chrismation. It is the gift of the Holy Spirit who "will guide you into all truth" (John 16:13). He is the Spirit of truth and the whole Truth is Jesus Christ himself (John 14:6) because He is the perfect image of the Father from whom the Spirit proceeds. The capacity to receive the fullness of revelation is actualized in the church's celebration of the eucharist which, as was said above, is a participation in the *eschata,* the feast of the kingdom.

Revisiting the notion of Tradition (with a capital "T") in this spirit should certainly help us in our attempts to discern the presence of the one faith in "traditions", which at first sight may seem alien to us. Is this not one of the primary tasks, if not *the* primary task, of the ecumenical movement today? For if we are able to discover, with the help of the

Holy Spirit, that our faith is truly one and that we can confess it together, from the Orthodox point of view, there will be no more impediments for the sharing of one eucharistic communion.

NOTES

[1] P. Serge Bulgakov, *Pravoslavie,* Paris, YMCA Press, 1935, p.1. ET: *The Orthodox Church,* London, 1935.

[2] *Louvain Studies,* 21, 2, 1996.

[3] L. Ouspensky and V. Lossky, *Der Sinn der Ikonen,* Neuchâtel, Urs Graf Verlag, 1952. ET: *The Meaning of Icons,* Olten, Switzerland, 1952 ("Tradition and traditions" reprinted in *A l'image et à la ressemblance de Dieu,* Paris, Aubier, 1967. ET: *In the Image and Likeness of God,* New York, SVS Press, 1974).

[4] *L'Eglise locale: ecclésiologie de communion et catholicité,* Paris, Cerf, 1995.

[5] See also Bishop Kallistos Ware's "Tradition and traditions", in the *Dictionary of the Ecumenical Movement,* N. Lossky et al, eds, Geneva, WCC, 1991, s.v.

[6] See e.g., *Essai sur la théologie mystique de l'Eglise d'Orient,* Paris, Aubier, 1944, p.48.

The Pneumatological Dimension in the Hermeneutical Task

MICHAEL PROKURAT

This essay will attempt to address the person of the Holy Spirit, holy Tradition (and the one gospel), and catholicity (here, a temporal understanding as well as a geographic one). Many Western theologies handle these topics differently from traditional Eastern Christian theology, and in this regard the Eastern understanding might serve to broaden Western theological sensibilities. On the other side of the coin, the Orthodox may learn the current point of departure, orientation and ecumenical worldview of their Western counterparts.

The task of our consultation at Bossey in June 1997 was to continue the work on ecumenical hermeneutics conducted by Faith and Order since 1995. In effect, the study had been attempting to formulate an "ecumenical hermeneutic", an interpretative theory and practice, which describes how Christian people get together and discuss their theological commonalties and differences. These commonalties and differences were found to be subject to confessional position, time, place, politics, and other factors, in spite of the fact that all recognize one God in Trinity, one Tradition, one gospel, and so on.

An ecumenical hermeneutic, or a clear hermeneutic for unity – never before defined – might seek to preserve the many traditions in the one Tradition, making God-established unity a visible goal. This conversation is valuable for Orthodox throughout the world, if for no other reason than that it could illuminate how current international and national divisions within groups might be approached and resolved. The study addresses one of the major difficulties confronting the Eastern churches in the 21st century: national distinctions and divisions. Of course, WCC participants were interested not only in the Orthodox ethnoses, but in issues affecting Christians throughout the world.

What might the term "ecumenical hermeneutic" mean?

The draft text[1] as it stood before the Bossey meeting contained no definition of the term "ecumenical hermeneutic". To me and some others, it was clear that a definition was absolutely necessary; a convenient distinction might be made between "hermeneutic" and "hermeneutics"; and conventional biblical hermeneutics needed to be related directly to "ecumenical hermeneutics". The reasons for these opinions were manifold. First, the project had previously included biblical hermeneutics as an integral component, one that was important to maintain; critical methodology in biblical studies could be challenged further, and positively so, by explicit reference to the ecumenical enterprise. Second, an ecumenical hermeneutic as it might be applied to biblical studies already appeared to be related intrinsically to canonical criticism. Canonical criticism is an established method of biblical exegesis with, among other concerns, a special focus on canonical scriptural texts within living Christian communities. Surely the relationship between the liturgical reading of canonical scriptural texts in communities of faith and the ecumenical interpretation of these texts cannot be overlooked. Finally, although some felt that no definitional distinction could be drawn between a general hermeneutic and an application to biblical studies, a comprehensive view might prove otherwise.

The question of a working definition of ecumenical hermeneutic met resistance over whether to have any definition at all and, if so, what the definition would be. The flexibility and advantage of not having a working definition subsequently gave way to the pressure and frustration of continually asking and explaining what one was talking about. Definitions came out of a maturation process, and lent specificity to further discourse.

The discussion surrounding the key question (What is an ecumenical hermeneutic?) was quite protracted and lively,[2] especially regarding "hermeneutic", but less so "ecumenical". After working through a reluctance to accept an American or British dictionary as authoritative, the definition was finally derived from several international theological authorities, and this wise compromise facilitated progressing beyond language.[3]

On the one hand, in American English a convention exists in biblical studies, wherein the word "hermeneutics" is used (in the plural) to describe methods of scriptural exegesis,[4] which in German are *die Geschichten*. "Hermeneutics" under this definition is based on a translation of the Greek *hermeneia*. On the other hand, in American English the singular "hermeneutic" may be used in a context broader than biblical studies to connote a generic philosophical or theological method. Frequently, such a hermeneutic is programmatic and associated with the approach taken by a particular philosopher or theologian, such as Jean-Paul Sartre's existentialism or Gustavo Gutiérrez's liberation theology.

The conventions described above appeared to me to be especially useful as applied to the ecumenical enterprise. Biblical hermeneutics is a wide and varied field that will doubtless not be tied for long to any single, overly specific method. "Ecumenical hermeneutics" seemed an apt choice as an overarching term among the many methodologies employed in contemporary biblical studies. The term "ecumenical hermeneutic" could be saved to apply not only to biblical studies, but also to the entire theological programme, including areas in the theological academic world outside of scriptural interpretation. Thus, the ecumenical hermeneutic would connote the general approach, as well as the particular application in areas such as parish ministry, ecclesiology, church history, etc. In addition, distinguishing "hermeneutic" from "hermeneutics" might facilitate the practical application of scriptural exegesis on the local level. The particularity of the task of scriptural exegesis – however long that might be productive – would be called "ecumenical hermeneutics". Working through a more general agenda of an "ecumenical hermeneutic" might well outlast the task of the specialized exegesis of scripture.

What is the "pneumatological dimension"?

How can one write of the Holy Spirit in so brief a space without simply acquiescing to wonderment? When and where was the Holy Spirit not present among the people of God? In classical theology it is commonplace to speak of the Holy Spirit in the Old Testament, in the New Testament, and in the church. From another perspective one might describe the Spirit as a person of the Trinity or speak of the personhood itself, taking either the Cappadocians or St Augustine as our point of departure. Whether we stand within the East or West, although there is a hiddenness to this person we agree that the Spirit is fully a person, immanent and transcendent.

The Holy Spirit is fully God, the Lord, the Life-Giver, and of one essence with the Father – from whom the Spirit proceeds according to the gospel of John. The Spirit is worshipped and glorified with the Father and the Son as the Life-Giver to creation and the Sanctifier of human nature. A favourite name is the Paraclete or Comforter, a treasury of blessings who is everywhere present and fills all things, taking part in the incarnation, but maintaining an apophatic nature even among cataphatic revelations, called a "chain" to the Father and the Son. The Holy Spirit is God of creation, salvation and transfiguration – and human nature is fulfilled in communion with the Spirit.

Depending upon one's frame of reference, the pneumatological dimension of ecumenical hermeneutics may be variously understood, as it was in committee. To begin with, one faces the question of the Holy Spirit in relation to the interpretation and formation of scripture, in other words, the canonization of texts. Since the formation of scripture necessarily involves interpretative action by the people of God in community, it might ultimately be that no canon of scripture is able to be formed without interpretation. The Spirit of truth is the guarantor of that interpretation and canon, but the Spirit must be discerned within both.[5] For example, the Nicene-Constantinopolitan Creed states that the Holy Spirit "spoke by the prophets". A contemporary reading limits "the prophets" to the three major and twelve minor prophets, or at most to the former prophets (Deuteronomistic history) and the latter prophets named in the Jewish canon. Let us consider another alternative suggested by this example.

Concerning interpretation and canon, we remember that at the end of the gospel of Luke the risen Lord refers to holy scripture as "the law of Moses, the prophets, and the psalms" (NRSV quoted here and in all passages following). Given the first-century believers' predilection for predictive prophecy and apocalyptic eschatology, one may legitimately label their understanding of the entirety of scripture as "prophecy", which is quite different from "the prophets" mentioned in the previous paragraph. In evidence of this more comprehensive understanding of prophecy we have the following. In the Lukan list above the "law of Moses" could be understood as prophecy, since Moses was acknowledged as the greatest prophet, and pseudepigraphal literature of the time reinforced this identification. Similarly, "the psalms" may also qualify as prophecy, because "the prophet David" was an established tradition at least as old as the Chronicles, when prophecy of that day was equated with temple singing, and David was credited with the writing and singing of psalms as well as founding the temple cult. We also read, "the Holy Spirit through David foretold" (Acts 1:16; similarly Acts 2:29-31) and analogous phrases in Luke. Additionally, "the psalms" might have connoted the entirety of "the Writings", since they were the first book in that corpus (literally, a scroll) and could have been used as a generic identification of the whole. Thus, in agreement with the implied Lukan understanding of "the law of Moses, the prophets, and the psalms" as prophecy inspired by the Holy Spirit, the Nicene-Constantinopolitan Creed seems to use the article on the Holy Spirit "who spoke by the prophets" to connote the Spirit in relation to the entirety of holy scripture. This is not merely what we regard as the prophets of the Old Testament.

Before the New Testament Pentecost, the Holy Spirit shows Jesus to be the Son of God at conception, baptism, ministry and resurrection. At Pentecost the Spirit is poured forth to enlighten not only the disciples – who become apostles – but all men and women to prophesy. Further, the New Testament coalesced as an interpretation of the Old Testament through the Holy Spirit. In the centuries following the writing of the

New Testament, more definition would be given to the canon through the inspiration and discernment of the Holy Spirit in the church.

An Eastern Orthodox contribution – the Holy Spirit and Tradition

For those acquainted with Eastern Orthodox theology, there is nothing novel in what follows. The topical approach taken falls under the category of "the Holy Spirit in Tradition", and is available in fuller, but more general, versions among several 20th-century Orthodox theologians.[6] For those unacquainted with Orthodox theology, what follows should begin to explain some of the ways of discerning the Holy Spirit in the life of the church, that is, the pneumatological dimension of an ecumenical hermeneutic.

For most if not all Christians, it is tautological to say that "Tradition" (with a capital "T" or "Holy Tradition") serves as the hermeneutic of the church. This is true especially for all the Orthodox. Many Christians have acknowledged the central role of Tradition for a long time, but difficulties remain with the term, difficulties of a technical definition as well as confusion with similar words. For the sake of convenience and clarity, we shall endeavour to present a rudimentary description and to explain related ideas and words.

For many Orthodox theologians of this century, Tradition has a very strong sense, so much so that speaking of Tradition is tantamount to speaking of the life of the church, always and everywhere. This is indeed a very strong identification between the entire life of the church and the term at hand, and is not characteristic of the way the word is commonly used by Western Christians or in the secular world. The life of the church, Holy Tradition, takes on the importance of an article of faith in the Nicene-Constantinopolitan Creed, the section occurring after Father, Son and Spirit. In the credal article it is described as an object of belief, as is the Trinity! Under the strong definition above, Holy Tradition bears the marks of the church itself: one, holy, catholic and apostolic. Having reached this juncture, Eastern Christians have something to bring to the table by way of discussion.

Holy Tradition is expressed within history, but is not easily reduced to a concept of systematic theology. The history within which Tradition is expressed is not restricted to past history. Holy Tradition includes the past history, the present history, and the future history of the life of the people of God, if not the eschatological sense of "history" as well. Thus, the catholicity of the church and its Tradition – well known in Western theology as geographically expressed – has a temporal dimension as important as its locative one. The catholicity of Holy Tradition as temporal and geographical seems to be expressed by means of formulas in both the Latin and Greek of the early eucharistic liturgies of the West and East. In these liturgies the gifts are described as being offered to God "at all times and in all places". Likewise, in the words of St Vincent of Lerins, "We must hold what has been believed, everywhere, always, and by all."

Let us take as a representative example of temporal catholicity a contemporary and emerging discipline, the history of exegesis. According to the Eastern church, in applying temporal catholicity this discipline could not be restricted only to eras favourite to traditional Western theological education. Thus, a biblical commentary that covers only sources from the "patristic era" might be very important and useful, but it ultimately falls short of being comprehensive by about a millennium and a half within the common era alone. Again, if Western scholars choose to call the period from the fall of Rome until the time of Charlemagne, Thomas Aquinas, or the Renaissance the "dark ages", they might acknowledge this as a provincial assessment, not one universally applicable. The full range of ecclesiastical witnesses through time (in other words, temporal catholicity) should always be allowed to speak. This includes what the Orthodox refer to as all the fathers and mothers of the church – and even before the church in first covenant times! – throughout the ages.

The strength and efficacy of Holy Tradition as the hermeneutic of (credal) faith and of holy scripture is not to be confused with local traditions or customs. Holy Tradition is of the type described by St Paul in 1 Corinthians, where he used technical, precise language in relation to the Lord's supper and the resurrection. "For I received from the Lord what I also handed on to you..." (1 Cor. 11:23; also 11:2; and 15:3 [2 Thess. 2:15]). St Irenaeus refers to the "rule of faith", *regula fidei*, by which every Christian openly confesses the Father, Son and Holy Spirit and interprets scripture. St Athanasius identifies the same by *skopos tes pisteos*, "the scope of faith", and similar identifications can be made within St Hilary of Poitiers, St Basil the Great, and so on.[7] Thus, Holy Tradition may be described as the life of the Holy Spirit within the church, the continuum of the church as the body of Christ, and the presence of the eschatological age.

Tradition (with a small "t"), for which I prefer the word "custom", consists of behaviour and attitudes attendant upon Holy Tradition throughout the centuries, bounded to and by time and place. We use the term "custom" rather than "tradition" here, not because it is historically correct – it is not – but to distinguish it from Holy Tradition.[8] Customs and indigenous local traditions might be harmonious with right belief, and certainly not in conflict with it, but are simply not to be identified with Holy Tradition. In fact some customs might tend to obscure Holy

Tradition; paradoxically, the defined distinctions might be clear in theory, but are less so in practice. This candid admission is found among Orthodox scholars of various ethnic backgrounds, but may be characteristic of any astute critic of culture and faith.

Understanding Holy Tradition as the life of the Holy Spirit within the church has parallels with several 20th-century theological themes, shedding some light on its meaning. For example, *oikonomia* in its larger sense of "divine economy" or divine providence is a synonym insofar as it pertains to all of God's actions on behalf of creation and its salvation. In Old Testament theology the term *Heilsgeschichte* or "salvation history" approximates this understanding, as does the term (gospel) *kerygma* in New Testament theology. However, each of these has necessary temporal limits particular to its discipline, which limits are not implied for the term Holy Tradition.

Conclusion

Discerning the Holy Spirit in the life of the church – in Holy Tradition – is a legitimate function of church history and doctrine, among other disciplines, and may be described as a "hermeneutic". The hermeneutic may be understood as a general philosophical, or rather theological, approach – the "agenda" of church history and other disciplines, so to speak. The Orthodox presuppose it is "ecumenical" in both the classical (referring to the orthodox Christian "oikoumene") and vernacular use of the word, and thus it may be called an "ecumenical hermeneutic". This programmatic agenda or ecumenical hermeneutic does not preclude, but rather necessarily includes, its specific application in all areas of church life. As discussed above, an ecumenical hermeneutic is something from which biblical studies, specifically exegesis, would profit greatly; being in that case referred to as (biblical) "ecumenical hermeneutics". Furthermore, an ecumenical hermeneutic might be applied to any of a number of ecclesiastical disciplines besides biblical studies and the others mentioned above.

Having said this, even the broad definition understates the case on two counts. First, Holy Tradition encompasses the "marks" of the church as one, holy, catholic and apostolic; and it constitutes the life of the church throughout history: past history, present history, and future history to its consummation – to the eschaton. In the Eastern church it is customary to speak of the totality of the experience of the church throughout time as Holy Tradition. Second, continually discerning the Holy Spirit is definitive and vital to the church itself. The self-identity of the church is intrinsically linked to the successful discernment and description of the work of the Holy Spirit, both within the church and outside its perceived formal limits. Therefore, describing the catholicity of the church through time as Holy Tradition and the identification of the workings of God, the Holy Spirit, in this same Tradition may aptly be called an ecumenical hermeneutic.

BIBLIOGRAPHY

Basil, Archbishop of Caesarea in Cappadocia, "On the Spirit", in *Nicene and Post-Nicene Fathers of the Christian Church*, vol. VIII, *St Basil: Letters and Select Works,* Philip Schaff and Henry Wace, eds, Grand Rapids, MI, Eerdmans, 1975, pp.1-50.

Bohachevsky-Chomiak, Martha, and Bernice Glatzer Rosenthal, eds, *A Revolution of the Spirit: Crisis of Value in Russia, 1890-1918,* tr. Maria Schwartz, Newtonville, MA, Oriental Research Partners, 1982.

Breck, John, "Orthodoxy and the Bible Today", in *The Legacy of St Vladimir,* J. Breck, J. Meyendorff and E. Silk, eds, Crestwood, NY, St Vladimir's Seminary Press, 1990, pp.141-57.

Breck, John, *The Shape of Biblical Language,* Crestwood, NY, St Vladimir's Seminary Press, 1994.

Congar, Yves, *I Believe in the Holy Spirit,* tr. David Smith, New York, Seabury, 1983.

Florovsky, Georges, *Bible, Church, Tradition: An Eastern Orthodox View,* vol. 1 in *The Collected Works of Georges Florovsky,* Belmont, MA, Nordland, 1972.

Golitzin, Alexander, "Spirituality: Eastern Christian", in *The Encyclopedia of Monasticism,* William M. Johnston, ed., Chicago, Fitzroy Dearborn, 2000.

Hildebrandt, Wilf, *An Old Testament Theology of the Spirit of God,* Peabody, MA, Hendrickson, 1995.

Hopko, Thomas, *The Spirit of God,* Wilton, CN, Morehouse-Barlow, 1976.

The Interpretation of the Bible in the Church, Rome, Pontifical Biblical Commission, 1993.

Ivanov, Vladimir, "The Doctrine of the Holy Spirit in Russian Theology", in *The Reconciling Power of the Trinity: Report of the Study Consultation of the Conference of European Churches,* Gosfar, FRG, CEC, 1983, pp.103-108.

Kesich, Veselin, *The Gospel Image of Christ,* rev. ed., Crestwood, NY, St Vladimir's Seminary Press, 1992.

Krašovec, Jože, ed., *The Interpretation of the Bible,* Sheffield, Sheffield Academic Press, 1998.

Levison, John R., *The Spirit in First Century Judaism,* Leiden, Brill, 1997.

Lossky, Vladimir, *In the Image and Likeness of God,* Crestwood, NY, St Vladimir's Seminary Press, 1985.

Lossky, Vladimir, *The Mystical Theology of the Eastern Church,* Cambridge, James Clarke, 1968.

Metzger, Bruce M., and Roland E. Murphy, eds, *The New Oxford Annotated Bible with the Apocryphal/Deuterocanonical Books,* New York, Oxford UP, 1994.

Meyendorff, John, *Living Tradition,* Crestwood, NY, St Vladimir's Seminary Press, 1978.

Meyendorff, John, *The Orthodox Church: Its Past and Its Role in the World Today,* rev. by Nicholas Lossky, 4th rev. ed., Crestwood, NY, St Vladimir's Seminary Press, 1996.

Meyendorff, John, *Orthodoxy and Catholicity,* New York, Sheed & Ward, 1966.

Norton, David, *A History of the Bible as Literature,* 2 vols, Cambridge, Cambridge UP, 1993.

On Spiritual Life in the Church, Encyclical Letter of the Holy Synod of Bishops of the Orthodox Church in America, Syosset, NY, Orthodox Church in America (undated, 1973?).

Pelikan, Jaroslav. *The Emergence of the Catholic Tradition (100-600),* and *The Spirit of Eastern Christendom (600-1700),* vols 1 and 2 of *The Christian Tradition,* Chicago, Univ. of Chicago Press, 1971, 1974.

Prokurat, Michael, Alexander Golitzin, and Michael D. Peterson. *Historical Dictionary of the Orthodox Church: Religions, Philosophies, and Movements, no. 9,* Lanham, MD, Scarecrow, 1996.

Prokurat, Michael, "Orthodox Interpretation of Scripture", in *The Bible in the Churches,* 3rd ed., Kenneth Hagen, ed., Marquette, WI, Marquette UP, 1998, pp.60-100.

Špidlik, Tomaš, *The Spirituality of the Christian East,* tr. Anthony P. Gythiel, Kalamazoo, MI, Cistercian Publications, 1986.

Stylianopoulos, Theodore G., *The New Testament: An Orthodox Perspective,* vol. I, *Scripture, Tradition, Hermeneutics,* Brookline, MA, Holy Cross Orthodox Press, 1997.

NOTES

[1] Cf. *Minutes of the Meeting of the Faith and Order Board, 8-15 January 1997*, Abbaye de Font-gombault, Faith and Order Paper no. 178, pp.77-95.

[2] Since my "social location" is not only related to Orthodox theology but also to American bibli-cal studies, my technical theological thinking and vocabulary was set in regard to the definition of "hermeneutic(s)" before this consultation.

[3] The reader may consult *A Treasure in Earthen Vessels: An Instrument for an Ecumenical Reflec-tion on Hermeneutics*, Faith and Order Paper no. 182, Geneva, WCC, 1998 (which is the final text in this study process and which is reprinted in this volume), §5 for the definitions finally decided upon.

[4] See J.A. Sanders, "Hermeneutics", in *The Interpreter's Dictionary of the Bible, Supplementary Volume*, Keith Crim, ed., Nashville, Abingdon, 1976, 402-407; Bernard C. Lategan, "Hermeneu-tics", in *The Anchor Bible Dictionary*, David Noel Freedman, ed., New York, Doubleday, 1992, 149-154.

[5] Albert C. Sundberg, Jr, "The Bible Canon and the Christian Doctrine of Inspiration", in *Inter-pretation*, 29, 1975, pp.352-71.

[6] See the works of G. Florovsky, V. Lossky and J. Meyendorff listed in the bibliography.

[7] Georges Florovsky, *Bible, Church, Tradition: An Eastern Orthodox View*, vol. 1 in *The Collected Works of Georges Florovsky*, Belmont, MA, Nordland, 1972, pp.73-92.

[8] I prefer the terms "Holy Tradition" and "custom" (cf. this usage in *The Historical Dictionary of the Orthodox Church*, 1996) out of a practical need to prevent confusion, although there has been no such distinction historically in regard to translating the words *paradidomi* and *trado*. The pre-sent-day confusion, circumvented by this suggested usage, is that "Tradition" (with a capital "T") cannot be distinguished from "tradition" (with a small "t") at the beginning of sentences or in speech. Difficulties in distinguishing meaning, with or without consistent capitalization or ref-erence to historical definitions, can even be found in reading recent authors, such as J. Meyen-dorff and J. Pelikan, et al. Furthermore, similar problems of vocabulary may be found in theo-logical discussions about "the canon within the canon" or "the Old Testament of the Old Testa-ment".

Ecumenical Hermeneutics:
Suspicion versus Coherence?

RUDOLF VON SINNER

Introduction: the problem of understanding each other in the ecumenical movement

"The debate now is no longer about the legitimacy of inculturation or contextualization. The burning issue today is: How to communicate between differently contextualized theologies, confessions and spiritualities? How to deal with the new diversity that is beginning to emerge?"[1]

This is the central question for the ecumenical movement today, put before us by World Council of Churches general secretary Konrad Raiser. In an article published just after the seventh assembly of the WCC in Canberra, Australia, in February 1991, he reflects on the controversy that arose around the presentation of Korean professor Chung Hyun Kyung.[2] In the end, he says, it revealed a deep gap between two kinds of hermeneutics:

> While Prof. Chung was guided in her presentation by a *contextual* hermeneutics, trusting that an interpretation that arose from the cultural context of Korea would evoke authentic responses from other contexts, even though the language would be radically different, the Orthodox reflections affirmed a *hermeneutics of tradition*, accepting the tradition of the apostolic faith as confessed by the early church as the normative criterion for ecumenical communication.[3]

Naturally, Chung's presentation aroused divergent reactions. What was worse, however, than the differing interpretations of her presentation was the fact that those who held opposing hermeneutics were unable to understand each other, let alone enter into dialogue. Thus, the necessity of a truly ecumenical[4] hermeneutics which would enable such dialogue and communication became obvious.

In this essay, I shall show how the question of an ecumenical hermeneutics was taken up in the Faith and Order world conference and the board and plenary commission. I shall then proceed to explore one of the crucial questions involved, that is, the alleged conflict between a hermeneutics of suspicion and a hermeneutics of coherence. Finally, I shall make some suggestions towards an ecumenical hermeneutics that could be helpful for clarifying the problems at stake and help us in growing together across confessions and contexts.

My reflections are based mainly on scholarly work, as the search for an ecumenical hermeneutics is also the perspective for my dissertation.[5] However, it is also influenced by my Reformed background in Switzerland on the one hand, and by my encounters with faith and life in the "South" – in Brazil and India respectively – on the other. These influences will be noticeable as we go along; this brief remark is meant to give a "hermeneutical key" for my reflections.

The search for an ecumenical hermeneutics in Faith and Order

The fifth world conference on Faith and Order in Santiago de Compostela, Spain, in 1993 restated the problem cited above and noted the need for an ecumenical hermeneutics. Again, it was Konrad Raiser who strongly emphasized the point in his address to the conference.[6] But also the section reports called for a study on hermeneutics:

> As we travel the way of pilgrimage, we will need to be able to understand each other's theological language and cultural ethos. We would be assisted in our journeying by intercontextual dialogues appropriately sponsored by regional ecumenical organizations, and in our interconfessional dialogues by a renewed Faith and Order study on hermeneutics, and new ways of doing theology which provide more adequate tools to express community on the way to the goal of visible unity.[7]

The question under discussion is not altogether new. For instance, Faith and Order had looked at intercontextuality in its meeting at Accra, Ghana, in 1974, where the issue of a "common language" and a "common frame of reference" for the expression of the Christian faith played a major role, presupposing that communication between theological formulations emerging out of different contexts is possible.[8] Various studies on a biblical hermeneutics and the authority of scripture have been carried out.[9] The Faith and Order commission meeting in Bangalore in 1978 pursued the question of "Sharing in One Hope".[10] However, the problem seems to have proved deeper than expected, as the Chung controversy shows.[11] That is why the Santiago conference made a strong plea for carrying out a study on ecumenical hermeneutics.

Three texts have been produced so far in the study. In 1994, a consultation in Dublin, Ireland, and a drafting meeting in Boston, USA, produced a first draft under the title: "According to the Scriptures: Towards a Hermeneutics for a Growing Koinonia".[12] A second consultation in Lyon, France, in March 1996 revised the text, which was then presented to the Faith and Order plenary commission meeting at Moshi, Tanzania, in August of the same year.[13]

A threefold structure had emerged that tried to deal with the matter involved in the following parts: the first part (a) dealing with the hermeneutics of scripture and Tradition, thereby also entering into confessional divergences; the second part (b) dealing with hermeneutics of contextuality and catholicity; and the third part (c) examining necessary forms of ecclesial discernment and the reception of ecumenical documents.

One question noted at the very beginning of the study process was that the responses to the widely distributed document *Baptism, Eucharist and Ministry (BEM)* showed that it was very differently understood. For example, M35 reads: "The orderly transmission of the ordained ministry is ... a powerful expression of the continuity of the church throughout history..."[14] The reactions to this showed that churches holding to the necessity of unbroken episcopal succession understood the paragraph to indicate that necessity, while those churches who do not hold this succession necessary understood the paragraph to indicate freedom in this matter.[15]

The plenary commission, reinforcing the need for the study but dissatisfied with its abstract and prescriptive language and lack of clarity, made a number of recommendations which were discussed at a third consultation in Bossey, Switzerland, in June 1997. The latter gathering produced a text under the title: *A Treasure in Earthen Vessels (2 Cor. 4:7): Towards a Hermeneutics for a Growing Koinonia* [a formes version of the text printed here, pp.134-60]. Taking into account the work done in the consultations on intercultural hermeneutics carried out by the WCC Programme Unit II, "The Churches in Mission", in 1994, published in 1996, part (b) on the necessary contextuality of every theology and their belonging together in catholicity was revised considerably.[16] It also tried to clarify its aims and sets of criteria offered, and to respond to the questions raised. It will be interesting and important to see how churches and theological institutions as well as individuals will respond to this revised text.

A hermeneutics of suspicion and a hermeneutics of coherence

One of the points raised at the 1996 Moshi meeting seems to be a crucial one. It shows a deep conflict within the ecumenical movement which, as I shall try to show, has been haunting it for some time. The text reads as follows: "The present text should be revised and developed so that... the relation between a social agenda and the quest for visible unity, a hermeneutics of suspicion and a hermeneutics of coherence be clarified and balanced."[17]

At first sight, the recommendation reads rather strangely. First of all, neither of the expressions used in the recommendation occurs in the Lyon text. Further, it seems to suggest antagonisms which are not, at least not explicitly, stated in the text. The two hermeneutics mentioned, a "hermeneutics of suspicion" and a "hermeneutics of coherence", appear in opposition, as if the latter sought to find coherence in its understanding and interpretation of scripture and Tradition, whereas the former aimed at dissolving it. Combined with the other pair of oppositions, a "hermeneutics of suspicion" seems to be connected to a "social agenda", while a "hermeneutics of coherence" seems to be the one needed in the "quest for visible unity". As it stands, for a reader engaged in the ecumenical movement there is a clear bias in favour of the second combination – the ecumenical project being itself the "quest for visible unity". A seemingly constructive "hermeneutics of coherence" of course would then have to be favoured, and an apparently destructive "hermeneutics of suspicion" linked to a merely "social" agenda, would have, at the very least, to be given less weight and priority.

In exploring what is meant by this formulation, it seems to me helpful to see where the naming of these two kinds of hermeneutics comes from. A person involved in the process of the ecumenical hermeneutics study, Anton Houtepen, made use of the term "hermeneutics of coherence" in an article in German published in 1990, where he says that an ecumenical hermeneutics should be designed to formulate common criteria of identity and coherence in Christianity, thus creating a wider framework for the presently used hermeneutics of consensus and convergence.[18] According to him, a fourfold ecumenical hermeneutics was operating in Faith and Order since Montreal 1963, including the formulation of BEM.[19] However, in the reception of BEM, other hermeneutics were used. Thus, the ecumenical movement had not been recognized in its quality as a "hermeneutical community". In Houtepen's view, the *sensus litteralis* proved stronger than a "hermeneutics of coherence". Against what he sees as a tendency in contemporary philosophy, namely "dissemination" (from Jacques Derrida), he refers to Paul Ricoeur for whom hermeneutics consisted in the "recollection of meaning".[20]

In fact, it is the same Ricoeur who brought up the notion of a "hermeneutics of suspicion". He spoke about the three "masters of suspicion", Karl Marx, Friedrich Nietzsche and Sigmund Freud.[21] From different angles, all three made a critique of religion,[22] claiming to lay bare unconscious factors influencing the interpreter which the three "attributed to the will to power, to the social being, or to the unconscious psyche" respectively.[23] However, according to Ricoeur, this suspicion is not to be taken as scepticism, because all three of its "masters" aim at the extension of consciousness, thus helping the process of interpretation. A hermeneutics of suspicion is, although opposed to a hermeneutics of the recollection or restoration of meaning, a necessary step in the process of interpretation.[24]

In a much more radical way, a "hermeneutics of suspicion" has been used in two streams of contemporary theology: liberation theology[25] and feminist theology.[26] In both cases, it essentially denotes a way of approaching scripture – and, for that matter, tradition – which sees scripture, and especially its use by Western academic male-dominated theology, as reflecting structures of power and domination. Therefore, every text has to be analyzed carefully in order to see whether the text itself is a witness to a group or person dominating another; moreover, it has also to be taken into account what the text does not say.[27] Domination is seen as non-compatible with the life and ministry of Jesus Christ. Therefore, any text or interpretation that is not liberating for men and women has to be viewed with suspicion.

This short exploration of the two terms as they are used by some contemporary theologians can help us in understanding the question at stake. For Ricoeur, both hermeneutics – although as such opposed to each other – seem to be necessary and important parts of the same process.[28] But what is meant by their opposition in the Moshi recommendation?

Two conflicting positions

The real question behind this dichotomy seems to be the longstanding conflict within the ecumenical movement between two strong positions, which are essentially those mentioned earlier by Raiser.

The first position, held mainly by theologians from the South, especially those connected to the Ecumenical Association of Third-World Theologians,[29] gives priority to the struggle of people and churches in their everyday life. In a context of poverty and oppression, they say, it is impossible to talk about doctrine without talking about life. In fact, the common struggle has brought many churches involved close to each other, although they might still differ on the doctrinal level. This position does not deny the importance of doctrine; it holds that a critical assessment of it and its relation to life is necessary. It is a *contextual* approach, as it is predominantly looking at the context in which the churches are living and trying to define the churches' task in it. It is this position, I believe, which is referred to by the terms "social agenda" and "hermeneutics of suspicion".

For the second position, the quest for visible unity is best served in theological discussions on the doctrinal level, as for those holding this view this is the place where divisions arise. If doctrinal problems were solved, visible unity between the churches could be established. While this position is not denying the need for practical action by the churches, and a necessary collaboration in that area, it prioritizes the doctrinal level. This position is held most clearly, but by no means exclusively, by the Orthodox churches.[30] It is a *confessional* or *traditional* approach. The rootedness in a fairly clearly defined tradition is predominant. It is this position which I see behind "the quest for visible unity" and a "hermeneutics of coherence" in the Moshi recommendation.

I am aware that these categories, simplified as they necessarily are, fall short of what they are pointing to, and other categories could be used. However, I believe that they are sufficiently adequate to denote the main conflict. The difference in the two positions or approaches should not be underestimated. In fact, it enters into questions of ecclesiology and authority. Who has the right to decide on which is the right perspective on scripture and Tradition? Who will say how the context is to be viewed and taken into consideration? The church with its leadership, the bishops or the primate? A group of theological experts? The human sciences in their perception of the world's agenda? The local congregation? The *sensus fidelium*? My thesis is that this basic conflict implies a deep difference in theological approach and hermeneutical perspective – and lies therefore at the heart of the very question of the study.

"Suspicion" and "coherence": two sides of the same coin

I would see both Tradition and context to be equally important in the way of discerning our standpoint as churches. Faith is always a fruit of the Holy Spirit, but it develops through our specific environment on the one hand, the whole of the life and tradition of the church on the other. There is neither a pure "tradition", nor a pure "context" which would not be viewed by a Christian in a faith perspective. Even the early church developed its doctrine through an intense interaction with its context – in other words, with Greek philosophy on the one hand, the Roman empire on the other. After all, it was the Roman Emperor Constantine, at that time not even baptized, who called and supervised the council of Nicea. This is not to deny that the Holy Spirit was at work in that council, but we cannot overlook that there were more factors involved than an interpretation of scripture and an "ecclesial process... for maintaining unity within diversity" (quoted from the Lyon text, I/6). Similar aspects can be shown at other stages of the development of tradition, including the 16th-century Reformation, which of course was strongly linked to political developments and forces. I would hold that even today we are always seeking the way of how to live out our common faith in a particular context, thus constantly contributing to the process of tradition.[31] The presupposition for this is, of course, the acknowledgment of all participants that "while no ecclesial community can claim to possess, to interpret and pass on the absolute and full comprehensive truth, each of them can pray for the Holy Spirit who discerns the spirits of truth and falsehood, even by speaking to one church through the insights of another" (quoted from the Lyon text, I/11).

In this process, we need both a hermeneutics of coherence and a hermeneutics of suspicion, to take up the formulation of the recommendation again, which in "the quest for visible unity" takes into serious consideration the "social agenda" that challenges the churches and calls for their action. However, I believe that the terminology itself is not helpful to our task. It in fact perpetuates ambivalent oppositions and undermines the necessary process of trying to understand and respect each other in our respective ways of doing theology and approaching the issue of unity in diversity.

I would rather say that what we need is a hermeneutics that takes both Tradition and context into consideration in its quest for visible unity. An ecumenical hermeneutics – a hermeneutics for a growing koinonia, rather than a "common" hermeneutics – would have to remind us that neither of these two aspects are to be left out. Without Tradition, our theology is without roots and in danger of becoming arbitrary. Without regard to the context, our theology is abstract and in danger of becoming irrelevant. In fact, there is a hermeneutical circle: it is through our perception of the context that we read the Bible, and it is through our reading that the Bible begins to read us (and our context), to take up a formulation used by Hans-Ruedi Weber.[32] And on this way of mutual reading, if we really consider ourselves – as churches in the ecumenical community – a "hermeneutic community" (Houtepen), we need the critique from others. These "others" include other Christians and other churches living in our time, as well as our forefathers and foremothers in the faith. It is there that an ecumenical hermeneutics could help us to see whether we are giving enough attention to scripture, Tradition, context and our hermeneutic community.

Towards a relevant and effective ecumenical hermeneutics: some suggestions

An ecumenical hermeneutics could surely help us in clarifying the points of convergence and divergence both across confessions and contexts. It could also help us in establishing a procedure for common discernment, if needed, and decision-making on theologies and practices of churches that seem to transgress the boundaries of the gospel. However, it has to be clear from the outset that an ecumenical hermeneutics is not to be mixed up with the decision to be taken. It can be necessary at times to take dogmatic or practical decisions, but an ecumenical hermeneutics can merely provide an instrument in going about this process. It can clar-

118 Interpreting Together

ify the problem set before us, but it cannot preclude the decision, which can only be taken in the actual dialogue between the churches or local congregations. As far as I can see, two sets of criteria could be provided by an ecumenical hermeneutics:

a) For the question whether a particular interpretation is to be declared illegitimate and contrary to the gospel. Such decisions, I would say, can only be made in a particular historical constellation and set of needs. Examples for this would be the councils of the ancient church which served as protection against what were considered to be serious heresies; the Barmen declaration of 1934 which was directed against the "German Christians" totally supporting Hitler and his racist ideology; the Dutch Reformed Churches in South Africa which were suspended from WARC membership due to their sanctioning of apartheid, and so on. Criteria of an ecumenical hermeneutics would have to provide not *material* decisions in advance, but a *procedure* on how to discern the (il)legitimacy of the stance concerned.[33] By procedure I mean a way by which the churches gathered in the WCC or in another ecumenical setting take a decision for or against a particular church or church practice which is deemed irreconcilable with the gospel, taking into account aspects like the local situation, the practice of the churches, the gospel message, and positions held in tradition as exposed in the creeds.

b) For the question of the establishment of a common understanding in terms of accepting the other's structures, liturgy, doctrine and so on as equivalent to one's own (see I/27). Criteria would then be needed to discover the one, holy, catholic and apostolic church in one another, presupposing a fundamental equality between the churches, and denoting the momentary amount of common ground. The way presented by Raiser in Moshi seems to me a valuable contribution to that end.[34]

On this way, it would seem to be fruitful to carry out case studies, dealing with the following questions:

a) How do different confessions react to the same context (for instance, the Roman Catholic, the Anglican, historical Protestant and Pentecostal churches in Brazil in reaction to poverty and injustice)?

b) How do churches of the same confession react to different contexts (for instance, the Greek Orthodox Church in Greece and in Africa)?

Reactions could be described on various levels, such as consequences drawn for church government, liturgical practice, social action, relating to other churches, relating to people of other faiths, and relating to "the world".

Furthermore, biblical stories should be explored and discussed from various confessional and contextual standpoints. The studies on acts that were done for the conference on world mission and evangelism in Salvador, Bahia, in 1996 are a good and valuable example. It is to be remembered that many people are criticizing the lack of biblical foundation of WCC studies. However, it is not enough to just quote biblical texts; the way of using them and the reason for it has to be made clear.[35]

These are a few tentative suggestions towards an ecumenical hermeneutics which I submit to the ongoing discussion. My hope is that they will aid in the growth of unity while preserving diversity as far as possible and necessary. Valuing diversity as a gift of God has been one of the major achievements of the ecumenical movement, especially in the last years. But the challenge of John 17:21 ("that they may all be one... so that the world may believe") remains. Both aspects play a major role as the Church of South India (CSI), a church united from among four confessional traditions and designed to be a sign and local embodiment of unity of the church worldwide, is celebrating its golden jubilee. In this year, apart from celebrating the unity achieved, this church's dealing with unity and diversity as well as problems in understanding each other within it are to be assessed anew. Both within the CSI and the wider ecumenical movement we would be greatly helped on the way towards unity if we could at least understand each other and be held accountable to each other as local expressions of the one body of Christ to which we belong.

NOTES

[1] Konrad Raiser, "Beyond Tradition and Context: In Search of an Ecumenical Framework of Hermeneutics", in *International Review of Mission,* vol. 80, 1991, nos 319-20, pp.347-54, quoted from p.351.
[2] For the text of her presentation see *Signs of the Spirit: Official Report, Seventh Assembly,* Michael Kinnamon, ed., Geneva, WCC, 1991, pp.37-47.
[3] Raiser, *op. cit.,* p.349; emphasis mine. The Orthodox reflections are to be found in *Signs of the Spirit, op. cit.,* pp.279-82.
[4] The word "ecumenical" in these reflections, as in the texts cited, refers exclusively to the relations between the Christian churches in the whole world, following diverse confessions and living in diverse contexts. The question of ecumenism with people of other faiths is not covered by the term, although the issue is mentioned as a contextual problem for many churches.
[5] Working title: "The Triune God in Context: Observations on Leonardo Boff (Brazil) and Raimundo Panikkar (India) as a Contribution to an Ecumenical Hermeneutics".
[6] "The Future of the World Council of Churches and the Role of Faith and Order within the Ecumenical Movement", in *On the Way to Fuller Koinonia,* official report of the fifth world conference on Faith and Order, Santiago de Compostela 1993, Thomas F. Best and Günther Gassmann, eds, Faith and Order Paper no. 166, Geneva, WCC, 1994, pp.168-74, esp. p.171.
[7] Report of Section I, §28, in *On the Way to Fuller Koinonia, op. cit.,* p.234.
[8] *Accra 1974,* minutes, Faith and Order Paper no. 71, Geneva, WCC, 1974, esp. p.78. See also the respective chapter in Tobias Brandner, *Einheit gegeben – verloren – erstrebt: Denkbewegungen von Glauben und Kirchenverfassung,* Göttingen, 1996, pp.252-66.
[9] See the compilation of Ellen Flesseman-van Leer, *The Bible: Its Authority and Interpretation in the Ecumenical Movement,* Faith and Order Paper no. 99, Geneva, WCC, 1980.
[10] *Sharing in One Hope: Reports and Documents from the Meeting of the Faith and Order Commission,* 15-30 Aug. 1978, Bangalore, Geneva, WCC, 1978.

120   Interpreting Together

[11] It is no wonder that the same controversy triggered off anew the old discussion of gospel and culture, which resulted in a four-year study process coordinated by Christopher Duraisingh at the WCC and culminated in the conference on world mission and evangelism at Salvador de Bahia, Brazil, Nov.-Dec. 1996. In the same process, a study on intercultural hermeneutics was carried out; see *International Review of Mission*, 85, 1996, no. 337, pp.241-52. In the world conference, the subject was taken up in section IV: "One Gospel – Diverse Expressions", part A, although the term is not explicitly used: see *Called to One Hope: The Gospel in Diverse Cultures*, Christopher Duraisingh, ed., Geneva, WCC, 1998.

[12] Published in *Minutes of the Meeting of the Faith and Order Standing Commission, 5-12 January 1995*, Aleppo, Syria, Faith and Order Paper no. 170, Geneva, WCC, 1995, pp.14-24.

[13] Published in *Faith and Order in Moshi*, Alan D. Falconer, ed., Geneva, WCC, 1998.

[14] *Baptism, Eucharist and Ministry*, Faith and Order Paper no. 111, Geneva, WCC, 1982, 29. The commentary (36) speaks of "the *sign* of apostolic succession"; emphasis mine.

[15] Excellent case studies on the different hermeneutics at work in the reception of BEM were carried out by William Henn and William Tabbernee, both published in this volume.

[16] See note 11 above. It seems, however, that the consultation found it difficult to fully grapple with their subject-matter; accordingly, the word "hermeneutics" does not come up anywhere in the text but once as "hermeneutical tools"! Except for the title, the text speaks about "intercultural communication", which is certainly part of, but not the whole field of, an intercultural hermeneutics.

[17] *Faith and Order in Moshi, op. cit.*

[18] A. Houtepen, "Ökumenische Hermeneutik. Auf der Suche nach Kriterien der Kohärenz im Christentum", in *Ökumenische Rundschau*, 39, 1990, pp.279-96, here p.279.

[19] *Baptism, Eucharist and Ministry, op. cit.*

[20] P. Ricoeur, *Freud and Philosophy: An Essay on Interpretation*, transl. Denis Savage, New Haven/London, Yale UP 1970, 5th ed. 1978, esp. pp.28-32. Konrad Raiser also referred to Ricoeur in this matter, in his paper presented at the Faith and Order plenary commission meeting in Moshi, Tanzania, in August 1996: "A Hermeneutics of Unity", in *Faith and Order in Moshi*, pp.115-27.

[21] *Ibid.*, pp.32-36. See also his *The Conflict of Interpretations*, Dan Ihde, ed., Evanston, Northwestern UP, 1974, pp.148-50, and "Hermeneutique philosophique et hermeneutique biblique", in *Du texte à l'action: Essais d'herméneutique II*, Paris, 1986, pp.99-133, esp. pp.131f.

[22] The first of these, Marx, called religion the "opium of the people", the second, Nietzsche, "platonism for the people", and the third, Freud, "collective neurosis", as Dorothee Sölle also put it in a recent article. For her, the feminist movement is another "master of suspicion", for whom religion is seen as the idealization of patriarchy: "Von der Hermeneutik des Verdachts zu einer des Hungers. Löst sich das Christentum in Ethik auf?", in A. Grözinger and J.Lott, eds, *Gelebte Religion. Im Brennpunkt praktisch-theologischen Denkens und Handelns*, Hermeneutica vol. 6, Practica, Rheinbach, 1997, pp.44-49, here p.47.

[23] Ricoeur, *The Conflict of Interpretations*, p.149.

[24] For a more elaborate and critical appraisal of Ricoeur's two notions see Hans Weder, "Kritik am Verdacht. Eine neutestamentliche Erprobung der neueren Hermeneutik des Verdachts", in *Zeitschrift für Theologie und Kirche*, 93, 1996, no. 1, pp.59-83, esp. p.60 (note 4) and pp.72-76, although I largely disagree with Weder's critique of Ricoeur and Schüssler-Fiorenza.

[25] See Juan Luis Segundo, *The Liberation of Theology*, Maryknoll, Orbis, 1976, esp. pp.7-38, who specifically speaks of an "ideological" and an "exegetical suspicion" in order to detect hidden power structures.

[26] See Elisabeth Schüssler-Fiorenza, *In Memory of Her: A Feminist Theological Reconstruction of Christian Origins*, London, 1986, e.g. p.56: "Considering this patriarchal context for the canonization process a hermeneutics of suspicion is called for. The information on women found in the surviving canonical texts and the writings of patristic orthodoxy are not value-neutral."

[27] When St Paul, for instance, who elsewhere highly values women's contributions, forbids women to speak in church (1 Cor. 14:33b-36), this might reflect that they held, in fact, an influential and strong position. Paul's verdict is an attempt to call them to order, so as not to upset the Hellenistic environment. Paul's major concern, therefore, is not the behaviour of women, but the protection of the Christian community, *ibid.*, pp.230-33.

[28] "Hermeneutics seems to me to be animated by this double motivation: willingness to suspect, willingness to listen; vow of rigour, vow of obedience. (...) it may be that extreme iconoclasm belongs to the restoration of meaning" (*Freud and Philosophy*, 27).

[29] The Ecumenical Association of Third-World Theologians, founded 1976 in Dar es Salaam, Tanzania. For a thorough assessment of EATWOT's positions, see Franklyn J. Balasundaram, *EATWOT in Asia*, Bangalore, 1993, esp. pp.282-93.

[30] See for instance *Orthodox Visions of Ecumenism, op. cit.*, p.189, para. 1, in the report of an inter-Orthodox consultation on "The Orthodox Churches and the WCC", Chambésy, Switzerland, Sept. 1991: "For the Orthodox, Eastern and Oriental, the primary purpose of the World Council of Churches is its work for the restoration of unity among Christians. In the Orthodox understanding, this means full ecclesial unity, that is, unity in doctrinal teaching, sacramental life and polity. The Orthodox recognize other important dimensions of ecumenical work and activity... But... the ultimate goal and justification of the ecumenical movement... is the full ecclesial unity of Christians."

[31] Robert J. Schreiter has greatly helped the understanding of that ongoing process; see his book on *Constructing Local Theologies,* London, 1985, esp. pp.95-121. This book is already a revised version of an earlier paper published in 1977. Such work should be further pursued, especially based as it is on the experience of people living in different contexts who entered into intense dialogue.

[32] Hans-Ruedi Weber, *The Book That Reads Me: A Handbook for Bible Study Enablers,* Geneva, WCC, 1995.

[33] This would be needed to discern illegitimacy of diversity, as mentioned – in a very general way – in Santiago, section II/17 and 18, see *On the Way to Fuller Koinonia, op. cit.*, p.241. However, while Santiago seems to seek more generally applicable criteria, I would see the necessity more in an ad-hoc-situation; this is also the assessment of O.V. Jathanna (UTC, Bangalore) in his reaction to the Lyon paper of 13 May 1997 (unpublished).

[34] See note 4. The following recommendations made in Santiago seem to me to ask for a study in this latter field, see sections I/28, II/12.1, II/15, pp.234, 240, 241.

[35] See William Tabbernee's remarks in regard to the use of Bible quotations in BEM's section on the eucharist, *op. cit.*

Hermeneutics: An Instrument for an Ecumenical Reflection on the Search for Church Unity

METROPOLITAN GENNADIOS (LIMOURIS) OF SASSIMA

Ecumenical history calls for a reflection on hermeneutics

Churches and Christians are in the midst of a decade-long crisis – a stagnation in the ecumenical movement and in the search for the unity of the church. Some churches, "traditional" or not, make strong complaints about the ecumenical movement. Others have abandoned their original commitment. Some cite new issues related to worldwide political, economic, socio-political and ethnic problems. Some, such as the Orthodox churches of Bulgaria and Georgia, have withdrawn their membership of the World Council of Churches. Amid all this is the recognition that at the eve of the third millennium Christendom – the church of Christ, his church, which we all proclaim and confess as the one, holy, catholic and apostolic church – is still divided .

This is a reality and a fact. It is true that many efforts have been undertaken during past decades on the part of the churches, through their multilateral and bilateral theological conversations and official dialogues, as well as on the part of the WCC, and the Faith and Order commission in particular. But the situation still remains unchanged. Is the quest for Christian unity still among the churches' priorities?

During the 1980s, and even before, there were many hopes that the convergence document on *Baptism, Eucharist and Ministry* would attract the churches to a closer rapprochement and to the study of divisive issues which could be identified with the help of that document. There was a hope, a deep desire, that something very significant and important might happen within the churches at the close of the 20th century. Others looked towards the recent eighth assembly, marking fifty years of the WCC's existence. Unfortunately, because of the *kairos* of human hostilities, these hopes as well as many others, emerging in theological multilateral conversations, have collapsed. Churches adhere still very strongly and solidly to their respective ecclesiological, confessional and denominational positions and presuppositions.

Nearly forty years ago, at the New Delhi assembly of 1961, the Orthodox[1] delegates suggested that the ecumenical endeavour could be characterized as *ecumenism in space*, aiming at agreement between various denominations, as they exist at present. They affirmed that the common ground, or rather the common background, of existing denominations, can and must be found in their common past history, in that common, ancient and apostolic tradition from which they all derive their existence. This kind of ecumenical endeavour can properly be called an *ecumenism in time*. The Faith and Order report to the New Delhi assembly speaks of agreement (in faith) with all ages, as one of the normative prerequisites of unity. The Orthodox in that report suggested a new method – which is still true for today – of ecumenical inquiry, and this new criterion on ecumenical evaluation, as a kingly rock, with the hope that unity may be recovered by the divided denominations by their return to their common past. By this way divergent denominations may meet each other on the unity of common tradition. No static restoration of old forms is anticipated, but rather a dynamic recovery of *perennial ethos*, which only can secure the true agreement of all ages. Nor should there be a rigid uniformity, since the same faith, mysterious in its essence and unfathomable adequately in the formulas of human reason, can be expressed accurately in different manners. The immediate objective of the ecumenical search, according to the traditional understanding, a reintegration of Christian mind, a recovery of apostolic tradition, a fullness of Christian vision and belief, in agreement with all ages.

The fifth world conference on Faith and Order at Santiago de Compostela, Spain, in 1993 initiated and encouraged Faith and Order to undertake a study on "Hermeneutics in Ecumenical Perspective". This new ecumenical venture created new difficulties for the churches and for theologians, at least those considered traditional, because the notion and the understanding of hermeneutics (*hermeneutiki* or *hermeneutica*) itself needs to be explored. The proposed studies for an ecumenical hermeneutics raised more important doctrinal issues, because the various church traditions have a different understanding, interpretation and ecclesial experience on hermeneutics on the one hand, and the expectations engendered by such studies on the other.

In Orthodox understanding, hermeneutics is considered to be the whole life of the church. There is not one hermeneutic for scripture and another for the patristic teachings, or another for the understanding of the church and holy sacraments. The "hermeneutics" of the Orthodox understanding is a holistic approach realizing the oneness of doctrine and dogma. On the other hand, if by interpretation we would try precisely to identify hermeneutics in this context we would be involved in an overly scholastic approach inappropriate to Orthodox theology.

Has the ecumenical reality expressed forty years ago in New Delhi changed? I do not think so, at any rate not completely. In the reports mentioned, what stands out is that the search for Christian unity identifies a *perennial ethos,* demanding the return of the churches to their common roots of the apostolic tradition which constitute our common background.

The French philosopher Ramonet describes today's world situation in terms of a certain *chaos,*[2] but he identifies *good* and *bad* chaos. Confronted by bad chaos, humankind can avoid isolation only through all possible efforts, supported by strong existential ideological and metaphysical presuppositions.

The dawn of a new century heralds the dawn of a new period for humanity, with hopes and expectations for the whole world. Likewise, the new period from Harare and beyond demands new efforts from all of us – church leaders and all those people committed to the sacred goal of the search for Christian unity. It demands new efforts on the part of Faith and Order, for its programmes are instruments for moving together in the pilgrimage towards a full communion/koinonia of humankind and the church of Christ.

First of all, existing programmes must continue in order to be finalized and to reach their convergence stage in the near future. But *how* must they continue? It is our duty to give them much-needed fresh blood, to offer new theological visions and new programmatic directions, not so much to satisfy our ecclesial and denominational traditions but rather in order to find ways of bringing the good news to people in their contemporary context and reality.

We need to rediscover Christ, to discover whether He as the Lord and Saviour is in the midst of us, somewhere where each of us can call upon him for very personal and human needs. Today, a christological crisis exists, a crisis of faith. Jesus Christ is neglected, his salvation is questioned and, even more, his existence as a divine-human person is questioned. A renewal of faith is demanded – a faith to be reaffirmed, which emerges from the ecclesial tradition, rooted in apostolic times and teachings. Our spiritual commitment should be enriched by our *metanoia,* a repentance for our divisions. Churches and Christians cannot continue to be divided; at the very least they should be able to share the common treasures and richness of our common roots of the ancient undivided church.

We must not continue to confess the divided body of Christ and to drink his blood which is the life of the church. Isolation and stagnation are bringing a kind of schizophrenia to human minds, and people are becoming eternal "earthen vessels" of a new paranoiac world which continues on another road – not the one leading to Emmaus and the kingdom of God, but to death.

Ecumenical history teaches us that we must learn to distinguish between the unity which exists and the fuller unity which should characterize the church of Christ and which it is our task to realize. There is the unity which holds us together right now and obliges us to go forward together. And there is the unity which is promised to us and which will be given to us in God's time if we respond obediently to do his will, to do his work of gathering. There is unity on the road and there is unity as the goal. The full unity of the church is something which still requires work, action and prayer. But there exists a unity in allegiance to our Lord for the manifestation of which we are all responsible. To paraphrase Archbishop William Temple, we should act upon it insofar as it is already a reality.[3]

Does a real unity exist already? The churches would not have declared that they "intend to stay together" if their common faith in Jesus Christ as God and Saviour, the bond of their common calling, was not real. The Amsterdam message to the churches and to the world describes that unity in these words: "... we are divided from one another, but Christ has made us his own and he is not divided". In a resolution concerning the nature of the World Council of Churches, also adopted by the first assembly, it was said of the churches: "They find their unity in him. They have not to create their unity; it is the gift of God."

Spirit and church: a hermeneutical Pentecostal image

The unity of the church is the necessary corollary to its calling. The church is the community of those who are called (1 Cor. 1:23). Thus, in the New Testament, calling does not refer only to individual callings, or vocations, but to the common calling in Christ (Rom. 8:30, 2 Tim. 1:9). And it is this common calling which binds Christians in an indestructible fellowship. They are united because they "share in a heavenly call" (Heb. 3:1), and there is one body because it can be said of them: "You were called to the one hope that belongs to your call" (Eph. 4:4). This calling could be considered as a biblical and ecclesiological hermeneutic. And it is not simply a privilege to be enjoyed; it demands a constantly renewed response (cf. 2 Pet. 1:10) in order to have a wider affirmation and implementation.

In the New Testament, from a hermeneutical perspective, unity is never static. Unity is always the result of the gathering and the search for the truth and love of our common roots in the Lord of the church. But in thinking of the church christologically, as the body of Christ, it is necessary to keep in mind the "image" of the church as the kingdom of the Holy Spirit. St Irenaeus spoke of the Son and the Spirit as the "two hands of God" which always work together. If the church is eucharistic, it is at the same time Pentecostal: it is an extension of the incarnation and of Pentecost.

In this gift of the Spirit at Pentecost, there are three elements of special importance.

First, the Spirit is not conferred solely upon a particular hierarchical order. It is a gift to the whole people of God: "they were all filled with the Holy Spirit". It is helpful to recall the distinction, emphasized by the Russian Orthodox theologian Vladimir Lossky, between the two givings of the Spirit. The first occurs on Easter day, when Jesus – risen but not yet ascended – breathes upon the disciples and says to them: "Receive the Holy Spirit. Whatsoever sins you remit, they are remitted; and whatsoever sins you retain, they are retained" (John 20:22-23). At this moment the apostles represent the hierarchy of the church: the gift of the Spirit is specifically linked with the authority to bind and loosen, and this particular power is not conferred upon the whole body of Christ but is transmitted through the apostolic college to the later form of the episcopate.

In the second giving of the Spirit, recorded in Acts 2 and following, the apostles no longer represent the hierarchy, but rather they constitute the entire body of the church as it then existed. The Spirit descends at Pentecost upon each and every member of the redeemed community, and this universality of the Pentecostal gift continues in the church throughout all ages. We are all baptized in the Holy Spirit and are spirit bearers: "You have been anointed by the Holy One and you all know" (1 John 2:20). Just as the eucharist is an action performed by all alike, so the Spirit is a gift to all alike.

Secondly, the gift of the Spirit at Pentecost is a gift of unity: in the words of Acts 2:1, "they were all with one accord in one place". It is the special task of the Spirit to draw humankind together. This aspect of the Spirit's work is vividly emphasized in Greek hymnography, when it contrasts God's descent at Pentecost with his descent at the building of the tower of Babel (Gen. 11:7). The God of old came down in order to divide humanity, but at Pentecost he came down in order to unite it. The festal hymn of Pentecost says the same: "When the Most High descended and confused the tongues, He divided the nations; but when He distributed the tongues of the fire, He called all to unity."

Yet the gift of the Spirit not only calls humankind to unity but it is also, and thirdly, a gift of differentiation. The tongues of fire are "divided" so that they rest upon each one personally. The Holy Spirit is a Spirit of freedom, and He bestows upon humankind an infinite diversity.

Unity and differentiation: such are the two aspects – contrasted but not opposed – of the gift of the Spirit to the church. The church is a mystery of unity in diversity and of diversity in unity. In the church a multitude of persons are united in one, and yet each of them preserves his personal integrity unimpaired. In our association on the purely human level there will always exist a tension between individual liberty and the demands of corporate solidarity. Only within the church, and through the gift of the Spirit, is the conflict between these two resolved. In the kingdom of the Holy Spirit there is neither totalitarianism nor individualism, neither dictatorship nor anarchy, but harmony and unanimity. Russian Orthodox thinkers since Khomiakov have used the word *sobornost,* "catholicity" to express this notion of unanimity in freedom.

The Pentecostal "image" or "icon" of the church and, together with it, our eucharistic "icon" form a salutary corrective to the first and inexact image, the image of earthly power and jurisdiction. "It shall not be so among you" because the church is not a kingdom of this world, but of the kingdom of the Holy Spirit, and therefore its rules and principles are not those of human government.

There is no way for churches which are neither fully united nor completely separated to arrive at real, concrete, manifest unity except the way of common obedience to the common calling. The ecumenical task is to go forward together in making a common response to the one christological calling. To act on unity, without using symbols or images, is to work towards the growth of this calling, which does not imply that any pressure is brought upon the churches other than the pressure which is inherent in their common calling and to which every church must make its own free response in accordance with the Tradition and the teaching of the undivided church.

The already existing "unity" which is expressed in various forms between churches yet divided, gives an opportunity to the World Council of Churches to be a unique ecumenical channel for the common witness and action of the churches in those matters in which they have to come to a common mind. In the words of Lesslie Newbigin, "we are in a transitory phase of the journey from disunity to unity".[4]

NOTES

[1] Cf. third assembly of the World Council of Churches, New Delhi, India, 1961, in *Orthodox Visions of Ecumenism,* Gennadios Limouris, ed., Geneva, WCC, 1994, pp.30-31.
[2] Cf. Ignacio Ramonet, *Le chaos et le monde,* Paris, 1999, p.45.
[3] Cf. his *The World Council of Churches: Its Process of Formation,* London, 1946, pp.172-73.
[4] *The Household of God,* London, 1953, p.21.

Reflections on "A Treasure in Earthen Vessels: An Instrument for an Ecumenical Reflection on Hermeneutics"

PABLO R. ANDIÑACH

The ecumenical task within the search for the visible unity of the church is one that envelops the whole life of the church. This life involves the church's actions and reflections, its past history and – perhaps most importantly – its present and future history. The task takes us on a long road, where light and darkness are intermixed. From time to time we must walk more slowly, perhaps to allow agreements to come into full light, agreements which may then facilitate more significant advances.

Along this road, the Faith and Order document *A Treasure in Earthen Vessels*[1] is a landmark which ought to be celebrated as a fundamental step. Reading the section on "past reflections on the theme" (§§14-20), or considering the itinerary through which the document arrived at its crystallization, reveals the diversity of opinions that were present in the document's development. This diversity is all the more significant for a document on hermeneutics. The task is not only a matter of reading scripture in the light of the different contexts in which the church is present. We must also test in a real way our judgment of the sometimes conflicting readings our brothers and sisters of other traditions make of the same texts, symbols and practices. Once we have been awakened to our neighbour's values, ecumenical hermeneutics should lead us to be able to criticize and to be criticized. (The former is a task for which we require no special qualifications, since we exercise it with energy and eagerness at every opportunity.) But going further, a study on ecumenical hermeneutics should lead us to be able to read our own tradition with critical eyes, to purify it from the inside, to make it more faithful to the scriptures, and finally, to be a part of a church more willing to extend its hand, to present the gospel in a way which is more genuine and more sensitive to the necessities of our times.

The task before us can be likened to crossing a river by stepping on stones: when we put our weight on a new stone we are overcoming one difficulty; at the same time we must summon the energy for the following leap. I have selected three concepts from the Faith and Order text that in my view reveal the point that has been reached. As a conclusion, I will propose three tasks which would continue the initial reflection, in order to begin thinking of the leap towards the next stone.

The document

The contextuality of texts, symbols and practices

    A Treasure in Earthen Vessels assumes that the scriptures were conceived in particular historical, social and cultural contexts. It is important to point out that this statement reflects a positive understanding of the contexts where the texts were produced and it should not be taken as to imply a defect or a limitation of the message. In a certain way, we are stating rather that it is thanks to the particular context that the word of God has come to us in a language that we can understand. Consequently the search to understand the objective social conditions being addressed by the text, the worldview that accompanies it and the struggles that it reflects, is an indispensable element in any serious reading of all writings. This leads us to wonder about our own theological output: is the context from which our theology arises a stumbling block against balance and authenticity, or on the contrary, is it an unavoidable condition for a meaningful message for women and men in our time? In other words, should we ignore the problems that arise from particular pastoral challenges because they are contextual – and therefore take us away from the so-called "universal thought" – or should we rather build our thought, understand our symbols and plan our practices in the same context in which we have been placed? It is remarkable that what we call "social context" is nothing other than that place where the church is called to exercise its ministry, and there is no possible alternative. It is there or it is nowhere.

    The document's brief meditation on the relationship between contextuality and catholicity (§§43ff.) is also helpful to our understanding of this essential issue. While contextuality refers to the proclamation of the gospel inside the life and culture of a particular community, catholicity applies to the participation of that community and that proclaimed Word, in the totality of life that is present through Christ in the church.

> When an interpretation of the gospel in a particular context points to injustice or liberation, this interpretation is not simply a contextual claim. It may provide an insight to be tested and amended or applied in other contexts (§47).

    In this sense we are opening our minds to discover universality in the particularity of our specific contexts.

Hermeneutical community

    If we can speak of a "hermeneutical community", as our document does, this is largely due to the theologies that have arisen primarily in the last thirty years in the so-called third-world countries. While the classic theologies understood that the interpreter of the scriptures was the church, and this was understood either as a *magisterium* separated from people, or as directed by a small group of scholars, the more recent theologies name the Christian community as the privileged space for the interpretation of the texts, symbols and practices. This doesn't mean that we have to discard the contribution of the specialists or that of the ecclesiastical bodies. Rather, these must develop their thought and actions in reference to people's necessities. They have to listen, in the first place, to the voice of those that are facing the problems of life, and from there they go to the texts to find orientation, support and hope. The raw material for a solid ecumenical hermeneutics should be the experiences and reflections that arise from the committed Christian community, with the challenges of its own time and place. This implies, on behalf of the theologians, the need to listen before speaking, but it also implies an approach to the texts – and our symbols and practices – that keeps in mind the necessities of the community surrounding the church, the community which it is called to serve.

In Latin America, as well as in other contexts, this reading from the base community has been a powerful tool to liberate our hermeneutics from prejudices, limitations and misreadings, although there is still a lot to be done. Such a methodology has been partly responsible for the movement called "popular reading of the Bible", or "reading the Bible with the people". It made us rethink our understanding of the scriptures, and it has opened our eyes to new interpretations. This reading of the texts from the community began to show us a liberationist perspective in the political field. We found ourselves discovering the reading from the minorities like natives or immigrants, or from those social outcasts as the unemployed or homeless, or from the excluded sectors as many minorities, or the fruitful readings from women's perspective in a patriarchal society. All of these are a growing contribution to the *re*-reading of the scriptures from the point of view of the poor and excluded. Such a re-reading is changing the life of the churches in a very hopeful way, bringing them to a more sensitive understanding of their relationship with the word. Even more, this new outlook in biblical understanding is helping the churches revise their dogmas and classical statements, challenging them with reality, and pushing them to face the real problems of our time with honesty.

Hermeneutics of coherence, suspicion and confidence

Another important achievement of the document under review is its acknowledgment of the necessary balance between a hermeneutics of coherence and of suspicion (§§6-8). Both approaches lose their ecumenical meaning if they are not made inside what the document calls hermeneutics of confidence. This is nothing other than the simple but profound attitude of listening to the other, and keeping in mind the possibility that the Spirit speaks in and through others (§8). Assuming, then, this general hermeneutic of confidence, I would like to discuss the relationship between coherence and suspicion.

The hermeneutic that seeks to find the coherence of the message, among all the believers of different ecclesiastical traditions, can only start with what has been given. Its goal is to allow the mutual recognition of the gifts of the Spirit present in each confessional expression, to exercise respect for the other, discovering that she or he can contribute to the improvement of our life. But it runs the risk of assuming that all that is received, whether from outside or from within our own tradition, is not only worthy in itself, but expresses faithfully the meaning of the gospels and the right understanding of them. However, we know that not all that our ecclesiastical traditions have bequeathed us is right and faithful to the scriptures. Neither should it be sustained if, after our reflections, we come to the conclusion that such a particular concept should be replaced, modernized or simply discarded.

But not everything *can* be disposed of. The church is a living body in which some cells are dying and others are born every day, with transformations that make it more mature, and expressions that ennoble it, and also expressions of which we have to feel ashamed. But we are not always so willing to admit our mistakes and our need to change. This is where the hermeneutic of suspicion comes in. It alerts us to the need to revise our understanding of the world and our reading of the gospel, our traditions and practices, those symbols that we want so much, although they can tie us up to inherited forms which need revision today. What place do the poor and the excluded have in our church? What use do we make of the scriptures when referring to minorities, women or rejected groups?

Going further

I want to conclude these brief remarks by suggesting three hermeneutical leaps towards further stones. They are linked with one another and in my view the Faith and Order text on hermeneutics calls us to face them.

1. The interpretations we have developed in the last two centuries give privilege to consideration of the history of the texts, their original context, and the author's intention. It is a kind of archeological work inside each text, looking for its past, its origin, and its previous traditions that led to the final version in our Bibles today. So the text is read from

behind the text. That task is unavoidable, for it prevents us from indulging in superficialities or mere literalism that deviate us from the meaning of the text. But we still face the challenge of reading the text from its front. That is to say, to locate the text in the enriching context of life, even overcoming the original intention and allowing the text to speak for itself starting from the concerns and questions that today's society is thinking about. The historical reading has shown us that the writing of the texts was a social process, with implications in the political and cultural realms. Our task is to return the scriptures to where they were created, where they have arisen and where they can show the maximum of their potential (cf. §23).

2. There exists neither a pure nor a completely objective reading. We always take sides when we face the interpretation of a text, or the evaluation of a practice. Whenever we read texts, symbols and practices we are called to do it from the perspective of the victims inside each society. They have different faces, different biographies and geographies, tears and acute pain which sometimes we do not understand; but they are those who suffer the consequences of other people's decisions, unjustifiable misery or discrimination. Jesus lived among them, and he was also a victim. To read the texts from and with the victims is to read them in their first and original social background. This reading should not simply be another perspective that we add to a colourful bunch of tools to use to understand the scriptures. It should be a privileged point from where other readings have to start, bearing in mind that the victims are always those who know (because they suffer the consequences) the true intention of any policy and the final effect of any economic decision. The victims have no influential friends, nor professional assistance, nor specialists in how to deal with the laws to explain why some are the winners and others are almost always the victims in an unbalanced world.

To read from the perspective of the victims is a challenge which should encourage us to go further in search of a more meaningful appreciation of the Bible and its message for today.

3. A *coherent* and *suspicious* reading of our time should look at two complementary aspects:

First, consider the future seen as a result of the decisions of the present. The biblical prophets, the gospel narratives, the apostle Paul: these reach their conclusions about the future by analyzing the present. It is biased to think that the biblical prophets foretold the future magically or through an internal and personal experience. All of them reached their conclusions after a careful analysis of the way in which the people of Israel and other societies acted. They understood the disasters as consequences of behavioural patterns. So they called the people to repent and to change even though history showed that people were more eager to kill prophets than to listen to them. This is an example of how God trusted in his people even when they did not deserve that confidence. Today – and this is our task – the same God still believes in the possibility of building a more humanitarian and less violent world.

Where is humanity going? What responsibility do we have today for the future of our increasingly threatened life?

Secondly, we need a hermeneutic where utopia is seen as possible. Many times in the gospel we find that the different and the distant are the vehicles that God provides to awaken new dreams of true freedom and justice among God's people. Today we realize that we are living in a society which is so bent on crystallizing a uniform way of life that it rejects fresh ideas and is far away from feeling itself enriched by what is different. What is more, it is promoting individualism and the suppression of other cultures. It is time to have a deeper insight of the texts, looking for a current of fresh air which can lead us to unpredictable places, to new skies, and to find the best words to announce that another reality is possible.

All this may sound strange. But the scriptures are full of such dreams. Ezekiel telling us of dry bones that are summoned to come to life again; ancient stories remind us of poor slaves that were miraculously freed from the hands of the most powerful king of that time; Luke tells us about jails that were opened to free the apostles in order to continue with their mission. These texts exultant with hope for the present and the future lead us in search of new horizons.

NOTE

[1] Geneva, WCC, 1999. Also reproduced here, pp.134-60.

A Treasure in Earthen Vessels:
An Instrument for an
Ecumenical Reflection on Hermeneutics

INTRODUCTION

1. The unsearchable mystery of God's love was made manifest, through the power of the Holy Spirit, in the covenant with Israel and fully revealed in the life, death and resurrection of Jesus Christ. This mystery has been proclaimed in the scriptures of the Old and New Testaments. Christian faith is the saving gift from God, which enables believers to receive the good news of God's love for all human beings and to become children of God and members of Christ's body the church. Faith in Christ gives life to the communion (koinonia) of the church. This faith has been handed on and received since apostolic times, from one generation to the next and from culture to culture.

2. This transmission takes place within the ambiguities of human history and the challenges of daily Christian life. So Paul can speak of us as having "this treasure in earthen vessels" (2 Cor. 4:7). Thus faith also relies upon human forms of expression and interpretation, dialogue and communication, all of which are fragile and all too often fragmented embodiments, none of which is completely adequate, of the mystery which has been revealed. These manifold human forms of expression include not only texts but also symbols and rites, stories and practices. Only at the end of time will the church's contemplation of God's revealed mystery go beyond a partial knowledge and arrive at that "knowing even as we are known" of which Paul writes in 1 Cor. 13:9-12.

3. Unity in confessing the faith is among the essential ways in which the koinonia of the church is made visible. The ecumenical movement has helped divided Christian communities to realize that even now they are united in a "growing, real though still imperfect koinonia" (Santiago de Compostela, 1993). This realization, however, cannot obscure the fact that significant differences in interpreting the faith still remain. In order to fulfil their vocation to grow in communion, the churches need to reflect together about the various ways in which the faith is expressed and interpreted.

4. The unprecedented changes occurring in our times because of the developments in mass media and in the means of communication make Christians more acutely aware of the religious, cultural, political and

economic diversities which characterize the human family. The community of believers must formulate its faith anew within such contexts. In this sense the mission to proclaim the gospel in terms meaningful to people of today is essentially an hermeneutical task. All churches share the challenge of proclaiming God's Word in credible ways within the diversity of contemporary cultures and by means of the oral and visual instruments of communication, be they traditional or those made available by contemporary technology.

1. The task of ecumenical hermeneutics

5. The particular purpose of this text is to explore the potential of *ecumenical* hermeneutics. Ecumenical hermeneutics shares with other forms of hermeneutics the goal of facilitating interpretation, communication and reception of texts, symbols and practices which give shape and meaning to particular communities. In recent years the definitions of hermeneutics have multiplied in philosophy and theology, and the scope of the term has been widened beyond giving principles for the interpretation of holy scripture. In this text we take the term hermeneutics to mean both *the art of interpretation and application of texts, symbols and practices in the present and from the past,* and *the theory about the methods of such interpretation and application.*[1]

More specifically, *theological* hermeneutics concerns itself with texts, symbols, and practices which have been inherited and shaped within a tradition of faith. For Christians this tradition of faith includes the scriptures of the Old and the New Testaments and the expressions of the Christian faith transmitted and re-expressed through the centuries. Within theological hermeneutics, *ecumenical* hermeneutics serves the specific task of focusing on how texts, symbols and practices in the various churches may be interpreted, communicated and mutually received as the churches engage in dialogue. In this sense it is a hermeneutics for the unity of the church.

6. The process of hermeneutical reflection impels and enables a living and faithful re-reading of any given text, symbol or practice. A hermeneutics for unity should:
- aim at greater coherence in the interpretation of the faith and in the community of all believers as their voices unite in common praise of God;
- make possible a mutually recognizable (re)appropriation of the sources of the Christian faith; and
- prepare ways of common confession and prayer in spirit and truth.

Such an interpretation, which seeks to manifest the integral unity of the Christian faith and community, has been called *"hermeneutics of coherence"*. At the same time the process of hermeneutical reflection reveals the time-bound character of the traditional forms and formulations as well as any ambiguous or vested interests on the part of the interpreters both past and present. This means that the interpreters should also be interpreted. This critical and testing aspect of the hermeneutical task is known as "hermeneutics of suspicion". In a constantly ongoing process, a responsible ecumenical hermeneutics will try to serve the truth, alerted by suspicion but always aiming at coherence.

7. The church is called to be an *hermeneutical community*, that is, a community within which there is a commitment to explore and interpret anew the given texts, symbols and practices. The tasks of an hermeneutical community also include overcoming misunderstandings, controversies and divisions; identifying dangers; resolving conflicts; and preventing schisms predicated on divisive interpretations of the Christian faith. The needs of the people of God in ever-new circumstances of faithful life and witness are also integral to this task. As an hermeneutical community, the church also submits itself to being interpreted by the ever-challenging Word of God.

8. This applies to each and every local church, and is a constant challenge within each confessional family of churches. As the churches engage in dialogue in the growing communion of churches in the ecumenical movement, a further and wider hermeneutical community is created. As it engages in ecumenical dialogue each church and tradition opens itself to being interpreted by other churches and traditions. To listen to the other does not necessarily mean to accept what other churches say, but to reckon with the possibility that the Spirit speaks within and through the others. This might be called *"hermeneutics of confidence"*. A hermeneutics for unity should entail an ecumenical method whereby Christians from various cultures and contexts, as well as different confessions, may encounter one another respectfully, always open to a *metanoia* which is a true "change of mind" and heart.

9. The ecumenical movement provides particular opportunities for the churches to reflect together on issues of interpretation and communication for the sake of ecclesial unity and the renewal of human community. But immediately it becomes clear that many Christian divisions are themselves based on conflicting interpretations of the texts, symbols and practices of the Christian faith. If we reflect together and agree on how traditions are to be interpreted, then the divisions of the churches – both those of longstanding character and new ones – might be better understood and even overcome. In this way, common reflection about our interpretations serves the "charism of truth" which has

been entrusted to the people of God and its apostolic ministry. As a common ecclesial exercise of the gift of discernment, this reflection reveals the salvific power of the Holy Spirit in making known the gospel and in uniting us with God. It brings into clearer focus the Spirit's own message, by resolving conflicts and preventing schisms, by sharing insights among churches, and by responding to the needs and questions of the people of God in our contemporary circumstances.

10. The need for hermeneutical reflection is not peculiar to our own age. Throughout the history of Christianity, diverse forms of interpretation have been used by different churches and denominations within various cultures and contexts. Given the wealth of cultural and linguistic differences, given the various structures of decision-making and the many ways of reading the scriptures which have appeared over time and, perhaps most importantly, given the unsearchable mystery of God which surpasses any human expression, one can only rejoice in much of the diversity in the interpretation and practice of the apostolic faith. We need to acknowledge that the hidden mystery of God is revealed to us in manifold ways and we need together to recognize the variety of ways in which that mystery has been and is understood, expressed and lived. At the same time, for the sake of coherence of the faith and the unity of the community, a common understanding of the interpretative process is crucial for enabling the churches to affirm together their common Christian identity and to be open to what the Spirit is saying through the faith, life and witness of one another.[2]

2. The origins of this study

11. Reflection about hermeneutics arises with fresh urgency at this moment in the history of the ecumenical movement. A new climate of trust and mutual accountability has been nurtured, but at the same time there are hesitations and even retreats because churches are not clear about the meaning of ongoing work towards visible unity. The past thirty years of Faith and Order dialogue, as well as the dialogues of other multi- and bi-lateral commissions, have produced numerous convergence texts and agreements directed towards a common understanding of the gospel and the church, including its creeds, sacraments and ministry. Yet many questions remain. In our present situation, the impossibility of eucharistic sharing is felt with pain by many Christians. In particular, the texts *Baptism, Eucharist and Ministry*; *Confessing the One Faith;* and *Church and World* have raised hermeneutical questions for the life of the churches. The process of officially responding to BEM has revealed many unexamined hermeneutical assumptions underlying not

only the churches' responses but also the very question concerning the extent to which they can recognize in the BEM text the faith of the church through the ages.[3] The fresh urgency to reflect together about hermeneutics is further heightened as new challenges of Christian living in today's world threaten to create new schisms within as well as among churches.

12. While describing the present situation among divided Christian communities as one of a "growing, real though still imperfect koinonia", the fifth world conference of Faith and Order in Santiago de Compostela (1993) pointed to three different, yet related tasks which are vital to furthering such growth:

- to overcome and to reconcile the criteriological differences with regard to a faithful interpretation of the one gospel, recognizing the multiform richness and diversity of the canon of the scriptures, as it is read, explicated and applied in the life of the churches, but at the same time strengthening the awareness of the one Tradition within the many traditions;[4]
- to express and communicate the one gospel in and across various, sometimes even conflicting contexts, cultures and locations;[5]
- to work towards mutual accountability, discernment and authoritative teaching and towards credibility in common witness before the world, and finally towards the eschatological fullness of the truth in the power of the Holy Spirit.[6]

13. The present text will address these three tasks in the following way:

- In the first section (A. Common Understanding of the One Tradition) an explicitly hermeneutical framework will be applied to the important themes raised by the Montreal study "Scripture, Tradition and traditions".[7] This reflection may take us beyond Montreal, as it considers the interpretation of scripture and Tradition in a more hermeneutically conscious way, especially with greater sensitivity to the conditions involved in interpretation.
- In the second section (B. One Gospel in Many Contexts) the text explores the hermeneutical and theological significance of the fact that the ecumenical movement includes the participation of communities from many differing cultures and contexts, and offers reflections which can lead to a more successful intercontextual dialogue.
- The third section (C. The Church as an Hermeneutical Community) explores three dimensions of the process of interpretation: the activity of discernment, the exercise of authority and the task of reception.

A. COMMON UNDERSTANDING OF THE ONE TRADITION

1. Past exploration of the theme
14. From the World Council of Churches, from the Christian World
Communions and from bilateral dialogues, as well as from the councils
of each church, a great deal of agreed theological reflection has been
produced in the past century. There is always a danger of ecumenical
"loss of memory". Those engaged in the interpreting process need to use
the original documents as well as the many explanatory books and pam-
phlets that make available ecumenical agreements. Particularly relevant
from past exploration for the present task is the fourth world conference
on Faith and Order.
15. The fourth world conference on Faith and Order at Montreal
(1963), was able to say:

> By *the Tradition* is meant the gospel itself, transmitted from generation to gen-
> eration in and by the church, Christ himself present in the life of the church.
> By *tradition* is meant the traditionary process. The term *traditions* is used... to
> indicate both the diversity of forms of expression and also what we call con-
> fessional traditions, for instance the Lutheran tradition or the Reformed tradi-
> tion... the word appears in a further sense, when we speak of cultural tradi-
> tions. (Section II, §39)
> Our starting point is that we as Christians are all living in a tradition which
> goes back to our Lord and has its roots in the Old Testament and are all
> indebted to that tradition inasmuch as we have received the revealed truth, the
> gospel, through its being transmitted from one generation to another. Thus we
> can say that we exist as Christians by the Tradition of the gospel (the *parado-
> sis* of the kerygma) testified in scripture, transmitted in and by the church,
> through the power of the Holy Spirit. (Section II, §45)
> The traditions in Christian history are distinct from, and yet connected
> with, the Tradition. They are the expressions and manifestations in diverse his-
> torical terms of the one truth and reality which is Christ. This evaluation of the
> traditions poses serious problems... How can we distinguish between tradi-
> tions embodying the true Tradition and merely human traditions? (Section II,
> §§47 and 48)

16. Montreal thereby helped the churches to begin to realize that the
one Tradition is witnessed to in scripture and transmitted by the Holy
Spirit through the church. This means the canon of scripture came into
being within the Tradition, which finds expression within the various traditions of the church. In this way Montreal helped to overcome the old
contrast between "sola scriptura" and "scripture and Tradition" and to
show that the different hermeneutical criteria in the different traditions
belong together. The ongoing interaction between Tradition and tradi-

tions enables faithful transmission, even though from time to time there have been distortions of the apostolic faith.

17. But Montreal did not fully explain what it means that the one Tradition is embodied in concrete traditions and cultures. Concerning the quest for an hermeneutical principle the conference listed the different ways in which the various churches deal with this problem but did not itself deal with criteriological questions, such as how to discern the authenticity of faith in a situation of conflicting cultural perspectives, frameworks or hermeneutical principles.[8] Finally, Montreal could go no further than the WCC's Toronto statement (1950), which deliberately provided no criteria beyond the Basis of the WCC[9] to assess the authenticity or fidelity of the traditions of its member churches, to say nothing of other human traditions. It could only point to the three main factors in the transmission process: the events and testimonies preceding and leading to scripture, scripture itself, and subsequent ecclesial preaching and teaching.

18. It must be recognized that Montreal left open the vital question of how churches can discern the one Tradition. Therefore there is a danger that churches identify the one Tradition exclusively with their own tradition. Even the discussion of this question in languages other than English is difficult, because the Montreal "solution" relied on English language conventions about the use of capital letters and these conventions can produce ambiguity, e.g. at the beginning of a sentence where it is not clear whether the capital letter distinguishes the one Tradition or simply marks the start of the sentence. These acknowledged limitations do not alter the fact that Montreal provided a valid set of distinctions, between Tradition as that which God intends to have handed on in the life of the church, tradition as the process by which this handing on takes place and traditions as particular expressions of Christian life and thought. These exist in some tension with one another but can also be the vehicles for developing a deeper grasp of the one Tradition, by which is meant the one gospel, the living Word of God.

19. After Montreal, Faith and Order undertook important studies on the hermeneutical significance of the councils of the early church.[10] Several reports on the authority of the Bible were assembled as a contribution to the hermeneutical discussions of that period.[11] The Odessa consultation (1977) on "How does the church teach authoritatively today?" addressed aspects of the hermeneutical problem, especially the question of continuity and change in the doctrinal tradition of the church. Also, after Accra (1974), Faith and Order began to collect newer expressions of faith and hope from around the world. These were published in a series, and also summarized at Bangalore (1978) in "A Common

Account of Hope". This work, which found continuation in the Faith and Order study on the apostolic faith, produced an awareness of the contextual aspects of confessions of faith, both in the sense of the original contexts in which they were made and of the effect on their use produced by the changing contexts of Christian discipleship.

20. The helpful results of these study processes did not prevent continuing conflicts, whether these were between traditions themselves, between the inherited traditions and newer contexts, or between various contextual approaches within each church or within the relationships of churches to one another. This was why Santiago felt the need to return once again to hermeneutical issues (cf. §11 above).

2. "According to the scriptures"

21. The primary authority of scripture within hermeneutical work is not weakened by our understanding of the way in which the text has been handed down within the church through the process of transmission. The texts of scripture thus received offer their revelatory character after a handing on through oral transmission. The written texts subsequently have been interpreted by means of diverse exegetical and scholarly methods. Wrestling with the principles and practice of interpretation, Faith and Order affirmed (Bristol, 1967-68) that the tools of modern exegetical scholarship are important if the biblical message is to speak with power and meaning today. These tools have contributed in vital ways to the present ecumenical convergence and growth in koinonia. The exegetical exploration of the process of tradition within the Bible itself, together with the recognition of multiple interpretations of God's saving actions in history within the unity of the early apostolic church, points to ways the Word of God is expressed in human language and by human witness. This is to say, the Word of God is expressed in language and by witnesses shaped amid diverse situations of human life, which are historically, culturally and socially conceived. This is also to say: "The very nature of biblical texts means that interpreting them will require continued use of the historical-critical method,... [since] the Bible does not present itself as a direct revelation of timeless truths, but as the written testimony to a series of interventions in which God reveals himself in human history."[12] Though some churches and individual Christians reject historical-critical interpretation, common study of the scriptures of the Old and New Testaments now has a long history of achieved agreement. Ecumenical hermeneutics can use the historical-critical method to establish, e.g., the background of the texts, the intentions of the authors, the inter-relationship of the different books.

22. Interpretation should not, however, depend only on this method, now shared by those of different traditions and theologies. Many other approaches to the text, both of long standing and of modern development, help in the recognition of the meaning of scripture for the churches today and for the many different situations of the world church. In particular the historical-critical method needs to be combined with a reading in critical interaction with experience, the experience both of individuals and of communities. Other methods are those inherent in traditional biblical interpretation including patristic, liturgical, homiletic, dogmatic and allegorical approaches to the text. Contemporary methods include those that focus on the original social setting of the texts (e.g. sociological methods); those that focus on the literary form of texts and the internal relationships within a text and between texts (e.g. semiotic and canonical methods); and those that focus on the potential of the text for readings generated by the encounter of the text with human reality (e.g. reader-response method). All these methods can also be used to deal with extra-biblical sources. Some methods help to open up neglected dimensions of the past from the perspective of marginalized groups. Examples of the latter are feminist or liberationist analyses of systems of power and patronage.

23. Nevertheless ecumenical hermeneutics cannot be reduced to the use of exegetical tools and methods isolated from the fullness of the experience of the interpreting community. A variety of factors are woven into that fullness, and these compose the hermeneutical locus within which scripture is interpreted. These factors include oral tradition, narratives, memories and liturgies, as well as the life, teachings and ethical decisions of the believing community. Thus, many dimensions of the life of the community are part of the context for interpreting the scriptural texts. Scripture emerges from episodes of life, a calendar of feasts, a scheme of history, and the witnessing account of the living people of God. In addition, scripture becomes alive once again as it engages the life, feasts, history and witness of faith communities today. From this perspective, the praxis of the Christian communities and people in different particular cultural and social contexts is itself a reading and an interpretation of the scriptural texts and not simply a position from which to approach the texts.

24. Because the biblical texts originated in concrete historical situations, they witness to the salvific presence of the triune God in those particular circumstances. However, the texts also transcend this particularity and become part of the world of the readers in each generation, of the witnessing community through the ages into the present. Although embedded in the life and times in which it was given written form, scrip-

ture, as inspired testimony, provides a measure for the truth and meaning of human stories today. In this sense, hermeneutical priority belongs to the Word of God, which has critical authority over all traditions.

25. The relation and sometimes also tension between past and present which exists when biblical texts are applied to our stories today reflects the eschatological dimension of scripture itself. Just as scripture constantly looks forward in hope to God's future, the interpreting activity of the church is also an anticipatory projection of the reality of the reign of God, which is both already present and yet to come. Reading "the signs of the times", both in the history of the past and in the events of the present, is to be done in the context of the announcement of "the new things to come"; this orientation to the future is part of the reality of the church as an hermeneutical community.[13] Therefore the struggle for peace, justice and the integrity of creation, the renewed sense of mission in witness and service, the liturgy in which the church proclaims and celebrates the promise of God's reign and its coming in the praxis of the faith, are all integral parts of the constant interpretative task of the church.

26. Ecumenical hermeneutics welcomes the diversity of insights that arise from biblical reflection of this broadly based kind. A scriptural text may be considered as authoritative for a particular matter of faith or practice, even if this text is interpreted differently by the dialogue partners. Thus agreement may be reached concerning a responsibility laid upon the church even though different hermeneutical methods were employed in deriving this sense of responsibility from scripture. On the other hand, the applicability of a text is not to be ruled out even if a specific interpretation is deemed by one of the dialogue partners to be irrelevant to a particular matter of faith or practice.

27. Common study of scripture has achieved ecumenical advance. However, it has not by itself led to the visible unity of the church. Interpreters from different churches and traditions have not been able to reach sufficient agreement for that. All Christians agree that scripture holds a unique place in the shaping of Christian faith and practice. Most agree that the expression of apostolic faith is not confined to the formulation of that faith expressed in scripture but that norms of faith have also been expressed in the life of the churches throughout the ages. The church receives the texts of scripture as part of the *paradosis* of the gospel. The texts are to be respected as coming from outside to the interpreter to be engaged dialogically. In the process of interpretation, which involves the particular experiences of the reader, scripture is the primary norm and criterion. Particular traditions need to be referred continuously to this norm by which they find their authenticity and validity. This response to scripture takes shape communally and ecclesially in worship, in the

sacramental life where hearing, touch and sight come together, in the *anamnesis* of the lives of biblical witnesses and in the lives of those who live the biblical message, inspired by the Holy Spirit. Scripture itself refers to the one Tradition, lived under the guidance of the Holy Spirit. The one Tradition, therefore, is the setting for the interpretation of scripture.

3. Interpreting the interpreters

28. Within the one Tradition, as Christians engage with scripture and their own traditions to understand God's will for the world and for the people called to be witnesses of God's love, they always need to interpret text and traditions anew. Amid this hermeneutical task, Christians are to be conscious that interpretations come out of special historical circumstances and that new issues may come out of various contexts. In considering these circumstances and issues, Christians involved in the hermeneutical task do well to investigate:
- the location from which the text is being interpreted;
- the choice of a specific text for interpretation;
- the involvement of power structures in the interpretation process;
- prejudices and presuppositions brought to bear on the interpretation process.

It is in the light of this understanding[14] that ecumenical hermeneutics needs to operate as a hermeneutics of coherence, showing the positive complementarity of traditions. It needs also to include a hermeneutics of suspicion. This does not mean the adoption of an attitude of mistrust but the application to oneself and one's dialogue partners of an approach which perceives how self-interest, power, national or ethnic or class or gender perspectives can affect the reading of texts and the understanding of symbols and practices. Positively, the recent work done by Protestants and Roman Catholics together on the Reformation debates about justification and sanctification has enabled fuller mutual understanding. Negatively, the way in which the Bible was used to justify apartheid is an example of a selective reading which was challenged by being confronted by these and other hermeneutical challenges. Safeguards against selective and prejudicial readings are also imperative in the realm of academic and scholarly interpretation, with particular attention to the wider testimony of scripture and the experience of the many oppressed.

29. Within the struggle for peace, justice and the integrity of creation the hermeneutical dimension of the quest for reconciliation and unity can be painful, especially when reconciliation involves those whose common past has been marked by injustice or violence. Interpreting a history

of this kind requires an hermeneutical awareness which enables one to renounce the stereotypes such histories can generate on both sides of a dispute. This hermeneutical process may call for repentance and forgiveness, since the reconciliation of injustice and violence requires a healing of memories, which is not the same as forgetfulness of the past. Much further work is clearly needed in this area of assessing the past. One must pray for the miracle of resurrection to new life, even if the marks of the crucifixion remain.

30. Hermeneutics in the service of unity must also proceed on the presumption that those who interpret the Christian tradition differently each have "right intention of faith".[15] It is not only a condition of dialogue, but a fruitful product of dialogue, that the partners come to appreciate and trust one another's sincerity and good intention. This means each is sincerely seeking to transmit that which God wishes to pass on through the church. It is important in conveying results of dialogue to the churches to transmit also the sense of mutual confidence. This is especially so where a painful shared history of conflict calls for the healing of memories. Since diversity can be an expression of the rich gifts of the Holy Spirit, the churches are called to become aware of the possibility of an abiding complementarity, i.e., of the values inherent in the "otherness" of one another and even of the right to be different from each other, when such differences are part of the exploration of the divine mystery and the divinely willed unity. Viewed in this way, differences can be an invitation and a starting point for the common search for the truth, in a spirit of koinonia that entails a disposition to *metanoia*, under the guidance of the Spirit of God.

31. When differences of interpretation and possible complementarity are being assessed, the question of authoritative interpretation arises. Part of the ecumenical method is to ensure that the partners in dialogue are made aware where authority resides in each church and how it is being understood and received by each participant. The process of ecumenical hermeneutics involves not only faithful understanding and interpretation of texts, symbols and practices but also analysis of the relative weight given to those texts, symbols and practices by the various churches in respect of the authoritative nature of sources themselves and the interpretations derived from them. Clarity about authority is a crucial element in that dimension of hermeneutics which concentrates on the faithful communication and reception of the meaning of texts, symbols and practices. Consequently, the relationship between scripture, Tradition and traditions and Christian experience arising from liturgical and other practices needs to be dealt with again and again within the hermeneutical process.

4. One Tradition and many traditions

32. The "one Tradition" signifies the redeeming presence of the resurrected Christ from generation to generation abiding in the community of faith, while the "many traditions" are particular modes and manifestations of that presence. God's self-disclosure transcends all expressions of it. How can Christians and churches share in the gift of the one Tradition as they confess and live according to scripture? How are they to read their own traditions in the light of the one Tradition? As has been noted above, the fourth world conference addressed the issue of hermeneutics in an ecumenical perspective, opening up the many traditions to the recognition of the one Tradition as a gift from God. Recognition of and continuity with the one Tradition, however, should not be confused with a mere repetition of the past without any recognition of the present. The Holy Spirit inspires and leads the churches each to rethink and reinterpret their tradition in conversation with each other, always aiming to embody the one Tradition in the unity of God's church. The churches of God as living communities, constituted by faith in Jesus Christ and empowered by the Holy Spirit, must always re-receive the gospel in ways that relate to their present experience of life. It is in this process of re-reception that the minds of Christian communities are enlightened by the Holy Spirit to discern truth from falsehood and to acknowledge both the richness and the limitedness of the diverse geographical, historical, religious and social circumstances in which the gospel is made manifest. Ecumenical hermeneutics is not an unaided human enterprise. It is an ecclesial act led by the Spirit and therefore it should be carried out in a setting of prayer.

33. The churches involved in the ecumenical movement recognize that by being in conversation with each other they learn to appreciate mutually each other's gifts, as well as to challenge limited or false understandings of what God expects churches to be and to do in the world. Thus they begin to move from identifying themselves in opposition to one another to identifying themselves in relation to one another. This opening to new understandings of the traditions of other churches – their history, their liturgies, their martyrs and saints, their sacraments and ministries – has changed the ecumenical climate since Montreal. The exchange of biblical exegesis, of systematic theological approaches, of historiographical studies, and practical-theological projects, has been a very enriching development. Exegetical research is undertaken on the basis of receptive as well as critical interconfessional discussion, fostered by ecumenical dialogue. Bible translations and commentaries have been published ecumenically, common liturgical calendars, lectionaries, hymn- and prayer-books have become the means of sharing spiritual resources with one another.

34. This ecumenical sharing has indeed created a new ecumenical situation, characterized by growth in mutual understanding across confessional boundaries predicated on a new appreciation of particular confessional traditions and witness. The challenge to move on from mutual understanding to mutual recognition is now before the churches in the search for visible unity. For example, ecumenical hermeneutics must also enable dialogue partners to declare their particular understanding of the relationship between "continuity" and "discontinuity" in the historic expression of the faith of the people of God. As one instance, the Reformation introduced changes in ministerial order which the Reformers perceived as a return to continuity with the early church whereas others felt the changes were an example of discontinuity.

35. Traditions are transmitted orally as well as through written texts. Ecumenical hermeneutics – as every hermeneutical task – is therefore a dynamic process concerned not only with written sources but also with oral tradition. In addition to textual and oral tradition, meaning is conveyed through non-verbal symbols: Christian art and music, liturgical gestures or colours, icons, the creation and use of sacred space and time, Christian symbols or signs are important aspects of the way in which the various dialogue partners understand and communicate their faith. Ecumenical hermeneutics needs to be intentional about incorporating this rich, but also neglected, source material for interpretation, communication and reception. As with symbols, Christian practices need to be taken into consideration by those engaged in ecumenical hermeneutics. Even when there is a basis for theological convergence on the meaning of, e.g. baptism or eucharist, attention needs to be given to the practices surrounding these rites in particular ecclesial communities. Here as elsewhere, hermeneutical reflection can serve as an aid in the process of recognizing the same faith underlying different practices.

36. As well as recognizing the new ecumenical situation, churches are also becoming more and more aware of shifts in perception and reception among their members which arise from changes in the media of communication. Spoken words and visual images are especially significant in the increasingly powerful multimedia culture of today's world. A renewed appreciation of narrative forms of transmission sheds new light on processes of interpretation and communication. It is also important to draw critically upon the perceptions of secular artists and film producers as they take up themes and symbols from Christian history.

37. Yet ultimately, amid the many ecclesial traditions, the one Tradition is revealed in the living presence of Christ in the world, but is not something to be captured and controlled by human discourse. It is a liv-

ing, eschatological reality, eluding all attempts at a final linguistic definition and conceptual disclosure. One way of describing the one Tradition is by speaking about the ecclesial capacity of *receiving* revelation. This capacity is nothing less than the gift of the Holy Spirit, received by the apostles at Pentecost and given to every Christian community and to every member of the community in the process of Christian initiation. This capacity is the gift of the Holy Spirit who "will guide you into all the truth" (John 16:13), who is the Spirit of truth; that truth is Jesus Christ himself (John 14:6), the perfect image of the Father from whom the Spirit proceeds. The capacity to receive the fullness of revelation is actualized in the church's celebration of the eucharist, which involves both a hearing and an embodying of the Word of God, a participation in the eschaton, the feast of the kingdom.

B. One gospel in many contexts

1. Living in diverse contexts

38. Christian communities live in particular places and times, defined culturally, economically, politically and religiously. These are the contexts in which their faith is lived and the gospel is interpreted and proclaimed. The diversity of contexts in which the churches live calls for engagement with the diverse riches of scripture. In other words, diverse contexts inform the selection, as well as the specific interpretation, of scripture. Selected passages of scripture, in turn, may challenge as well as affirm diverse contexts:

- In a context of social injustice, Mary's Magnificat (Luke 1:46-55; cf. 1 Sam. 2:1-10) and Jesus' inaugural sermon (Luke 4:18, quoting Isa. 42:7) may become a word of hope for the poor and the oppressed. And, at the same time, these may be a word of judgment to oppressors.
- In a context where Christians are a tiny minority among people of other faiths, the affirmation of the common humanity of all women and men as created in God's image may turn attention to the presence of the Spirit outside the Christian churches. As reflected in the story of Paul's sermon in Athens (Acts 17:16ff.), this awareness of common humanity and of the Spirit's presence may be both affirming and challenging in relation to peoples of other living faith traditions.
- In a context of resurgent nationalism, Jesus' commandment to love even our enemies (Matt. 5:44; cf. Lev. 19:34) and to distinguish between loyalty to God and the emperor (Mark 12:17) may at once challenge the inherent danger of nations becoming exclusive and

totalitarian, and affirm the Christian responsibility to upbuild or rebuild the nations by and for the sake of the participation and reconciliation of all people (Rom. 13:5-10).

– In a context of what some call post-modern pluralism, where individual choice is so emphasized that common points of reference are obscured, an affirmation of commitment and of communion may become life-giving. This affirmation need not deny the value of personal freedom but rather recognizes the tension Paul addresses when he wrote to the Corinthians: "'All things are lawful', but not all things build up. Do not seek your own advantage, but that of the other" (1 Cor. 10:23f.).

39. Dialogue among Christian communities of different confessions as well as contexts calls for respect and openness. Partners are, first of all, called to respect one another, recognizing the temptation to reduce one another to one's own confessional categories or to the cultural, economic, political and religious categories that interweave to define one's own context. This call entails an openness to *metanoia*. Such openness includes a willingness to see the limitations of one's own perspective as well as to listen actively to and communicate with one's own dialogue partners. Encounters characterized by respect and openness are often enriching. These encounters may also give rise to disagreements that become conflictual.

40. Amid these complex interactions, Christian churches should welcome faithful and fruitful encounters of the gospel and contexts. Churches should also recognize and repent of false interpretations of the gospel that may be occasioned by contextual influences. This is to say that while the gospel proclaimed in local languages and music and customs may enliven people's faith, there are also contexts in which racist ideologies and their attendant political institutions have been justified by churches and said to be compatible with the gospel. Likewise, churches and societies have both, consciously and unconsciously, discriminated against or oppressed women in contradiction to the gospel's message of liberation for all people. Wherever the gospel is authentically engaged by diverse cultures, its interpretation and proclamation will be life-giving for men and women, young and old, sick and healthy, rich and poor, uneducated and educated.

41. Missionary activity especially exemplifies the complex interactions of churches and contexts. Some Christian missionaries have greatly helped local peoples and societies to affirm and express themselves in their own cultural media. Others have been reluctant or unable to engage local contexts and peoples respectfully and openly. Historically, many missionaries were bound up with imperialist impulses and consequently

became colonialist. Christianity has continued to be alien and alienating in many places, even as it has initiated life-giving change in many other places. In every context there is a potential ambiguity about the way in which the gospel is proclaimed. Every Christian community needs to repent of what is alienating in the way in which the gospel continues to be proclaimed, and to recommit themselves to ensuring that the gospel that is proclaimed is life-giving.

42. All these encounters make it clear just how complex are the inter-actions within and among diverse confessions and contexts. Contextual differences have helped shape confessional divisions. Correlatively, communities of the same confessional family have taken on different faces in different contexts. For example, it makes a great difference whether a church has long been present in a country where it is a major-ity or whether it is made up of migrants living in another country. More-over, confessionally different communities have reacted differently to the same context in which they are living together. Some have opposed particular forms of nationalism; others have legitimized and supported them. Although these examples turn attention to contextual challenges, confessional challenges do not disappear. Indeed, it is important to rec-ognize the ways in which new churches have arisen precisely because of different responses to particular contextual challenges.

2. Contextuality and catholicity

43. The many local communities of Christians throughout the world, each within their own context, perceive themselves as embodiments of the one catholic church. They belong to one another in a profound way because of their relationship to God through Jesus Christ. They make up one family, having been "born of water and the Spirit" (John 3:5). For the apostle Paul, this unity is rooted in Jesus himself. He therefore chal-lenges the Corinthians to avoid factions by asking them: "Is Christ divided?" (1 Cor. 1:13). Later, in the same letter, Paul compares the Christian communities to the members of a body, each one needing the others, none enjoying special status above the rest (cf. 1 Cor. 12:12-26). This unity and diversity of Christian communities flows together from the Holy Spirit. It is one and the same Spirit who bestows the marvellous variety of gifts and ministries (cf. 1 Cor. 12:1-11). These gifts and min-istries work together to build up the bonds of faith and love which allow the church to grow in communion day by day, until the full realization of communion in the kingdom of God.

44. In order to reflect theologically upon both the diversity of and the relationships among local Christian communities, the terms "contextual-ity" and "catholicity" are especially helpful. The dimension of *contextu-*

ality refers to the interpretation and the proclamation of the gospel within the life and culture of a specific people and community. Such a proclamation of the gospel can seek to judge the cultural context, it can seek to separate itself from the culture in which the church is set and it can seek to transform culture. As the WCC Jerusalem consultation "On Intercultural Hermeneutics" stated, contextuality "appears whenever the gospel works like salt and leaven, not overwhelming a context, but permeating and enlivening it in distinctive ways. When the church's faith is genuinely contextual, the shame and stigma imposed on oppressed people begins to be lifted. They find a new dignity as they see not only their own lives but also their culture in God's redeeming light. When faith is contextual, there is a recognition that the gospel speaks to Christians in their language, connects with their symbols, addresses their needs and awakens their creative energies."[16]

45. The term "catholicity" derives from the Greek words *kath' holon*, which mean "according to the whole". This word refers to the fullness, integrity and totality of life in Christ and the inclusiveness and wholeness of the Christian community.[17] Catholicity, according to the ancient creeds, is one of the primary qualities of the church. It is ascribed, first of all, to each local community, inasmuch as each community expresses in its faith, life and witness this fullness that is not yet fully realized. Churches are called to grow in God's gift of catholicity by engaging one another in collegial and conciliar structures, by mutual accountability to the gospel, and by prayer for the eschatological work of the Holy Spirit. As churches look forward to the future of eschatological promise, they also look back to the apostolic community assembled on the morning of Pentecost. This sense of catholicity across the ages, as well as among local Christian communities of diverse contexts in any given age, sustains hope for the full realization of common life in Christ.

46. By its very nature, the eucharist is to be the celebration of a local community and the manifestation of its unity; at the same time it expresses the communion of the local church with other churches that celebrate the same eucharist and with all those who have celebrated it throughout the ages. Thus the local church experiences the fullness of the church, the catholicity of the church. Therefore, the eucharistic celebration itself urges every church, on the one hand, to share the needs and hopes of the people in the place where it lives and to speak their language, and, on the other hand, to overcome the divisions that prevent the common celebration of the Lord's supper, in order to enjoy the unity for which Jesus prayed (John 17:21).

47. To speak of contextuality and catholicity together clarifies the relationship between the local community and the wider communion of

all local communities. Contextual interpretations can contribute to a fuller interpretation of the gospel and can thereby speak to the Christian community as a whole. When an interpretation of the gospel in a particular context points to injustice or to liberation, this interpretation is not simply a contextual claim. It may provide an insight to be tested and amended or applied in other contexts. Accordingly, catholicity binds all local communities together, thereby allowing them to contribute to one another's understandings and to broaden their horizons.

48. Interpretation of the gospel has to be relevant to particular believing communities in particular contexts in order to be both pastoral and prophetic. But no interpretation can claim to be absolute. All must be aware of the limitations of any perspective or position. The catholicity that binds communities together makes possible this awareness of limitation as well as a mutual acknowledgment of contribution to one another's interpretation. In this way, catholicity enables communities to free one another from one-sidedness or from over-emphasis on only one aspect of the gospel. Catholicity enables communities to liberate one another from being blinded or bound by any one context and so to embody across and among diverse contexts the solidarity that is a special mark of Christian koinonia.

C. THE CHURCH AS AN HERMENEUTICAL COMMUNITY

1. Ecclesial discernment and the truth of the gospel

49. This ongoing dialogue involving both catholicity and contextuality characterizes the church as a "hermeneutical community". The church, whether embodied in a local congregation, episcopal diocese, or a Christian World Communion, is called to interpret texts, symbols and practices so as to discern the Word of God as a word of life amid ever-changing times and places. This hermeneutical task undertaken by the church, with the guidance of the Holy Spirit, is a condition for apostolic mission in and for the world. To speak of the church as an hermeneutical community is also to say that this community is a proper locus for the interpretation and the proclamation of the gospel.

50. Hermeneutics, perhaps especially ecumenical hermeneutics, is not the work of specialists. Ecumenical hermeneutics, in the pursuit of visible church unity, is first and foremost the work of the whole people gathered in believing communities in diverse contexts. Believers, pastors, theologians and biblical exegetes each have distinctive gifts to bring to the hermeneutical task. These gifts are most appropriately brought together and exercised within the various settings in which the church carries out its work as an hermeneutical community.

51. For the sake of this work, churches need to renew their responsibility for the formation of their members as faithful hearers and interpreters. This formation is embedded in the life of worship[18] and is nurtured by conciliar teaching, the writings of the early church, and the witness of saints and martyrs. All these testimonies to the apostolic faith disclose the faithful and fruitful interpretation of God's Word through Christian history. They also testify to the ways in which non-theological issues, e.g., the struggle to attain or maintain ecclesiastical or political power, may influence or distort interpretation. Finally, these witnesses teach that temporary divisions may in the end, in God's time, be more fruitful for mutual and respectful understanding than an enforcement of unity when and where there is no unity. Such a formation will enable believers of diverse confessions and contexts to enter into respectful and open relationships. With the Spirit's guidance, these relationships may lead to fruitful dialogue concerning the interpretation of the gospel, as well as concerning the interpretation of ecumenical documents dedicated to the search for visible church unity.

52. The church as hermeneutical community must beware of false interpretations of the gospel that may have life-denying contextual consequences, for example, interpretations legitimizing racism or economic exploitation as noted above. The church as hermeneutical community must also beware of false interpretations of the gospel that threaten or destroy the fullness of life together in Christ. At the same time, faithful interpretation of the gospel also may give rise to conflict and critical tension, both within believing communities and between the church and the world. The church is called to offer a pastoral response to those who doubt or who raise disturbing questions and to those who suffer amid deep disagreements. The church thereby carries out the ministry of reconciliation to which it is called.

53. Ecumenical hermeneutics takes as its starting point the reality that conversations aiming at greater unity are carried out by representatives of the various churches and that their contributions are mediated through particular ecclesial, cultural, social, economic, geographical and historical backgrounds.

– For dialogue to be genuine, these representatives need to see each other as equal partners.
– They must, on the one hand, speak to each other from the perspective of their traditional interpretations of the apostolic faith as articulated in their confessional documents, their liturgies and their experience.
– But they must do so with a willingness to view their own interpretations from the vantage point of those with whom they are in dialogue. This involves being attentive to the insights provided by the dialogue

partner, taking care to take into account one's own unwitting prejudices and limited perspectives.

2. Authority, apostolicity and mutual accountability

54. The church as an hermeneutical community is responsible for the
faithful transmission of the inherited gospel in different times and places.
In that process the Holy Spirit guides the churches in discerning, receiving and communicating the will of God in the ever-changing circumstances of life. The churches have developed in their histories specific
and differentiated ministerial structures by which they preserve their
apostolicity, unity and mission. Despite the different configurations of
these ministerial structures that the churches have developed in their separation from each other, it is widely recognized that ministerial structures must serve the purpose of the church, to lead all into unity with
God by the power of the Holy Spirit.

55. The Holy Spirit maintains the churches of God in truth and guides
all the faithful into unity with Jesus Christ (John 16:13), distributes the
ministry of Christ to all believers and empowers them to participate in
God's mission for the salvation of the world. All ministries in the church
are related to each other and their authority is derived from their identification with Christ's ministry. In the ongoing ecclesiology discussion of
Faith and Order it has been affirmed that the church is a communion of
co-responsible persons. No function, no gift, no charisma is exercised
outside or above this communion. All are related through the one Spirit
in the one body. All believers, because of their unity with Jesus Christ
and the indwelling of the Holy Spirit, have the potential to receive God's
word, to discern God's will, and to proclaim the gospel. Those whose
call by God to exercise the ministry of oversight *(episkope)* is recognized
by the church must enable the people of God to recognize and actualize
the gifts that the Holy Spirit has bestowed upon them for the fulfilment
of the church's life and mission. This means that the ministry of oversight must include an hermeneutical function. The vitality of the
church's life and mission depends upon the actualization of these gifts.

56. While the Holy Spirit distributes the ministry of Christ to all
believers, the same Spirit unites all ministries by means of the ministry
of *episkope*. The function of *episkope* is to sustain and nourish the unity
of the local church, to maintain its communion in faith, life and witness
with all other local churches; to safeguard the apostolicity and catholicity of the local church; and to empower the local church to discern God's
will, to proclaim the gospel and to be a credible witness of God's presence in the world. Although the forms of *episkope* have developed differently within various ecclesial traditions, the functions of such a min-

istry have been widely recognized to be of fundamental importance for ecclesial unity. Christian churches continue to explore the appropriate forms of *episkope* for this unity. As is the case with all ministries, *episkope* can only be exercised within and in relation to the whole church. It needs, as all other ministries, the recognition, collaboration, support and assent of the whole community. The authority of *episkope* is grounded upon the authority of Christ's sacrificial love and humility (Luke 22:25-27). If *episkope* becomes oppressive, overlooks the charisms or hinders rightful communication among the ministries, it becomes an exercise of power alien to the authority of Christ.

57. An important visible expression of the unity of God's church occurs whenever those who have been entrusted with the oversight of the churches are gathered to support one another, to strengthen and give account of the faith, life and witness that unites them in Christ. Collegiality is at work wherever those entrusted with oversight gather, discern, speak and act as one on behalf of the whole church. This entails leading the church by means of the wisdom gained by corporate prayer, study and reflection, drawing on scripture, Tradition and reason with attention to the wisdom and experience of all church communities and of the contemporary world. Such collegial exercise of oversight is exercised at the present time by those churches who are united in faith, life and service to the world. In some parts of the world, the ecumenical movement has encouraged and brought into existence shared oversight on matters of Christian faith and witness by churches who are not yet visibly united.[19]

58. The ecumenical recognition that those who have been baptized in the name of the triune God are brought into unity with Christ, with each other and with the church of every time and place challenges the churches to overcome their divisions and visibly manifest their communion in faith and in all aspects of Christian life and witness. Towards the realization of this goal, churches are encouraged to increase their consultation with other churches, at all levels, regarding important questions of faith and discipline. Any church which is not prepared to listen to the voices of other churches runs the danger of missing the truth of the Spirit as it operates in the other churches.

59. Within the ecumenical movement, a number of structures which foster encounters between divided churches help them work together as a common hermeneutical community characterized by mutual accountability. For example, the various areas of activity within the World Council of Churches provide a wide range of opportunities for common interpretation and praxis of the gospel message. Bilateral relationships concerned with theological dialogue, work for justice, peace and the

integrity of creation and collaboration in mission, education and charitable works, offer similar opportunities. As churches find these and other means of communion across confessional and cultural lines fruitful, they may also benefit by improving communication with their own community.

60. An ecumenical exercise of teaching authority is already beginning to develop in some respects. It is hoped that ways of common decision-making can be developed, even as there is allowance for certain decisions a church must take without or even against the opinion of others. All must be aware of the fact that new expressions of the faith often emerge from the talents and needs of a local church. Accordingly, the need for decisive judgments from time to time at local or regional levels must be acknowledged. It is, after all, the local churches which are challenged directly by the possibilities and the failures of their contexts and cultures. There is a need to hold together the freedom for diverse expressions and the necessity to confess together for the sake of unity, in the spirit of mutual love and patience.

61. The Christian churches cherish their conciliar tradition which goes back to their very beginning (Acts 15). They have come together in synods and councils throughout the centuries. The ecumenical movement considers its dialogues and preliminary structures of deliberation and consultation to be not only instruments for the fulfilment of its hermeneutical task but also a patient preparation for coming together in a genuine ecumenical council able to restore full koinonia as God wills. Ecumenical dialogues and deliberative consultations are, in this preliminary and preparatory sense, aspects of the church's conciliarity. Ecumenical structures may already help churches communicate to one another decisions taken in matters of faith and discipline, and to prepare for decisions to be made, so that what relates to all should be dealt with by all. Such gradual steps prepare the churches for sharing common structures of decision-making, as well as for engaging the significant qualities of their diverse modes of authoritative teaching.

62. The quality of the churches' authoritative teaching depends very much upon commonly accepted hermeneutical procedures with regard to the traditions and formulations inherited from the past. Mutual knowledge of the criteriological principles guiding one another's authoritative teaching (cf. note 8) is an important contribution to mutual understanding. It is to be hoped that these developments will, in God's time, help the churches together to make decisive judgments in matters of faith. After due reception, these judgments may become part of their common witness, according to scripture. More work needs to be done to find common ground on which to test the authoritative nature of the teaching.

3. Reception as an hermeneutical process

63. The search for the unity of Christians divided by cultural or social differences, or by the separate development of confessions and denominations, requires attentive reception of each other. This reception, in turn, requires recognition of the dignity of all as human beings and, within the Christian community, as sisters and brothers in Christ. This mutual reception by Christians amid cultural, social and confessional differences is addressed by apostle Paul when he writes: "Therefore receive one another, as Christ also has received us to the glory of God" (Rom. 15:7). The hermeneutical implications of this reception of one another are manifold and bear upon the way churches relate to one another's traditions of texts, symbols, rites and practices. Reception of ecumenical agreements thus involves the reception of other persons; it may require a transformation of one's own life and of relations with others.

64. The church is a communion of persons in relation; thus active participation and dialogue between communities, and within each community at all levels, is one expression of the church's nature. The divine being of the triune God is the source and the exemplar of communion. The Holy Spirit is sent to create communion bestowing the gift of faith upon each believer. Likewise, the Holy Spirit empowers each one to understand more fully the revealed Word of God and to apply it more fruitfully to the concrete situations of daily life. As a "royal priesthood" (1 Pet. 2:9), the community of the baptized engages in the active reception of the gospel. Churches acknowledge the need to consult all levels of their constituency in matters of doctrine. Historically, even the reception of ecumenical councils was a process that extended through a considerable period of time, and employed a wide variety of means, such as the liturgy, catechesis, theology, the teaching of pastors, and popular piety. This process of reception called upon the participation of all church members, according to the charisms and ministries of each.

65. In recent times, growing agreements between the churches have improved the climate for mutual consultation, reception and accountability. At the same time, the reception of these agreements in some churches has been far from complete. The reception of ecumenical documents, which have the distinct purpose of helping to reunify divided Christian communities, is part of the ecumenical task of the church as an hermeneutical community. The process of responses to BEM, for example, sheds light on this form of reception, indicating in particular the diversity of criteria by which churches read and evaluate ecumenical documents. The BEM responses further show that reception is more than simply a church's official response to a document. Churches were asked

to respond not only to a text, but beyond that to consider changes in their own life and finally to change in their relations with others who could also recognize in the text the faith of the church through the ages. Reception is therefore also a process that extends over time and involves many factors, including a certain level of ecumenical education, the accessibility of the texts, resources for their distribution and help of theologians and local ministers to explicate their content and implications. The forums on bilateral dialogues have contributed much to a more adequate understanding of these factors.[20]

66. A practical application of ecumenical hermeneutics occurs both in the production and reception of ecumenical documents. It is important to recognize, however, an important difference between these two spheres. Ecumenical documents are *written* jointly in the context of active discussion during which the dialogue partners may question each other with regard to respective interpretations, challenging each other's positions and developing insights that point to convergence. On the other hand, ecumenical documents are *read* by people who must enter into the dialogue without having been part of the initial discussion and who did not have the opportunity to present their own views in their own terms or to check their perceptions of the views being presented by others. Moreover, ecumenical documents are often produced through multilateral dialogue, whereas these documents are normally read from the point of view of a single tradition. Consequently, it is crucial that special care is taken by those who produce ecumenical documents to ensure that meaningful exchange is facilitated at all levels by adequate attention to those dimensions of ecumenical hermeneutics that result in accurate communication and reception.

CONCLUSION

67. Under the power of the Holy Spirit the church is intended to be God's special instrument for bringing about the encounter between the Word of Life and human beings. When this Word is received, it nourishes as the living bread, which "gives life to the world", for which Jesus' listeners asked: "Lord, give us this bread always" (John 6:33-34).

68. In and through diverse historical and contemporary forms of inculturation and contextualization the bread of life, which is to be broken and distributed, remains one bread. Although the Word enters history, this historicity does not limit it to any single historical form or formulation. Yet this insight leads neither to limitless diversity nor to ecumenical complacency. Rather, as an hermeneutical community, the

church is called to grow into full koinonia by Spirit-guided discernment of the living Tradition. The church should not be imprisoned by holding on to inadequate answers from the past, nor should it silence the Word of God by endlessly putting off a clear recognition of the way this Word continues to impart meaning and orientation for human life. Under the guidance of the Holy Spirit, in faithfulness to the living Tradition, and through genuine ecumenical forms of conciliar deliberation and reception, the church is called to "interpret the signs of the times" (Matt. 16:3) by looking to the One who is both in and beyond time, to the One "who is the same, yesterday, today and forever" (Heb. 13:8).

NOTES

[1] The following definitions, drawn from recently published scholarly dictionaries of philosophy, illustrate a certain degree of consensus within the scientific literature on the topic. E.g., hermeneutics: "The method of interpretation, first of texts, and secondly of the whole social, historical and psychological world" (*Oxford Dictionary of Philosophy*, Oxford, 1994); "The art or theory of interpretation, or... the interaction between interpreter and text that is part of the history of what is understood" (*Cambridge Dictionary of Philosophy*, Cambridge, 1995); "A methodology of the right understanding and the meaningful explication and application of texts" (*Europäische Enzyklopädie zu Philosophie und Wissenschaften*, Hamburg, 1990).

[2] Cf. BEM, Ministry 52.

[3] Cf. *Baptism, Eucharist and Ministry 1982-1990: Report on the Process and the Responses*, Faith and Order Paper no. 149, Geneva, WCC, 1990, pp.32-35.

[4] Cf. *On the Way to Fuller Koinonia: Official Report of the Fifth World Conference on Faith and Order*, Thomas F. Best and Günther Gassmann, eds, Faith and Order Paper no. 166, Geneva, WCC, 1994, Section II, §18, p.241.

[5] *Ibid.*, Section I, §§15-16, p.232.

[6] *Ibid.*, Section III, §31, pp.251f., and Section IV, §3, p.254.

[7] Cf. below at §15.

[8] Cf. Scripture, Tradition and traditions, §53, in *The Fourth World Conference on Faith and Order, Montreal 1963*, P.C. Rodger and L. Vischer, eds, Faith and Order Paper no. 42, London, SCM Press, 1964, p.53: "In some confessional traditions the accepted hermeneutical principle has been that any portion of scripture is to be interpreted in the light of scripture as a whole. In others the key has been sought in what is considered to be the centre of holy scripture, and the emphasis has been primarily on the incarnation, or on the atonement and redemption, or on justification by faith, or again on the message of the nearness of the kingdom of God, or on the ethical teachings of Jesus. In yet others, all emphasis is laid upon what scripture says to the individual conscience, under the guidance of the Holy Spirit. In the Orthodox church the hermeneutical key is found in the mind of the church, especially as expressed in the fathers of the church and in the ecumenical councils. In the Roman Catholic Church the key is found in the deposit of faith, of which the church's magisterium is the guardian. In other traditions again the creeds, complemented by confessional documents or by the definitions of ecumenical councils and the witness of the fathers, are considered to give the right key to the understanding of scripture. In none of these cases where the principle of interpretation is found elsewhere than in scripture is the authority thought to be alien to the central concept of holy scripture. On the contrary, it is considered as providing just a key to the understanding of what is said in scripture."

[9] The Basis of the WCC's constitution reads: "The World Council of Churches is a fellowship of churches which confess the Lord Jesus Christ as God and Saviour according to the scriptures and therefore seek to fulfil together their common calling to the glory of the one God, Father, Son and Holy Spirit."

[10] "The Importance of the Conciliar Process in the Ancient Church for the Ecumenical Movement", in *New Directions in Faith and Order, Bristol 1967*, Faith and Order Paper no. 50, Geneva, WCC, 1968, pp.49-59 (also in *Councils and the Ecumenical Movement*, World Council Studies no. 5, Geneva, WCC, 1968).

[11] "The Authority of the Bible, Louvain, 1971", in *The Bible: Its Authority and Interpretation in the Ecumenical Movement*, Ellen Flesseman-van Leer, ed., Faith and Order Paper no. 99, Geneva, WCC, 1983 (2nd ed.), pp.42-57.

[12] "The Interpretation of the Bible in the Church", Pontifical Biblical Commission 1993, pp.128-29.

[13] Cf. below, Part C.

[14] Cf. §6 above.

[15] Cf. BEM, Ministry 52.

[16] *International Review of Mission*, 85, 1996, no. 337, p.245.

[17] These senses of "catholicity" have been accounted for in the modern ecumenical movement; cf. e.g., "The Holy Spirit and the Catholicity of the Church", in *The Uppsala Report 1968: Official Report of the Fourth Assembly of the World Council of Churches, Uppsala July 4-20, 1968,* Norman Goodall, ed., Geneva, WCC, 1968.

[18] Cf. *So We Believe, So We Pray: Towards Koinonia in Worship,* Thomas F. Best and Dagmar Heller, eds, Geneva, WCC, 1995.

[19] A useful report on emerging patterns of shared oversight can be found in the Faith and Order report on *Episkopé and Episcopacy within the Quest for Visible Unity,* Faith and Order Paper no. 183, Geneva, WCC, 1999.

[20] Cf. esp. *Sixth Forum on Bilateral Dialogues,* Faith and Order Paper no. 168, 1995.

Contributors

Dr Pablo Andiñach (Evangelical Methodist Church) is dean of ISEDET in Buenos Aires, Argentina, and a member of the standing commission on Faith and Order.

Rev. Martin Cressey (United Reformed Church) is retired principal of Westminster College, Cambridge, UK, a former moderator of the United Reformed Church in the UK, and a former member of the standing commission on Faith and Order.

Metropolitan Prof. Dr Gennadios of Sassima (Ecumenical Patriarchate of Constantinople) is co-president of the International Joint Commission on Lutheran-Orthodox Dialogue, co-secretary of the International Joint Commission on Theological Dialogue between the Orthodox Churches and the Roman Catholic Church, and vice-moderator of the Faith and Order commission.

Rev. Prof. William Henn (Roman Catholic Church) is professor of theology at the Gregorian University in Rome, Italy, specializing in ecclesiology and ecumenism, and a member of the plenary commission on Faith and Order.

Prof. Anton Houtepen (Roman Catholic Church) is director of the Interuniversity Institute for Missiology and Ecumenical Research in Utrecht, and professor of ecumenics at the theological faculty of Utrecht University, Netherlands.

Prof. Nicholas Lossky (Russian Orthodox Church) is professor of English intellectual history at the University of Paris-Nanterre, professor of church history at the Orthodox Theological Institute of St Sergius in Paris, and director of the Institut supérieur d'études œcuméniques at the Catholic Institute in Paris, France.

Very Rev. Dr Michael Prokurat (Orthodox Church in America) is associate professor of sacred scripture at the school of theology of the University of St Thomas, Houston, Texas, USA.

Rev. Rudolf von Sinner (Swiss Protestant Church Federation) is assistant lecturer and doctoral student in ecumenics and missiology at the theological faculty of the University of Basel, Switzerland, and a member of the commission on Faith and Order.

Prof. William Tabbernee (Christian Church-Disciples of Christ) is Stephen J. England professor of Christian thought and history at

Phillips Theological Seminary, Tulsa, Oklahoma, USA, and a member of the standing commission on Faith and Order.

Participants in the Consultations

During the Study Process on Ecumenical Hermeneutics

D = consultation in Dublin 1994
BN = drafting meeting in Boston 1994
L = consultation in Lyon 1997
BY = consultation in Bossey 1998
F = drafting meeting in Faverges 1999

Moderators
Prof. Turid Karlsen Seim (Lutheran), Norway (D, BN, L, BY, F)
Prof. Emmanuel Clapsis (Eastern Orthodox), USA (D, BN, F)

Participants
Rev. Dr Hilarion Alfeyev (Eastern Orthodox), Russia (L)
Rev. Dr Pablo Andiñach (Methodist), Argentina (L)
Dr Edward Antonio (Methodist), Zimbabwe/South Africa (L, BY)
Mr Christian K. Ayivi (Evangelical), Togo/Germany (D)
Rev. Frans Bouwen (Roman Catholic), Israel (D)
Dr Nicholas Constas (Eastern Orthodox), USA (L)
Rev. Martin Cressey (Reformed), UK (BY, F)
Rev. Gao Ying (Postdenominational), China (BY)
Prof. Dr William Henn, OFM Cap (Roman Catholic), USA/Italy
    (L, BY, F)
Prof. Dr Anton Houtepen (Roman Catholic), Netherlands (D, BY)
Bishop Thomas Hoyt (Methodist Episcopal), USA (D)
Dr Nam-Soon Kang (Methodist), Korea (L)
Rev. Fr. Johns Abraham Konat (Oriental Orthodox), India (D)
Rev. Dr Abraham Kuruvilla (Mar Thoma), Australia/India (D, BN, L)
Prof. Kyung Sook Lee (Methodist), Korea (BY)
Prof. George A. Lindbeck (Lutheran), USA (BN)
Rev. Dr Melanie May (Brethren), USA (BY, F)
Dr Antonio C. de Melo Magalhaes (Baptist), Germany/Brazil (D)
Rev. Dr Nestor Miguez (Methodist), Argentina (D, BN)
Rev. Prof. Angelo Maffeis (Roman Catholic), Italy (D, BY)
Dr Kirsten Busch Nielsen (Lutheran), Denmark (D)
Rev. Prof. Martin Parmentier (Old Catholic), Netherlands (D)
Sr Maria Pascuzzi CSJ (Roman Catholic), USA/Italy (L)

V. Rev. Michael Prokurat (Orthodox), USA (BY)
Rev. Araceli Rocchietti (Methodist), Uruguay (BY)
Rev. Dr Barbara Schwahn (United), Germany (L)
Rev. Rudolf von Sinner (Reformed), Switzerland (BY)
Dr William Tabbernee (Disciples of Christ), Australia/USA (L)
Prof. Petros Vassiliadis (Eastern Orthodox), Greece (BY)
Dr Gerald West (Anglican), South Africa (L)

Staff
Dr Peter Bouteneff (Orthodox), USA (D, L, BY, F)
Rev. Dr Dagmar Heller (United), Germany (D, BN, L, BY, F)
Mrs Carolyn McComish (Reformed), England (BY, F)
Mrs Renate Sbeghen (United), Germany/Switzerland (D)
Ms Monica Schreil (Roman Catholic), Sweden (L)